WILLIAM E. DONOGHUE'S
GUIDE TO
FINDING MONEY TO INVEST

By William E. Donoghue with Thomas Tilling

William E. Donoghue's Complete Money Market Guide
William E. Donoghue's No-Load Mutual Fund Guide

By William E. Donoghue

Donoghue's Mutual Fund Almanac

William E. Donoghue's

GUIDE TO FINDING MONEY TO INVEST

Building a Lifetime Savings Program with Your Hidden Cash Resources

WILLIAM E. DONOGHUE

HARPER & ROW, PUBLISHERS, New York

Cambridge, Philadelphia, San Francisco, London

Mexico City, São Paulo, Singapore, Sydney

1817

Grateful acknowledgment is made for permission to reprint the list of when to buy excerpted from *Sylvia Porter's New Money Book for the 80's* by Sylvia Porter. Copyright © 1975 by Sylvia Porter. Reprinted by permission of Doubleday & Company, Inc.

FIRST EDITION

Designer: Sidney Feinberg

Library of Congress Cataloging in Publication Data

Donoghue, William E.
    William E. Donoghue's Guide to finding money to
invest.

    Bibliography: p.
    Includes index
    1. Investments—United States—Handbooks, manuals,
etc. 2. Finance, Personal—United States—Handbooks,
manuals, etc. I. Title. II. Title: Guide to finding
money to invest.
HG4921.D65   1985   332.024'01   84-48155
ISBN 0-06-015393-8

---

85 86 87 88 89 10 9 8 7 6 5 4 3 2 1

Contents

Preface   xiii

Acknowledgments   xv

1. You Are Richer Than You Think   1

Money Funds Have Come a Long, Long Way in a Few Years   2
Where Is All This Money You Say I Have to Invest?   2
You Can Start With as Little as $1—But You'll Have More   3
How Good Can It Be?   3
Forced Savings Mean Forced Losings   6
Do-It-Yourself Is the Only Way to Go   6
You Won't Have to Go It Alone   7
Doing It Yourself Means Fewer Hassles   7
Your Hidden Gold Mines—A Closer Look   7
A Strategy for All Seasons   10
Onward and Upward   10

2. Getting to "Know Thyself" and the "Tools of Thy Trade"   11

Where Do You Stand in the Investors' Hall of Fame?   11
Rip Van Winkle—The Banker's Friend   12
Good Old Rip's Not Alone   12
Sophie the Sensible Saver   13
Rocky had the Super-SLY Smile of a Winner   13
"Get Rich Quick" Richard and "Sounds Good to Me"
    Sam—The Stockbroker's Delights   14
Super-SLYC Sallie's Simple Secret   14
Which Type of Investor Are You?   15
A Short Quiz   16

Now You Can Set Financial Goals   17
The Far Future: Your Children and Your Retirement   17
What's Really Important to You?   18
Filling Your Financial Tool Kit   18
Tool 1: Looking for Mr. Goodbank   18
Tool 2: Money Market Mutual Funds   25
Tool 3: A Major Credit Card   29
Tool 4: Why You Need a Retirement Plan—Today   30
Tool 5: Trust Accounts for Your Children   31
Tools You Don't Need   31
Stockbrokers Are Often Just Salespeople   32
You Bet Your Life, but Will You Be There to Win?   32
Pack Up Your Tool Kit, Hop on Your Ship of Savings, and Sail On   32

3. Liberate the Lemons: Spring Cleaning Your Financial House   33

Rethinking, Reworking, and Retooling   33
Build Yourself a Balance Sheet   34
Let's See Where You Stand   34
Striking a Good Balance   35
Are You Richer than You Thought?   37
   1. "Cash on Hand" That Most Folks Don't Count   37
   2. Accounts You Can Bank On   38
   3. Are You Stuck on Your Stocks?   38
   4. Don't Lose with Savings Bonds   39
   5. Company Thrift Plan Accounts, Money Fund Accounts,
      and Other Mutual Fund Accounts   40
   6. Get the Whole Benefit from Whole Life   40
   7. Other Liquid Assets   41
   8. Is It Time to Liberate Your Home?   44
   9. Automobiles   44
  10. Check Your Home—Room by Room   44
  11. "Neither a Borrower nor a Lender Be . . ."   49
  12. Minding Your Own Business   49
  13. If the Vest Fits, Wear It—It's Tailored for You   51
  14. Liberate Your IRA   51
  15. Tax Refunds Due—Don't Forget 'Em   52
  16. What Else You Got?   52
You're Rich (More or Less)! Now What Do You Do?   53
   1. Credit Card Bills   53
   2. Real Estate Taxes Due   53
   3. Income Taxes Due   54

4. Installment Loans and Other Short-Term Loans   54
5. Mortgages   54
6. Other Long-Term Debt   54
Donoghue's Rule for Savers   55
What's Your Net Worth?   55
Your First Steps   55
Now Invest that Cash—Quickly   55
Liberating Lemons—The First Key to Finding Money to Invest   56

4. Cutting Down Your Major Expenses   57

Renovating Your Mortgage Loan   57
The Joys of Refinancing—Sometimes   58
Adjustable Rates Will Turn Against You   59
How to Save Thousands in Interest—Without Refinancing   60
Is It Time to Move?   60
Escaping the Debt Traps   61
The Rule of 78s: When the Early Bird Lays an Egg   62
Coolly Cut Credit Card Costs   62
Careful Credit Card Shopping Is Smart   63
Insure Yourself—But Don't Cheat Yourself   64
Agents of the Money Market Revolution   64
New Policies—And New Complications   65
Know What You Really Need   65
The Rest of Your Insurance Bill   67
Automatically Check Your Auto Insurance   68
Don't Forget Discounts   68
Insure Your Children the Right Way   69
The Lowest Priced Company Isn't Necessarily the Cheapest   69
Protecting Your Home   69
Don't Take Everything the Doctor Orders   70
The New Opportunity in Health Care   70
Drugs Needn't Be Downers   70
A Little Energy Will Cut Energy Bills   71
The Right Time to Buy   72
Is All This Enough to Help You Find Money to Invest?   73

5. Cash Planning: Your Way to a Better Life   74

You Can Budget a Failure, but You Have to Plan Success   74
Cash Is the Name of the Game   75
Planning the Ways and Means   75
Developing a Family "Business Plan"   76

viii   **Contents**

Would All This Be More Fun with a Computer?   76
Getting Down to It   77
The First Step: Defining the Means   77
Salaries: The Wages of Win   77
What Other Income Do You Have?   78
Drain Dollars Out of Your Savings Accounts   79
Interrogating Your Investment Income   79
Recognize the Rainy Day You Have Been Saving For   80
Fixing Up the Fixed Expenses   80
Now for the Tough Stuff to Budget—Your Living Expenses   85
Putting the Puzzle Together   95
So! Where Do You Cut?   96
Now You're Ready to Roll   97

6. "Brilliant Deductions, Sherlock," or Getting Out from Under a Tax   98

To Fund or Refund, That Is the Question   98
Turning the Tables on the Tax Man   98
A Refund Is Fun for a Day, Invested Cash Is a Blessing All Year   99
Withhold on Your Withholding   100
Getting Some Help to Pay for Your House   100
Just One More Question about This Withholding Business   102
How to Find an Investment on Your Return   102
Adjusting Your Gross Income   103
Figuring Your Adjusted Gross Income   106
Itemizing Your Way to Investment Cash   106
Don't Be Afraid to Take What's Coming to You   107
Tax Credits   111
How to Make a Good Year Better   115
A Caveat about Taxes   115
Less Taxes Mean More Money to Invest   116

7. Deep in the Heart of Taxes: A Primer on How to Keep Your Investment Returns   117

How to Avoid Taxes Without Evading Them   117
What's Taxable and What's Not Makes a Big Difference   118
Six Kinds of Investment "Income"—and Two Kinds That Aren't
    Income at All   118
Know When Cash Flow Isn't Income—When It's Money That is Yours,
    but You Haven't Seen it for a While   128
Choose the Right Kind of Income and You'll Come Out Way Ahead   129

Tricks of the Tax Shelter Trade   129
You're Sleeping in a Pile of Cash   133
When the Tax Man Cometh . . . He's Gonna Leave Still Hungry   134

8. Tax Shelters for Very Important Investors   135

Old-Style Tax Shelters Were Designed to Keep Lawyers Employed   135
You're on Your Own, so Listen Close   136
The Deal of the Century for VIIs   136
Tax-Deferred Magic   136
Tax-Deferred Compounding: Even More Magic   137
Meet SARA, the Tax Shelter of the '80s   138
IRA, SARA's Older Brother   141
Looking into a Keogh   143
A Warning—You Must Withdraw from Your Tax Shelter or
    Pay the Consequences   145
An Alternative: Variable Annuities   145
How to Make the Most of Your Tax-Deferred Investments   147
The Rate's the Key   147
Guaranteed Rates Guarantee Less   147
If You're Young, Don't Be Afraid to Take Some Risks   150
If You Can't Afford an IRA or Keogh, It Can Pay to Borrow   150
Know When to Hold 'Em and When To Fold 'Em   150
Tax Shelters for Very Important Investors: Keystones to Savings Plans 153

9. Super-SLY Money Market Investing   154

We've Come a Long Way, Baby   154
What Does Super-SLY Stand For?   155
The Deregulation Derby   155
Safety Is a Prime Concern . . .   156
. . . But Know the Rules of the Road   156
Insurance You're a Fool Not to Buy   157
Safety Without Insurance   158
Liquidity: When You Need It in a Hurry   159
Yield: The Right Way   159
The $19.5 Billion Rip-Off—Still in Progress   159
Down-to-Earth Advice From the "Guru"   160
You've Made a Good First Move   161
Paying Too Much in Taxes Is Not SLY, It's Dumb   162
People Who Have Money Like to Keep It   162
Less Can Be More—Sometimes   162
Somebody Does It Better—But Only in Three Great States   163

What About Other States?   163
When You Invest Can Be as Important as Where   164
What to Do When Interest Rates Rise   164
Questions and Answers for the Curious   165
How to Get a Handle on Money Market Trends   167
Turning the SLY Indicator into a Super-SLY Indicator   170
Investing 'After the Fall'—or What to Do When Interest Rates Decline   171
Riding the Yield Curve   171
The Two Best Choices   172
Now You CDs, Now You Don't   173
A Liquid Alternative   174
Are You Ready for Super-SLY Now?   176

10. Super-SLYC Investing for Patriotic Investors   177

What Does SLYC Stand For?   177
The SLYC Funds: All in the Family   177
Safety and Liquidity First   178
Yields Are Getting More Than Your Money Back   179
Catastrophe-Proofing: Creative Paranoia   179
Where to Store Your Gold Reserves   180
Beating the Hyperdeflation Hype   180
Back to SLYC   181
When Rates Fall, Opportunities Rise   182
How Do I Know When to Switch Investments?   182
Where Does the 'Super' in Super-SLYC Come In?   183
How Much Better Is Super-SLYC?   184
When the Market Dives, Head for the Shore   184
Customizing SLYC   185
When You Make the Plunge—Look Before You Leap   187
Patience Is Prudence and Consistency Can Be a Blessing   188
Sell High—On an After-Tax Basis   189
Spreading Your Risk   189
Now It's Time to Start Waving the Patriotic Flag   189
Investing for Growth and Avoiding Taxes   189
Some More Super-SLYC Common Sense   190
Patience Pays   190
Don't Take the SLY Out of SLYC   191

11. Your Guide to Commonsense Investing   192

The Wrong Place at the Wrong Time   192
Commonsense Investing Is the Way to Go—You "Auto" Get That Right   193

The VIP Treatment: Learning to Tax-Shelter What You Earn   194
When to Borrow to Invest—Supercharging the Superchargers   197
Where to Borrow to Invest   198
When to Repay Loans   198
Knowing Why You Are Investing Can Make a Big Difference in How You
     Invest   199
Check-a-Month Plans Work Both Ways   201
What about Those Catastrophe-Proofing Investments?   202
The Wisened Old Philosopher Muses for the Masses   203
The Five Best Risk-Reduction Strategies   203
Getting the Family in on Your CASHPLAN   205
One Final Warning   206
You've Got the Route and the Loot to Boot   206

Glossary   209

Market Indexes   218

Suggested Reading   220

Addresses & Phone Numbers   223

Appendix 1   236

Rate of Return (ROR) for Cash Value Life Insurance

Appendix 2   239

Life Insurance Comparison

Appendix 3   243

Sample List of Tax Publications

Appendix 4   245

3% Real Rate of Return

Appendix 5   247

IRA Breakeven

Appendix 6   249

SLYC Funds

xii   **Contents**

Appendix 7   251

Rule of 72: "How Long to Double Your Money?"

Appendix 8   253

1984 Tax Rate Schedules

Index   255

Preface

This Book Can Change Your Life

The two keys to building a lifetime savings program are: (1) staying with it long enough to learn from your mistakes and (2) finding enough money to do (1). That's why this book is called *Guide to Finding Money to Invest*. It's a two-way street—you have to know how to invest wisely and you have to know where to find the money to invest wisely.

How to Read This Book

Read the whole book before you do anything. Then read it again. This could well be the most important single effort you undertake in your life, because it will determine how well you live and how comfortably you retire.

As you read, keep a note pad alongside of you and start building up your "to do" list—actions you will be taking to generate money to invest and investment information you will want to obtain. When you get finished, rewrite the list on another piece of paper. That very act will help you make sure you understand exactly what you want to do. Prioritize your list as you copy it. What will you do first? What will generate the most cash for *you?*

You Only Get Two Chances

Remember, for most of us, there are only two kinds of chances in life to free up our biggest hidden cash reserves: (1) the one-time opportunities to redirect those easy-to-find-and-liberate passbook savings accounts, cash value of whole life insurance policies, the proceeds of the garage sale, etc., and (2) the slow-but-sure process of squeezing cash from a paycheck, reducing living expenses, earning new investment profits, cutting taxes, and the like.

If you take the money and blow it on something you can't afford—throw it away on lottery tickets or your stockbroker's latest hot tip, or simply fritter it away—that's the ball game.

The "Easy Way Out" Can Be Expensive

Once you start building your plans, you must stay alert to threats to your core investments. Resist the temptation to let others make your decisions for you, at *your* expense. Take the time to gain the confidence to make your own decisions. After all, it's your money.

We've Done Our Share . . .

The extensive list of realistic and practical techniques for finding money to invest will amaze you. Our researchers have searched high and low to discover techniques for prying loose investible money which the average individual can actually apply with the minimum of hassles and surprises. You are, indeed, *much* richer than you think.

The team of investment advisers who worked with me in developing the seemingly simple investment strategies outlined in this book have a total of over seventy-five years of experience with mutual funds. Our no-nonsense approach to do-it-yourself investing can work for you.

The rules are simple, realistic, and sound: Pay yourself first, manage your own money confidently, don't invest in anything you don't understand, stay liquid, and, most important of all, remember that the purpose of investing is to live better, and that you can do that only if you are in charge of your finances.

You are in for a very special treat. This may be the most exciting, entertaining, and inspiring financial book you will ever read. It just may change your life. I hope you enjoy reading it half as much as I enjoyed writing it.

Acknowledgments

Writing is a uniquely personal task. When you can surround yourself with a top-flight team of advisers, editors, and researchers, as I have, it becomes an exciting creative experience. Now you know why I seem always to be enjoying myself so much. My staff and I are especially proud of this book, which we, the toughest critics we know, think is our best effort to date.

Special thanks go to those who worked directly on this project. John Waggoner, my senior editor, who managed the project, suggested many fresh approaches to the subject matter, contributed some of the most outrageous puns, and sweated out the long hours of writing, rewriting, and editing with me. The charts and tables are the work of research assistant Beverly Rowe. Michael Healy, our attorney, and Robert Charron, our accountant, helped us with many of the finer points of tax law (although we are ultimately responsible for any errors or omissions). Robert "Woody" Wood, an editorial consultant, helped us break through some important creative logjams that always plague a project of this scope. Elizabeth Skinner King, managing editor, saw the manuscript through the vital final stages.

At Harper & Row, I would like to thank publisher Edward Burlingame and associate editor Sallie Coolidge. Their friendship, encouragement, and confidence in my abilities as an author helped me survive the always challenging process of writing not just a book but a bestseller (which is another task indeed). Gone from Harper & Row, but not forgotten, is Nancy Crawford, who discovered me as an author and brought me together with my former coauthor, Thomas Tilling, who provided a fine literary example and helped with my first two books.

Many of the ideas for this book have come from the pages of our newsletters, primarily, *Donoghue's MONEYLETTER,* edited by Kathleen Victory, who succeeded Jim Henderson. Editors Connie Bugbee, Lisa Sheeran, and Jennifer Brown, research director Alan Lavine, and economist Conrad Grundlehner contributed many fresh ideas and research.

I would also like to thank my administrative staff and advisers, whose support has been a source of inspiration: Frank Harrison, our able and dedicated vice president; Debra Strafuss, our resourceful controller and office manager; Lynda Morgan, my assistant and confidante; and B. P. Fulmer and Allen Grieve, two trusted advisers, close friends, and sounding boards, both creative banking professionals.

Last but not least, I would like to thank Marie Cardinal Hansen, who has been encouraging me to write this book for the past five years. "Here 'tis, Marie."

WILLIAM E. DONOGHUE'S
GUIDE TO
FINDING MONEY TO INVEST

1

You Are Richer than You Think

Everywhere I go, people tell me, "Bill, your investment advice sounds great, but I just don't have any money that I can afford to lock up in an investment." Are they in for a surprise! They simply don't realize the power of their hidden cash resources and—corny as it may sound—the virtue of simple thrift. If you learn to "pay yourself first," you will never be poor.

You see, most people accumulate assets the way I accumulate junk in my office: they just spend their money on things and leave them lying around in the hope that someday they'll be useful. Even the most destitute among us have some hidden assets lying around that they can turn into investable cash. And whatever money you can find lying around unproductively, you can turn into hard-working investment money.

This isn't one of those "get-rich-quick" schemes that you're always reading about. But it could be your chance of a lifetime: Once you have spent your hidden cash resources, you won't have them again. So make them work for you this time.

It takes money to make money, and I'm going to show you how even a little money can grow into a substantial nest egg. It just takes time, patience, and confidence.

There has never been a better time in history to build wealth through simple thrift, or a better time to be a saver. Not only do investment opportunities abound, but the financial world has finally opened up for the small saver.

Money Funds Have Come a Long, Long Way in a Few Years

When I wrote my first book, *William E. Donoghue's Complete Money Market Guide,* in 1980, there was really only one sensible place for small savers to put their hard-earned cash: money market mutual funds (money funds). But even then only a few million smart investors had taken advantage of them. Now over 12 million investors use money funds, and many millions more are invested in bank and thrift institution money market accounts.

Money funds did much more for small savers than give them a fair rate of return. Money funds, with their excellent safety record, their convenient accessibility, and their high money market yields, set a shining example for the financial world to follow. Soon banks, stockbrokers, insurance companies, mutual fund families, and even Sears department stores and Kroger supermarkets were taking small investors seriously and offering a wide range of attractive investment services.

Better still, the financial revolution didn't stop with the money market. Wall Street jumped onto the small saver bandwagon, lowering the minimum investments for growth stock mutual funds, bond mutual funds, and a whole array of attractive mutual fund services. No-load mutual funds, with no sales charges (loads), are becoming much more accessible and convenient, allowing investors to avoid those expensive and unnecessary services most brokers sell.

Even more importantly, more no-load mutual fund families are offering the best deal of the '80s: the ability to become your own investment manager and use their free telephone "switching" service to exchange your shares of a fund that is not performing well for shares of a better-performing one—all with a tollfree telephone call.

Where Is All This Money You Say I Have to Invest?

You can squeeze investable cash from nearly everything you have and from nearly all the cash that passes through your hands. As you read through the pages of this book, you will discover how to teach your checking account to pay you money, how to turn the junk in your attic into cash, how to make money from the cash value of your life insurance policy, how to increase your take-home pay, how to cut your insurance bills, how to save money when you buy a home or car, and how to pay less taxes on what you earn and avoid taxes on some of your new income.

It is your responsibility to make every asset you have and every dollar you earn work as hard and as long as you do to make your life easier and fuller.

You Can Start with as Little as $1—But You'll Have More

In fact, if you have just $1 in your pocket, you can start a lifetime savings plan. There are money funds which will open an account with, and pay money market rates on, as little as $1.

For another dollar, many money funds will allow you to open an Individual Retirement Account (IRA) for your long-term savings. That way you have a tax-sheltered savings account, a new deduction on your tax return, and a solid "starter" investment. Then you are really on your way to starting a lifetime savings program.

Do you still have any excuses for not saving? (See Table 1 for money funds permitting initial investments of $500 or less.)

How Good Can It Be?

As I described in my last book, *William E. Donoghue's No-Load Mutual Fund Guide,* mutual fund families that allow you to use the services of a whole family of funds can produce results that are absolutely amazing—and easy to achieve, if you're willing to take some risk. How amazing? Would you like to average a return of over 20 percent a year?

Let's take a look at what I call the 10–20–30 plan. And let's say that each week you saved $10 and invested it in a mutual fund. That's the first part of the 10–20–30 plan.

Now suppose you used the Super-SLYC (pronounced "slick") system I describe in Chapter 10 for building both growth stock mutual funds and money funds into your investment strategy. Over the past five years, my system averaged 23 percent. But we'll say that you'll average 20 percent—just to make allowance for future unknowns and occasional bad moves. That's the 20 part of the 10–20–30 plan.

Now let's say that you carried out this plan for 30 years or so, which is the final part of the 10–20–30 plan. That's a reasonable amount of time for the average retirement plan. You could start at age thirty-five and still have plenty of time to prepare to retire at age sixty-five.

Now, if you'd saved $10 per week and stuffed it in your mattress, you'd have $15,060 for your retirement kitty at the end of a little more than thirty years—an amount that won't last you very long. But if you averaged 20 percent over that amount of time and tax-sheltered it in your IRA, you'd be sitting on top of more than $1 million. That's nothing to sneeze at. (See Table 2.)

Now, no one can guarantee you a 20 percent annual return. But with a

Table 1   Money Funds Permitting Initial Investments of $500 or Less

Name of Fund	Type of Fund*	Investments (Initial/Subsequent)	Check Minimum
CAM Fund Consolidated Money Management Inc. (PA) (800) 423-2345	GP	None/None	None
First Trust MMF (general purpose)	GP	None/None	$100
First Trust MMF (government portfolio)	GP/GO	None/None	$100
First Trust tax-free fund Principal Protection Adv. Services (IL) (800) 621-4770	GP/TF	None/None	$100
Brown (R. C.) MMF Brown (R. C.) & Co. (CA) (800) 221-9855	GP	$100/None	$100
AARP U.S. government MMF Institutional Research Corp. (PA) (800) 245-4770	GP/GO	$500/$100	$500
American Treasury Shares American Shares Management (FL) (800) 237-0738	GP/GO	$500/$500	$500
Daily Cash Accumulation	GP	$500/$100	$250
Daily Cash Government Fund Centennial Capital Corp. (CO) (800) 525-7048	GP/GO	$500/$100	$250
FBL Money Market Fund Farm Bureau Mutual Funds (IA) (800) 247-4170	GP	$500/None	$500

Table 1 *(Continued)*

Name of Fund	Type of Fund*	Investments (Initial/Subsequent)	Check Minimum
Financial Planner's Federal Securities Steadman Security Corp. (DC) (800) 424-8570	GP/GO	$500/None	$500
Franklin Federal Money Fund	GP/GO	$500/$25	$100
Franklin Money Fund	GP	$500/$25	$100
Franklin Tax-Exempt MMF Franklin Distributors, Inc. (CA) (800) 227-6781	GP/TF	$500/$25	$100
Sigma Government Securities Fund	GP/GO	$500/$100	$500
Sigma Money Market Fund Delfi Management Inc. (DE) (800) 441-9490	GP	$500/$100	$500
Transamerica Cash Reserve Transamerica Investment Services (CA) (800) 631-0749	GP	$500/$100	$250

*GP=general purpose; GO=government only; TF=tax-free.
Source: Donoghue's Mutual Fund Almanac (15th ed.).

Table 2

If You Save This Much Each Month . . .	. . . You'll Have This Much*					
	in 1 Year		in 10 Years		in 30 Years	
	10%†	20%†	10%†	20%†	10%†	20%†
$ 40	$ 507	$ 535	$ 8,262	$15,295	$ 91,173	$ 934,432
50	634	699	10,328	19,118	113,966	1,168,040
60	760	803	12,393	22,942	136,760	1,401,648
70	887	937	14,459	26,765	159,553	1,635,256
80	1,014	1,071	16,524	30,589	182,346	1,868,864
90	1,140	1,204	18,590	34,413	205,139	2,102,472
100	1,267	1,338	20,655	38,236	227,933	2,336,080

*Before taxes.   †Interest rate.

little prudence, my Super-SLYC plan will beat the doubloons off anything you can get in the money market alone.

If you're a more conservative investor (and there's no need to be ashamed of being one), you can still average upward of 10 percent on your savings without sacrificing safety by using my new Super-SLY strategy. In fact, if you know when to lock in the high yields and when to let your savings float upward with interest rates in liquid asset accounts, you can do even better than 10 percent. All it takes is a little thought and the right moves at the right time.

Forced Savings Mean Forced Losings

Now, there's one catch to this plan: you've got to do the saving yourself. Why? Because if you fall for a forced savings plan, such as a Christmas club, a whole life insurance policy, or even some of the check-a-month plans offered by stockbrokers, you can watch your savings go down the drain of inflation or, worse still, of a stock market gone sour.

For example, let's take a look at that venerable institution, the Christmas club. Every year, banks and thrifts (savings & loans and mutual savings banks) offer this turkey, ostensibly to help people to save for the holiday season. Each week, the bank takes a certain amount of money from your checking account and puts it into a "Christmas club account."

Ebenezer Scrooge never had it so good. A Christmas club is just a passbook savings account in disguise. You get a measly 5.25 percent on your savings, if you're lucky. Some Christmas clubs don't pay anything. When inflation is running around 6 percent, all a Christmas club does is force you to watch your money lose its value.

There are lots of other ways that the financial world takes advantage of people who want to be forced to save: Some whole life insurance policies, for example, often lock you into a rate that rivals that of the passbook, and service fees and sales charges eat away at the poor rate you get.

Do-It-Yourself Is the Only Way to Go

So if you want to be a saver, the best way is to do it yourself. If you take the time to direct your own savings, you'll avoid all those nasty fees that forced savings plans charge. Fewer fees for them means more money for you and a better overall return on your investments—even with occasional miscues.

Now, don't tell me you don't know anything about investing. You were smart enough to buy this book, weren't you? Don't tell me you can't learn how to invest your money, either. I just don't buy that. I'll bet you learned how to drive a car. Like some investments, a car can be very dangerous, but somehow you learned to turn what can be a very dangerous weapon into a very useful and essential part of your everyday life. You can do that with your investments, if you want to.

You Won't Have to Go It Alone

If you're still leery of managing your money yourself, you shouldn't be. Financial information is easily available from many reputable sources. For example, if you can't make heads or tails of a mutual fund prospectus, you can always call the fund's customer service representative to get the answer to your questions. Or you can turn to any one of a great number of consumer organizations, newsletters, and newspapers to get much of the information you need. In fact, there's a list of my recommended sources in the back of this book, so you'll know where to get started.

Doing It Yourself Means Fewer Hassles

Another good reason for managing your own savings is that you can change your mind about your investment without fees or penalties. If you follow my advice, you won't be forced to borrow back your own money, as you must with most insurance products, or, even worse, pay a penalty to get your own money out of one investment and into another.

The reason you'll have this flexibility is liquidity. Now, liquidity doesn't mean that you'll be floating a loan, nor does it mean that you'll wind up all wet. It means that you'll be able to get at your investment money, in most cases, within twenty-four hours. You can either have the money sent to your bank account or switch it into another investment. If the stock market turns sour or if you have a personal emergency, you'll be able to move your money quickly—and without paying a penalty.

It's not hard to cultivate good savings habits, and in later chapters I'll show you just how to do it without feeling deprived or impoverished. But if you need just a bit of incentive, look at Table 2, which shows you how much you can save in one year by putting a little away each month.

Your Hidden Gold Mines—A Closer Look

Are you interested yet? If not, keep in mind that this gives you only a small idea of what saving can do for you if you have absolutely no money whatsoever to invest. But nine out of ten people are sitting on top of hidden assets that they never tap.

If you're shaking your head and doubting me, here's just a partial list of the places I'll show you where your hidden assets are.

1. Liberate the lemons. Free up those idle assets and unproductive investments you have accumulated over the years, such as passbook savings accounts, Christmas clubs, those old coin and stamp collections that are gathering dust, and all that junk in the garage and the attic that would make a good tag sale. Then put that money where it belongs—hard at work for you and your family.

2. Slash your major expenses. How much money do you spend on your insurance, your mortgage, your credit cards? Wouldn't you love to cut those expenses to the bone? Well, you can—if you know how.

For example, did you know that most conventional mortgages allow you to make voluntary contributions of principal with each mortgage payment? No? That's because it's buried in the fine print. Now most bankers won't tell you about it, but if you pay as little as $25 extra per month, you can save as much as $59,000 in interest over the course of a $75,000, thirty-year mortgage.

I'll be telling you other ways to slash those expenses and improve your weekly cash flow—without getting you in trouble with the bank or losing any insurance protection for you and your loved ones.

3. Squeeze your budget—without getting squashed. Most people would rather spend a weekend at the dentist than sit down and create a budget. But I'll show you how a little creative scrimping can give you money to invest without cramping your lifestyle.

For example, how much do you pay for your checking account each month after the fees and charges? $10? $15? If you find the right bank or make the right arrangements with your employer, you can skip those fees— and save between $120 and $150 every year.

4. Reduce the thighs of your tax bill with accounting aerobics. If you get a tax refund each year you are probably overwithholding your taxes and you're lending the government money interest-free. Would Uncle Sam lend *you* money interest-free? No way.

But you can get that money to work for you with your next paycheck. For example, how would you like to get the IRS to contribute to your IRA? It's easy, and it works like this: Suppose you intend to put $2,000 into your Individual Retirement Account (IRA) this year, and that you make $20,000 per year. Since you can deduct your IRA contribution from your federal taxes, you should be paying taxes on $18,000, not $20,000, right?

All you have to do is adjust the amount of taxes your employer takes out of your weekly paycheck. It takes about five minutes of your time—and you'll get a bigger paycheck each month. If you put that extra money into your IRA, you've gotten the IRS to contribute to your IRA—and who could resist that?

There are lots of other ways you can detect, record, and deduct for rewards. If you can discipline yourself to keep a few simple records, you will find that you will have more legitimate expenses to deduct on your tax return and reduce your taxes. Reduced taxes mean more money to put to work for you and less for the government—and that sounds like a good deal to me. If you are in the 20 percent tax bracket, each dollar you deduct will mean a twenty-cent savings in your pocket.

5. *Double the rate you get on your savings—without risk.* If you're one of the millions out there with a passbook savings account, you're getting rooked out of at least 5 percent on your savings annually. By investing in safe, liquid, and high-yielding money funds or bank money market deposit accounts, you can make your money work twice as hard as it is now. According to my calculations, shifting from passbook savings to money funds would make American consumers about another $14.6 billion a year.

If you're willing to take a bit of risk, you can do even better by investing in the stock or bond market at the right time. I'll tell you how to invest in the money market and the stock market—and when to switch between them for maximum earnings.

6. *Adopt nonfriction investing.* "Friction costs," as a good friend of mine loves to call them, are those insidious "extra charges" that seem to crop up everywhere, especially in the investment field—commissions, "loads," setup charges, and whatever.

A knowledgeable investor knows which of these friction costs are unnecessary and which are good values. For example, "loads," or commissions, on most mutual funds sold by stockbrokers are a waste. You would have to come up with some pretty convoluted reasoning to believe that a mutual fund will perform better just because you paid a broker an exorbitant fee (up to 8.5 percent) to fill out a few forms.

If you're a saver, you should use your investment money for *you*—not to support salespeople. The less you spend in wasteful friction costs, the more you can keep and enjoy for yourself. There's a whole world of investments out there—such as money funds and no-load mutual funds—that cost you nothing more than some reading time and a twenty-cent stamp. Why settle for anything less? Besides, if you decide to take my advice, this book may then qualify for the "nonfriction bestseller list."

7. *Turn fifty-cent pieces into eighty-cent pieces.* Once in a while, as in the past few years, investors have had the opportunity to turn fifty-cent dollars into eighty-cent dollars. People who recognize that opportunity can save a whole lot in taxes.

You see, if you can hold onto an investment for over six months before you sell it, the profit qualifies for long-term capital gains treatment. That means the maximum tax you will have to pay on that profit is 20 percent instead of 50 percent. If you are in a lower tax bracket, the tax is, of course, still lower. Eighty percent tax-free money is a gift from the gods.

Wonderful as capital gains are, they're just one way to reduce the tax bite on your hard-earned savings. I'll tell you how to beat the taxman to your savings—without getting into trouble with the IRS.

8. Common cents add up to dollar savings. Using a bit of common sense in investing can save you money and get you more investment for your money.

Some examples of common sense? Dollar cost averaging is a simple way to make sure that your average cost per share on your investments is lower. You simply invest a little at a time instead of all of your money at once and your average cost per share will be less.

More common sense? Know when to take a loss instead of hanging onto a losing investment. It's better to lose a few dollars and start getting some of the money back by deducting it from your taxes than hang on waiting for an upturn that may never come.

A Strategy for All Seasons

As you can tell from the list above, not all the money you find to invest will be lying about your attic. You'll earn much of your savings money the old-fashioned way: by accumulating it slowly, investing it, and preserving it.

So your first strategy will be how to accumulate money slowly and steadily. You will learn how to be a disciplined saver, and how to trim your budget without trimming your lifestyle. And you'll learn the pleasure of watching your savings grow.

Your second strategy will be how to invest your money assertively with a few simple tools: a checking account, a mutual fund family, a tax-deferred retirement account, a major credit card, and a trust account for each child. You'll learn what the best investments are for rising interest rates, falling interest rates, and long-term goals. Whether you're a Super-SLYC or Super-SLY investor, you'll get the best returns available on the financial markets—without gambling with your hard-earned cash.

Your third strategy will be preserving your money: how to pay as few taxes as legally possible, how to keep one step ahead of inflation, and how to protect your hard-earned cash from economic catastrophe.

Onward and Upward

Are you ready to dig deep into your hidden cash reserves and start your life as an investor? Are you prepared to take a hard look at the way you handle your money and start a lifetime savings program? Do you want to watch your savings grow? If so, then you're ready to find money to invest.

2

Getting to "Know Thyself" and the "Tools of Thy Trade"

If you're the disciplined type—and lucky—you could become rich without even reading the rest of this book. But if you stop reading now, you'll undoubtedly miss out on thousands of dollars' worth of additional money to invest every year. In fact, if you're as undisciplined as I used to be, you'll probably give up on the whole project before you've even learned how easy it is to make a lifetime investment plan succeed.

So take the time right now to set your program up right. You'll want to keep refining it for as long as you live, but this chapter will help you on your way to fortune, if not fame.

Where Do You Stand in the Investors' Hall of Fame?

It's now time to decide what you are willing to do with this hard-earned money you are liberating.

Are you going to hide it under the mattress? Are you going to give it to a stockbroker or banker and say, "Do something with it and don't tell me about it—I don't understand this whole investment scene, you're the expert"? Or are you going to stand up and say, "I learned how to make money. By jingo, I am going to learn how to teach my money to make money for me!"

If the last is what you want to do—skip ahead to Chapters 9 and 10. If you're not sure, read on as we profile some of today's typical investors. You might recognize some friends, even yourself.

Rip Van Winkle—The Banker's Friend

Asleep at the wheel, the good Mr. Van Winkle has never paid even the slightest attention to his finances. He dutifully puts his paycheck into his checking account (when he gets around to it) and, once every twenty years when he awakens from his trance, he decides to put some money into his passbook savings account to save for the future. However, he makes his son and daughter put $5 each month into their 5.5 percent passbook savings account so they can learn the wonders of thrift.

Whenever his checking account gets just too embarrassingly bloated, he goes down to his local stockbroker, who talks him into investing in something like Nocturnal Aviation, Inc. (a fly-by-night firm if I ever heard of one). The stock promptly makes the broker a commission and then takes a nosedive, never to be seen again except as cheap wallpaper.

Our good friend Rip will soon retire among the millions who think that Social Security will provide for them in their old age, through a good portion of which Rip will, no doubt, sleep fitfully in his normal unconscious state.

Good Old Rip's Not Alone

If this all sounds farfetched, allow me to enlighten you a bit. I used to work as a chief internal auditor for a firm with a large clerical work force that was at least a bit out of tune with the times, as were many of our other employees.

After management finally talked our workers into accepting checks each week—until 1965 or so they were still being paid in cash, something on which the local muggers simply thrived—we were still surprised at the number of clerks who would deposit their weekly paychecks once a quarter or once a year. We actually had to ask them to deposit the checks. The company, of course, enjoyed the use of the funds until the checks cleared.

Today, after all the money market hoopla, there is still nearly twice as much money in passbook savings accounts earning 5.5 percent at most as there is in money market mutual funds. Those folks must be Rip Van Winkle's cousins. Even today, too many bankers count on this source of cheap money for their profits. It's time *you* profited from your money.

Even worse is teaching your children to save their money in passbook savings accounts. There are money market mutual funds with no minimum investment requirements which pay two to three times the rate of passbook savings. To start them off on a lifetime savings program making the same mistakes you did is nearly criminal.

Of course, the folks who turn their money over to a stockbroker never to see much of it again are legion. But after all, that is part of the reason you bought this book—to learn to do better.

So much for suckers like Rip. You are not *that* bad, are you?

Sophie the Sensible Saver

Over the past seven years, sensible savers like Sophie have learned about the money market. First it was money market mutual funds, and then the banks came along with six-month money market certificates, liquid money market accounts, certificates, and a wide range of money market services. Sophie figured out this new kind of saving pretty early.

Sophie now deposits her paycheck each week into her insured bank money market deposit account (it only takes $1,000 to start one and she has earned that on her savings over the past few years), transfers money into her checking account once or twice a month to pay her bills, uses the new auto-mated teller machines to get cash when she needs it, and keeps some of the excess money she has saved in a longer-term certificate. She set up an Individ-ual Retirement Account last year (she could afford to put in only $500 the first year instead of the full $2,000 permitted, but it was a start) and she saved some money on her taxes by doing so.

Sophie has got the basic idea and is living a bit better because of it.

Rocky Had the Super-SLY Smile of a Winner

Just like Sylvester "Sly" Stallone's character Rocky Balboa, you too can break out of the crowd to become a recognized winner. All you have to do is believe in yourself.

SLY investors (who learned their money market investment strategies in my first book) will be glad to hear that, like Rocky I, II, and III, we have a new chapter in investment strategies for money market investors—Super-SLY.

SLY stands for Safety, Liquidity, and Yield, the investment goals for most investors. First, you want safe investments that help you protect your hard-earned money. Second, you want liquid investments, so you can always get at your hard-earned money. Finally, you want those investments to earn the highest yields consistent with the first two goals.

If you have noticed that some money market investors have a particularly SLY smile on their faces, that is because they have incorporated some special information into their investment strategies that allows them to earn a bit higher returns. They are willing to understand the various money market instruments, how they work, how to get the highest yields, and most impor-tantly when to invest in which instrument.

If you want to become one of the SLYly smiling investors who is willing to do a little research, think about what you are doing, and earn higher returns in the process, then you are ready to read Chapter 9 on Super-SLY money market investing.

Rip Van Winkles or speculators need not apply, but Sophie is always welcome to join the ranks of our friends.

"Get Rich Quick" Richard and "Sounds Good to Me" Sam —The Stockbroker's Delights

Richard and Sam are two of my favorite characters.

Rich is a sucker for a good investment story. He will invest in anything that "someone says" is a good deal. He has always "heard about it somewhere" when you ask him about his latest stock purchase. To hear him tell it, he heard someone made a killing on this stock or that one. He would have made millions if he could have invested in it last year. He seems to want to make cocktail conversation, not money. In fact, I overheard his stockbroker, who needed to make some money to pay for his vacation, say (to his compatriot, who asked where he was going to find the money), "Get Rich quick. He'll buy anything."

Sam is another case. If Rich buys it, Sam buys it, he thinks. Actually he buys "something just like it" from Rich's stockbroker. In fact, he buys something from Rich's stockbroker every time he calls because he thinks Rich is rich. Actually, Rich just owes a lot of money.

Rich is an excellent example of someone to whom a little information can be very dangerous. Sam is someone who never seems to understand any information. He just trusts his banker or stockbroker to "do the right thing" for him.

Neither has yet figured out that Sophie's sister, Super-SLYC Sallie, is the real winner in this race.

Super-SLYC Sallie's Simple Secret

Sallie is someone we should all admire. She is the model of the assertive liberated woman (of course, a man could figure this out too). Sallie never studied finance at Harvard, she never seems to get a "hot tip" from "the boys downtown," she never gets last-minute calls from her broker about the "last chance" to get in on the latest tax-sheltered deal, and she doesn't even know where to find the latest copy of the *Wall Street Journal, Barron*'s, or investment guru Joe Granville's latest forecasts of bull markets and earthquakes.

A while ago, Sallie found out about no-load mutual funds. No-load mutual funds fit Sallie's lifestyle. There are no pushy salespeople, no sales commissions (loads) to pay, and no investment secrets or "hot tips" about which only "the boys downtown" know. What there is are professionally managed investment pools that are open to everybody who wants to join, public performance track records, easy, convenient investment services to get your money in and out of the funds, friendly well-educated customer service people on the telephone to help you at every turn (except giving you investment advice), and fully detailed regular statements so you know what is happening to your investments.

One of the things Sallie likes best is that she can watch the value of her investments grow simply by reading the morning paper, and if the stock market is taking a nosedive all she has to do is make a tollfree telephone call and move her investments back into the shelter of her money fund account.

It sounds good, doesn't it? Well, folks, it *is* simple, but you do need to know the rules and have a strategy. There is some risk involved, but if you are willing to trade some short-term risk for long-term profits, if you are willing to pay attention to your investments and manage your money as you try to manage your life, and if you are willing to take responsibility for your own finances, you can make your money find more money for you to invest.

How much more? How does a five-year track record of an average annual rate of over 20 percent sound? You will never get that much even by using the Super-SLY system. You need to be Super-SLYC and a Patriotic Investor at the same time.

Super-SLYC investors who want to learn how to get high long-term returns with the minimum of hassle should turn to Chapter 10 to read about the newly revamped SLYC investment strategy—Super-SLYC.

Patriotic Investing, on the other hand, is designed to allow you to keep more of your hard-won investment returns. You see, if we pay unnecessary and excess taxes (and many of us do) we are giving Congress more money to spend. If you give Congress a dollar they will likely spend a dollar and a half. That is inflationary, and inflation is *un-American*. So avoiding taxes is patriotic and profitable.

Which Type of Investor Are You?

Did you recognize yourself? Are you a Rip Van Winkle, Sophie the Sensible Saver, "Get Rich Quick" Rich, or "Sounds Good to Me" Sam? Or are you a Super-SLY Rocky or a Super-SLYC Sallie? If you want to become a Patriotic Investor like Rocky and Sallie, read on.

The "eye of the tiger (or tigress)" is all you need to become an assertive investor and grow rich through simple, systematic thrift.

A Short Quiz

If you're still not sure what kind of investor you are, answer the following questions as honestly as you can:

1. Do you genuinely want to be rich and live a fuller and more comfortable life?
2. Are you willing to accept the risk that your investment plan might turn out badly and you might have to give up a few goals in life because of losses?
3. Can you make a plan and stick with it?
4. Can you accept occasional temporary setbacks without losing sleep?
5. Can you read a few well-selected books and try to understand the investment world?
6. Can you keep a cool head and a clear eye on your goals when an investment loses money?

If you can answer "Yes" to five or six of these questions, you're well on your way to becoming an assertive, successful Super-SLYC investor. If you answered "Yes" to three or four, you should seriously consider the Super-SLYC strategy. Not only is assertive investing likely to make much more money for you in the long run, but it's better for America: The nation needs people who are willing to take reasonable risks.

If, on the other hand, you answered "Yes" to only one or two questions, you'd better stick to Super-SLY investments for now. You may never get truly rich, but I'll show you how to build up a nice cushion against poverty.

Whether you decide you are a Super-SLY or Super-SLYC investor—or even if you feel you can't tell yet—you now know enough about financial management and investing to do some creative dreaming and goal setting.

How would you like to live the rest of your life? What are "musts" (money for your kids' education, a decent amount put aside for retirement)? What goals, if any, will you take risks for? The riskiest approach to investment is *not* to have any well-defined approach. For yourself and your family, you've *got* to define what you want out of life and what risks you're willing to take to achieve it.

Start by making a list of the major purchases and other big expenses you want to be able to meet between now and age seventy. Also, how much do you want to have accumulated by that age for your golden years and to pass along to your heirs?

Ignore inflation in these calculations for now. Inflation varies enormously from year to year, and money market yields tend to compensate for inflation because they are high when inflation is high. We'll also try to compensate for inflation below by projecting "real"—that is, after inflation—investment yields.

Don't worry about neatness or even practicality as you compile your list of big expenses. You're dreaming now—you can bring the dreams into line with reality later.

Your lists should include your children's education, the down payment on a house, trips to places you want to visit, and such purchases as expensive new cars and a boat. Also estimate the assets you'd like to possess one year, three years, five years, ten years from now, and at retirement.

Now You Can Set Financial Goals

Can your dreams be translated into realistic goals? Start by adding up how much you need over the next year for major purchases. Then ask yourself how much wealth you would like to have on hand one year from today. If you divide the sum of those two amounts by 13 (allowing some room for earnings), you have a good approximation of how much you should be putting into your money fund account every month.

What's the right amount of wealth to try to accumulate over the next year? Well, you can expect investment income as well as your savings to help you meet your longer-term goals. Assuming only the expected returns from a very cautious Super-SLY investment program, and allowing for inflation and taxes, a good set of assumptions is that your one-year wealth-accumulation goals should be:

- About one-fourth of the sum of the major purchases you want to make each year and the amount of wealth you want on hand after three years
- About one-seventh of the major purchases you want to make each year and the amount of wealth you want on hand after five years
- About one-eighteenth of the major purchases you want to make each year and the amount of wealth you want on hand after ten years

If you're going to adopt a more assertive Super-SLYC investment program, you should figure out which of your goals you're willing to take risks for and which you're not. You should be putting aside enough so that you'll cover the "musts" even if you achieve investment yields a bit less than the SLYC investor expects. But for the goals you honestly could give up, you can assume a much higher investment yield and thus begin putting aside significantly less.

The Far Future: Your Children and Your Retirement

You should also set financial goals for your children's education and, if you're close enough to start working on it, for your retirement. You can count on a higher return on money invested in your children's trust accounts because they won't have to pay much in current taxes and in your Individual Retirement Accounts because you won't pay taxes on the investment income until you begin to draw on it, at which point you'll probably be in a lower tax bracket.

Retirement planning can be complex, but a good rule of thumb is to put aside enough so that with Social Security, pensions, and income from your investments you will receive 60–80 percent of your preretirement income. Your local Social Security office and your company can tell you how much to expect from Social Security and pensions. Then you'll know how much you need to accumulate to have a nest egg sufficient to give you the income you need in addition to Social Security and pensions. Begin depositing in your retirement plan immediately to build that nest egg.

What's Really Important to You?

As you think about a lifetime investment plan, and as you look for money to invest, keep asking one key question: "How do I want to spend the rest of my life?" With a lifetime savings and investment plan built around the right tools and a realistic assessment of your needs, chances are you can meet most of your goals. Without one, life just won't be the satisfying experience that it could be.

Filling Your Financial Tool Kit

Now that you've figured out what kind of investor you are, and what some of your goals are as well, you'll need just a few tools to launch you on your way:

1. The *right* kind of bank checking account
2. The *right* kind of money market mutual fund account
3. The *right* kind of major credit card
4. The *right* kind of retirement plan
5. The *right* kind of trust accounts for your children

Tool 1: Looking for Mr. Goodbank

The first place to look for money to invest is in your checkbook. Now, don't get offended. I know what you're thinking: "I don't have any money in my checkbook, Bill. That's why I bought this book." But if you look a little closer, you might find that there's money to invest in even the most closely balanced checkbook.

How much money passes through your hands in a year? $15,000?

$30,000? More? Well, if you're not earning a market rate of interest on all of that money—even the money that's only in your account overnight—then you're losing money that you could use to invest.

You could be losing a few hundred dollars a year—not enough to let you retire a millionaire, but enough to make a big difference in the long run if it were properly invested. The problem is that it's harder than it appears to get a fair rate of return from either a bank or a "thrift institution" (that is, a mutual savings bank, savings and loan association, or credit union).

Your first step to tapping the cash in your cash flow is finding a low-cost (or better yet, free) checking account. I'll tell you how it can earn money market interest. But for now, we'll look for the best type of checking account.

NOW Accounts: See You Later. One choice from your bank is a NOW account, which is actually a cross between a passbook savings account and a checking account. The NOW stands for Negotiable Order of Withdrawal, which means, technically, that the check you write is a withdrawal slip from a savings account.

The negotiable part stands for the ability to negotiate or transfer ownership of the "checks" by endorsing them on the back. (The reason NOWs are offered is that it's still illegal for a bank to pay you interest on an ordinary checking account—but Congress may soon change that.)

The best feature of a NOW account is also its worst feature. With a NOW account, you can get interest on your checking—a whole 5.25 percent. If that sounds good to you, think again. With an inflation rate of 6 percent or higher expected this year, you still look almost as dumb as Aunt Agatha, who keeps her money in a mattress.

The deal gets even worse if your bank charges you transaction fees. At, say, twenty cents per check, your earnings on your savings start looking pretty small pretty quickly. What's worse, some banks require you to keep as much as $1,000 just to earn a piddling 5.25 percent on your NOW account. Is the amount of money you tie up worth such a rotten rate of return? Of course not. So stay away from the NOW account.

One final warning about NOW accounts that few people know about. In order to qualify as a savings account rather than as a checking account, there must be a provision for the bank to place a hold on your money. Banks and thrifts reserve the right (but are highly unlikely to exercise it) to refuse to pay your NOW "checks" for up to fourteen days. How would your landlord like that one?

When Is "Super" Not So "Super"? When It's a Super NOW. Your bank also offers something called a Super NOW account, which will pay you an alleged money market rate of interest. Sound good? Well, in most cases it isn't. Why? Because Super NOWs offer generally lousy rates. In addition, most Super NOWs have hidden service charges, and tax surprises.

What was supposed to make a Super NOW account better than a regular NOW account? A Super NOW account doesn't have a maximum interest rate ceiling, although you must keep a minimum balance of at least $1,000 to earn the full rate. When the federal regulators authorized this account, they reasoned that banks would offer high rates to draw new deposits to their banks.

Unfortunately, most banks and thrift institutions find it hard to make a profit on the Super NOW account when they pay a genuinely competitive return. Checking accounts are expensive to operate. Some banks simply don't offer Super NOW accounts because they can be so costly. Many banks that do offer the account trim their costs by paying less than money market rates or by other annoying tricks.

You see, banks and thrifts aren't required to pay you the actual money market value of your money—they are *allowed* to but they are not *required* to. They can pay you any rate they want and they are allowed to call it a "money market rate."

What this means to you is that Super NOW accounts pay, on the average, about 2 percentage points less than other investments that are just as liquid. Don't worry—we'll get to the good ones in a moment.

As If That Weren't Bad Enough. You're in for another shock if you don't get free checking on your Super NOW account. Watch what happens to the net return on a Super NOW with a twenty-cent fee per check, assuming that twenty checks are written per month: If the account had an average balance of $3,000 at an annual rate of 8 percent, the gross interest earned would be $20 per month. Thirty checks in one month at twenty cents each will cost you $6, leaving $14 of earned interest for that month or an effective interest rate of 5.6 percent.

As if the service charges weren't enough, the government taxes the interest on Super NOW accounts as well. The interest on Super NOW accounts is fully taxable as income. Because individuals may not deduct their bank's service charges on their income tax return, you get taxed on the full interest without being able to deduct the money paid for service charges. That's like burning up your money and paying taxes on the ashes. (See Table 3 for selected pricing on three types of checking.)

Money Market Deposit Accounts. Another little offering from the banks is the Money Market Deposit Account (MMDA). Some of these accounts can be a good deal for some people. With $1,000 at most banks, you can open an MMDA, which, like the Super NOW, has no interest rate ceiling. You can also write three checks per month. If you don't need many checks, and want the safety of federal deposit insurance, an MMDA can be worthwhile.

You have to keep an eye on some of your MMDAs, however. Sometimes banks introduce MMDAs with great fanfare, paying whopping interest rates, then gradually let their rates slip down as their customers' attention drifts away from the money they've deposited. Sound unbelievable? It happened when these new accounts first came on the scene, and it could happen again.

Where's the Beef?—Knowing What's Fair Can Help You Avoid Having One. How do you find out whether you're getting a fair market rate from one of these new deregulated bank accounts? Well, one of the best ways is to look in your local paper for Donoghue's Money Fund Table, an essential source of information for anyone interested in the money market. (See Figure 1.) You can find it every week in most leading newspapers (or at least sixty-five of them). Look for it on Thursdays, although some run it later. If you have any trouble finding it in your newspaper, it's also in *Barron's,* the national financial weekly, every Saturday.

At any rate, look for the figure at the bottom of the table that gives the average yield for all taxable money market funds.

If your bank is offering at least as much as the average taxable money fund for its MMDA, well, that's not too bad. It's above average for an MMDA (most banks average 1.25 percentage points less on their MMDAs). If your bank is offering more, great. But keep an eye on your MMDA. Remember, banking rules are set up for the benefit of the bank, not for you—so approach any MMDA warily, and be prepared to drop it like a hand grenade if the rates fall much below Donoghue's Money Fund Average.

The Best Bet for Most People. By this time, you must be getting discouraged. It seems that every checking account that banks or thrift institutions offer has some way of keeping you from getting a fair rate of return. Fortunately, there is a better way—although it may surprise you.

I think most people should look for a free checking account at a bank or thrift institution which requires a low minimum balance and won't charge outrageous fees if you accidentally slip below the minimum. Shop around a bit, you can probably find one.

Banks' promotions about "interest on checking" and "money market rates" usually just create diversions to disguise the fact that, over the long haul, they won't offer the best returns. So just find a free checking account which requires a low minimum balance. Check out the level of fees for special services.

Now, finding a good, low-minimum, free checking account is just the first

Table 3 Selected Pricing on Three Types of Checking

Institution	Non-Interest-Bearing Checking	NOW	Super NOW
Bank of New England, Boston	Any opening amount. $2/mo. + 15¢/check if bal. below $300 (may combine with savings)	Any amount to $2/mo. + 15¢/check below $500 (may combine with savings)	8.10% $2/mo. + 15¢/check + 25¢/deposit. 7¢/check over 5. 5¼% below
Citytrust, Bridgeport, Conn.	$10 to open. $5/mo. per statement. $5/mo. if bal. below $1,000 + 25¢/check. $25/overdraft. F: Waived w/min. $1,500 in savings (may combine w/savings).	$1,500 to open. $5/mo. + 25¢/check below $1,500. F: Waived w/$1,500 savings.	7.00%. $6/mo. + 25¢/check for $1–$2,499; $3/mo. + 25¢/check for $2,500–$4,999; 25¢/check for $5,000–$9,999
First National Bank of Mobile, Alabama	$50 to open. $6.50/mo. for $0–$199; $5.50/mo. for $200–$299; $4.50/mo. for $300–$399; $3.50/mo. for $400–$499;	N.A.	8.35%. $1,000–$1,499: 20¢/check to max. of $5; $500–$999, $3/mo. + 20¢/check to max. of $7; $500 or less, reverts to regular checking with no interest
Commerce Union Bank, Nashville, Tenn.	$100 to open. $5/mo. if below $500. 10¢/check over 20	$100 to open. $6/mo. if below $2,000. 10¢/check over 20	6.75%. "Relationship banking": Fees based on balances in other accounts, but charged to this account. $1,000–$4,999—$6/mo. + 10¢/check over 20; under $1,000 or with no other accounts—$8/mo. + 20¢/check over 20. "Free" checks, no fees on MasterCard or Visa, etc

National City Bank, Cleveland	Any opening amount. $2/mo. maint. fee + 25¢/check paid + 25¢/deposit. 15¢/electronic debit + credit	No minimum. $5/mo. maint. fee; same debit + credit charges as reg. checking. Fees waived w/$1,000 min. or $1,200 avg. monthly bal. or $2,000 in savings	6.85%. $5/mo. maint. fee; same debit + credit charges as reg. checking. Fees waived if $2,500 avg. monthly bal., or $2,500 in savings
Lincoln National Bank & Trust, Ft. Wayne, Ind.	$50 to open. $400 above—no service charge; below $400, $3/mo.; below $200, $3/mo. + 10¢/check	$1,500, or $2,500 in savings, to open. $7.50/mo. if either account below $1,500 or $2,500, respectively	6.35%. 5¼% if bal. below $2,500. $10/mo. if below $1,500; $5/mo. if $1,500–$34,999; no charge if $35,000 above
American Fletcher National Bank, Indianapolis	$25 to open. No charge if $500 on deposit or if the avg. monthly bal. is $1,000. Charge based on min. bal. and number/checks written per statement cycle. F: 12¢/check or other debits. "Electronicheck": $25 to open, 15¢/check or other debit, $1.25/statement period	N.A.	6.80%. $6/mo. + 15¢/check if bal. below $999 during statement cycle.
First Indiana Federal S&L, Indianapolis	N.A.	$1 to open. $5/mo. if avg. bal. below $500	8.10%. No charges
First Texas Savings Association, Dallas	$200 to open. $4/mo. if daily bal. below $500, or if avg. bal. below $750, at customer's option. 25¢/check	N.A.	7.50% 7.75%—$10,000–$24,999. 8.00%—$25,000–$49,999. 8.25%—$50,000 above

Unless otherwise specified, the Super NOW minimum required balance was $2,500, and below that the rate reverts to 5¼%.
Source: Bank Rate Monitor, Miami Beach, FL 33140, April 2, 1984.

Money Market Mutual Funds

Money Funds with assets of $100 million or more that are available to individual investors.
For the week ended June 20, 1984

Fund	Assets ($ million)	Average Maturity (Days)	7-day Average Yield (%)	30-day Average Yield (%)	Fund	Assets ($ million)	Average Maturity (Days)	7-day Average Yield (%)	30-day Average Yield (%)
AARP U.S. Gov't M.M.T.	3,067.5	41	9.6	9.3	Mass Cash Management Trust	764.2	30	10.1	10.0
Alex. Brown Prime	600.8	29	10.2	10.1	McDonald Money Market	143.7	44	9.8	9.7
Alliance Group					Merrill Lynch				
Capital Reserves	807.0	35	9.8	9.7	CMA Gov't Securities	1,400.1	45	9.2	9.5
Gov't Reserves	163.2	37	9.3	9.1	CMA Money Fund	13,360.8	44	9.6	10.1
American Capital Reserve	392.4	17	10.4	10.1	Gov't	1,394.4	45	9.7	9.8
Boston Company Cash Mgt	222.7	34	10.2	10.0	Institutional	977.9	36	10.6	10.2
Bull & Bear Dollar Reserves	103.4	14	9.9	9.8	Ready Assets	11,226.7	48	9.5	10.0
Capital Cash Mgt Trust	120.3	16	10.3	10.2	Ret. Res. M.F. (r)	1,293.6	34	9.6	10.0
Capital Preservation	1,646.7	36	9.2	9.2	USA Gov't Res.	132.2	45	9.2	9.8
Capital Preservation Fund II	586.8	2	9.8	9.4	Midwest Income ST Gov't	151.3	24	9.6	9.3
Cardinal Gov't Securities	335.7	24	10.4	10.1	Money Market Instruments	188.3	25	9.6	9.3
Carnegie Gov't Sec Trust	169.9	20	9.9	9.7	Money Market Management	266.9	35	10.0	9.8
Cash Equivalent Fund	3,945.3	29	10.4	10.2	Mutual of Omaha M.M.A.	269.2	36	10.0	9.8
Cash Equivalent Gov't Only	433.5	22	10.0	9.8	NEL Cash Management Trust	727.4	30	10.4	10.2
Cash Management Trust	662.8	17	10.2	10.4	NLR Cash Portfolio	1,382.5	33	10.2	10.0
Centennial Money Mkt Trust	182.2	23	9.9	9.9	Nationwide M.M.F.	415.8	35	10.1	10.1
Columbia Daily Income	460.8	26	9.8	9.7	Oppenheimer M.M.F., Inc.	1,409.5	27	10.1	10.1
Composite Cash Mgt Co.	150.1	30	10.0	9.7	Oxford Cash Management	101.9	27	10.4	10.1
Current Interest M.M.F.	742.7	41	9.6	9.5	Paine Webber				
Daily Cash Accumulation	2,931.0	24	10.0	9.9	CASHFUND	4,023.5	39	10.2	10.0
Daily Income	469.2	36	10.0	9.8	RMA M.F.-M.M. Port.	775.9	39	10.3	10.1
Dean Witter					RMA M.F.-U.S. Gov't	136.1	41	9.8	9.5
Active Assets Gov't Sec.	119.5	38	9.6	9.5	Parkway Cash Fund, Inc.	360.6	30	10.1	9.9
Active Assets MT	1,483.6	42	10.2	10.1	Prime Cash Fund	128.3	27	10.3	10.1
Sears Liq. Asset	5,608.6	42	10.2	10.2	Prudential-Bache Securities				
Sears U.S. Gov't M.M.T.	328.6	39	9.5	9.4	Command Money Fund	765.9	29	10.4	10.3
Delaware Cash Reserve	1,434.4	32	10.3	10.1	MoneyMart Assets	2,949.0	27	10.5	10.5
Drexel Burnham Lambert, Inc.					Gov't Sec. Trust	205.9	28	9.9	9.8
Cash Fund Gov't Sec. Port.	183.1	39	9.9	9.5	Putnam Daily Dividend Trust	276.8	38	10.2	10.0
Cash Fund M.M. Portfolio	933.9	41	10.1	10.0	Reserve Fund - Gov't	271.3	9	9.7	9.4
Dreyfus					Reserve Fund - Primary	1,740.2	40	10.1	9.9
Liquid Assets	7,795.9	57	10.3	10.1	Rothschild Earnings & Liq.	320.2	37	10.1	10.0
M.M. Instruments Gov't	885.8	63	9.8	9.5	Scudder				
ED Jones Daily Passport	529.3	39	10.0	9.7	Cash Investment Trust	1,001.3	30	10.0	9.9
Eaton Vance Cash Mgt Fund	190.5	25	10.1	10.0	Gov't Money Fund	130.3	38	9.6	9.6
Equitable Money Mkt Account	253.8	34	10.1	9.8	Seligman C.M. Fund Prime	444.5	20	10.4	10.1
Fahnestock Daily Income	122.6	36	9.9	9.7	Shearson Lehman-Amex				
Fidelity Group					FedFund	1,341.7	34	10.1	9.9
Cash Reserves	4,024.5	35	10.2	10.1	Daily Dividend	3,608.5	14	10.6	10.1
Daily Income	2,682.3	34	10.1	10.0	FMA Cash	662.0	15	10.5	10.1
U.S. Gov't Res.	374.5	33	9.8	9.4	FMA Government	112.1	27	9.6	9.3
Financial Daily Income	244.3	28	10.5	10.4	Gov't & Agencies	935.7	29	9.9	9.5
First Investors Cash Mgt	356.8	24	10.2	10.1	T-Fund	957.2	32	10.2	9.8
1st Variable Rate	618.5	15*	10.0	9.9	TempFund	4,244.3	30	10.6	10.3
Franklin Federal M.F.	140.2	3	10.1	9.3	Short Term Income Fund	241.4	34	9.9	9.8
Franklin Money Fund	921.1	27	9.7	9.8	Standby Reserve Fund, Inc.	223.5	26	10.2	10.1
Fund-Gov't Investors	984.6	40	9.8	9.7	SteinRoe Cash Reserves	966.8	32	10.3	10.1
General Money Market Fund	214.5	77	10.0	9.8	Summit Cash Res.	421.7	43	9.8	10.2
Government Investors Trust	322.8	20	10.1	9.9	T. Rowe Price				
Gradison Cash Reserves	411.8	28	10.0	9.8	Prime Reserve	2,922.8	30	10.2	10.1
Hilliard Lyons Gov't Fund, Inc.	114.8	18	9.9	9.5	U.S. Treas. M.F.	166.8	38	9.8	9.3
Hutton, E.F.					Transamerica Cash Reserve	372.1	21	10.6	10.3
Cash Reserve Management	4,180.9	37	10.6	10.3	Trinity Liquid Assets Trust	242.9	18	10.5	10.3
AMA Cash Fund	897.2	34	10.4	10.1	Trust-Cash Reserves	148.1	43	9.9	9.6
Gov't Fund	817.9	37	10.2	9.8	Tucker Anthony Cash Mgt	335.4	33	10.1	9.9
IDS Cash Management	938.0	41	10.3	10.2	USAA Money Market Fund	223.5	38	10.5	10.3
John Hancock Cash Mgt	383.2	26	9.8	9.7	United Cash Management	347.4	43	10.1	9.9
Kemper Money Market	4,032.0	29	10.6	10.4	Value Line Cash Fund	542.1	26	10.2	10.2
Keystone Liquid Trust	313.6	25	9.9	9.7	Vanguard M.M.T. Federal	425.4	34	10.0	9.9
Kidder Peabody Premium	245.0	38	10.3	10.1	Vanguard M.M.T. Prime	1,310.8	35	10.6	10.3
Legg Mason Cash Res. Trust	188.3	34	9.9	9.6	Vantage Cash M.M.F.	157.8	34	10.2	10.1
Lehman Cash Management	970.2	25	10.5	10.3	Webster Cash Reserve	1,126.6	36	10.3	10.1
Lehman Gov't Fund, Inc.	355.6	6	10.2	10.0	Donoghue's Money Fund Average				
Lexington Money Market	229.3	57	10.2	10.0	(Averages for all 256 taxable funds)				
Liquid Capital Income	1,305.7	18	10.1	10.1			36	10.00	9.79
Liquid Green Trust	155.9	35	10.1	10.0					
Lord Abbett Cash Reserve	218.7	36	10.1	9.9					
Lutheran Brotherhood MMF (r)	460.4	39	10.2	9.9					
Mariner									
Cash Mgt Fund	193.7	17	10.4	10.3					
Gov't Fund	130.4	5	10.3	9.9					
U.S. Treasury	101.9	3	10.2	9.7					

Yields represent annualized total return to shareholders for past seven- and 30-day period. Past returns not necessarily indicative of future yields.
* Average term to next rate adjustment date.
(r) Restricted availability.
Source: Donoghue's Money Fund Report, Holliston, Mass. 01746
© 1984 by the Tribune Company Syndicate Inc.

Figure 1. Donoghue's money market mutual table. *(Source: Donoghue's Money Fund Report)*

step in getting cash out of your cash flow. For the second step, you'll need our second tool—a money market mutual fund.

Tool 2: Money Market Mutual Funds

When you put your money into a bank, the bank lends it out—to home buyers, consumers, corporations, other banks, the government, and even other countries. Even money that the bank has for only one day (such as large parts of your paycheck) is loaned out overnight. This lending of short-term money makes up much of the "money market."

Until a few years ago only banks, large corporations, and very wealthy individuals could use the money market. But thanks to money market mutual funds, you too can earn interest on your money every day without sacrificing safety, yield, or the use of your money when you need it and without paying excessive service charges.

This new market for your money is what I call the retail money market—the money market that is available to all savers and investors, even those with only small amounts to invest.

Lending Your Money at Retail. In the retail money market, the price for the use of your money—that is, the interest rate you are paid—changes every day, depending on such factors as the way the government is managing the economy, the federal deficit, and borrowers' needs for money. But whatever the current price of money, it's probably more than you're getting from your bank.

How much is your money worth? Take a look at Table 4. That was what money was worth on that day. Today you will find different rates.

The problem with many of these money market investments is that you must tie up your money for a period of time. But with two of the investments listed below, the money market mutual fund (money funds) and the MMDA,

Table 4   Current Interest Rates for Short-Term Money Market Instruments

Friday, June 15, 1984	Rate (percent)
Money market mutual funds	9.87
3-month Treasury bills	10.07
6-month Treasury bills	10.66
Money market deposit accounts	9.00
6-month bank and thrift certificates of deposit	10.34
1-year bank and thrift certificates of deposit	10.64
2½-year bank and thrift certificates of deposit	11.02
5-year bank and thrift certificates of deposit	11.46

you can make money from the money that passes through your hands. That means your cash flow will generate a significant investment yield—even if you have no regular savings program at all.

So What's a Money Fund? If you've read any of my previous books—or even if you've been paying close attention through the first few pages of this one—you know how I feel about money funds. I love them. And if you want a full, detailed explanation of them you'll have to read my first book, *William E. Donoghue's Complete Money Market Guide.* Here, however, is a quick rundown of what money funds are and how they can help you get your money's worth from the money you use to pay your bills.

A money fund is a mutual fund that pools funds from many investors and invests them exclusively in short-term loans to the U.S. government and to the largest and safest banks and corporations in the world. Most funds' charters let them invest only in Treasury bills, commercial bank certificates of deposit, and top-rated short-term investments such as bankers' acceptances and commercial paper.

What Do Money Funds Do with Your Money? Because money funds invest in such high-quality investments, they are extremely safe. Money funds are also highly diversified, which spreads the low risks even thinner. The Securities and Exchange Commission (SEC), which regulates money funds, requires that for the first 75 percent of their assets they cannot invest more than 5 percent of total assets in the obligations of any single issuer other than the government. Nearly all funds limit their nongovernment securities investments even more strictly than the SEC requirements.

A Clean Track Record Makes Insurance Unnecessary. While money funds are not insured by federal deposit insurance, it's hard to imagine how you could lose money in one. Money funds have a track record that the banking system doesn't have: No one has ever lost money in a modern money fund.

Bankers must envy that track record. Hundreds of credit unions, banks, and thrifts have failed in recent years, and hundreds of other credit unions, banks, and thrifts have owned CDs of those that failed. Not one money fund has ever invested in any money market instrument that didn't pay off at maturity. Give me a money fund anytime.

All This and Liquidity, Too. Aside from their safety, money funds also boast liquidity. Now, a liquid investment is usually defined as one that can be converted into cash within thirty days. But money funds are so liquid that you can convert your shares into cash by simply writing a check or having the fund transfer all or part of your money directly to your bank. On some funds you can even write a check for as little as $1, and the checks are usually free of charge. Further, no one will give you any grief about cashing a money fund check—after all, it is really a check on the money fund's bank account. Banks have given up trying to make you think a money fund check is different.

What this means to you is that you can use your money fund account in much the same way as you would a bank account. The main difference is that you'll earn a fair market rate of interest on every cent you send to your money fund—without having to tie up your money.

Table 5 lists the money funds which permit check-writing of $100 or less.

Banks seem to set interest rates in ways deliberately designed to confuse you. Money market funds, on the other hand, pay investors all the income the funds' portfolios earn, after subtracting only a small fee—usually about 0.5 percent per year—for management and administrative expenses.

In short, then, a money fund is what I call a SLY investment: you get Safety, Liquidity, and Yield. Best of all, you can start a money fund account at several money funds for less than $500. In fact, a few money funds—First Trust Money Market Fund is one—have no minimum investment requirements, which means that you can open a money fund account for as little as $1.

An Easy Trick for Maximum Yields. Even if the money fund you select has a $100, $250, or larger minimum check size, you can still earn some easy money with a very simple maneuver.

Simply adjust your cash flow so that you pay your bills on one day of the month—preferably the last possible moment that won't impair your credit rating. Keep a small amount of money in a bank checking account, and deposit each paycheck directly to the money fund (or money market deposit account, if you've found one that gives you a good deal).

When you write the checks that will pay your bills each month, simply write a money fund check or MMDA check and deposit it in your ordinary bank checking account in time to clear before the checks you wrote to your creditors arrive. You'll find you earn high money-market interest on your paycheck for about 250 days a year.

When you've found Mr. Goodbank, you can keep a small amount of money in the checking account and earn a market rate of interest on the rest of your money in a money market mutual fund. You won't sacrifice safety or give up the convenience of a checking account.

Shifting money intelligently between bank and money fund may take some effort—from, say, a few hours a year to a few minutes to write a check. But if you learn to manage your money actively, you'll get the real value out of every dollar and be on the road to better saving and investing.

Table 5   Money Funds Allowing Check-Writing for $100 or less

Name of Money Fund	Minimum Check Amount	Initial Investment
American Express Money Fund	100	1,000
American Express Government Fund	100	1,000
Boston Company Advisors		
Boston Company Cash Management	100	1,000
Boston Company Government Money Fund	100	1,000
Boston Company Advisors		
Brown (R. C.) Money Market Fund	100	100
Brown (R. C.) & Co.		
CAM Fund	0	0
Consolidated Money		
Capital Preservation	0	1,000
Capital Preservation Fund II	0	5,000
Benham Management Corp.		
Carnegie Government Securities Trust	100	1,000
Carnegie Management Corp.		
Daily Dollar Reserves	0	5,000
Reich & Tang, Inc.		
First Trust MMF (general purpose)	0	0
First Trust MMF (government portfolio)	0	0
Principal Protection Adv. Services		
Franklin Federal Money Fund	100	500
Franklin Money Fund	100	500
Franklin Distributors, Inc.		
GIT Cash Trust Government	0	1,000
GIT Cash Trust Regular	0	1,000
Bankers Finance Investment Management		
Lexington Government, Securities MMF	100	1,000
Lexington Money Market Trust	100	1,000
Lexington Management Corp.		
Liquid Capital Income Trust	100	1,000
Carnegie Capital Management Co.		
Liquid Green Trust	0	1,000
Unified Management Corp.		
Merrill Lynch Retirement Res. MF	0	0
Merrill Lynch Asset Management		
Midwest Income Cash Management	100	1,000
Midwest Income ST Government	100	1,000
Midwest Advisory Services		

Table 5 (Continued)

Name of Money Fund	Minimum Check Amount	Initial Investment
Reserve CPA Fund (government portfolio)	0	1,000
Reserve CPA Fund (primary portfolio)	0	1,000
Reserve Management Co.		
So. Farm Bureau Cash Fund	100	500
So. Farm Bureau Advisor, Inc.		
SteinRoe Cash Reserves	100	2,500
SteinRoe Government Reserves	100	2,500
Stein Roe & Farnham		

Source: Donoghue's Mutual Funds Almanac (15th ed.).

Which Money Fund Is Right for You? There are over 350 money funds in the United States. You're looking for one with:

- Check-writing privileges (with a check minimum as low as possible, preferably no minimum).
- Initial and subsequent investment minimums that are convenient for you.
- A check-a-month plan, if you have a hard time remembering to save, under which your money fund will automatically withdraw a specified amount from your checking account. (It saves you the monthly bother of sending a check, and it's cheaper than writing a check, too.)
- If you're a Super-SLYC investor, in stock or bond funds, you should look for a fund in a no-load mutual fund "family" that will let you switch your investment easily by telephone among several funds with different investment strategies and objectives.

Lots of funds meet these criteria. If you need a list, check Appendix 6 of this book or, for more information, see *Donoghue's Mutual Fund Almanac*— $23, including first-class shipping—available from the Donoghue Organization, Inc. (Box 540, Holliston, Mass. 01746, or by phone at 1-800-343-5413.)

Tool 3: A Major Credit Card

"I want to have some money handy for emergencies." That's a major reason many people cite for keeping an overstuffed checking account or a passbook savings account, two very poor investments.

Well, if you think about it a bit, there are few emergencies that you can't charge on your VISA, MasterCard, or American Express card. You can go into nearly any bank or thrift in the country and get a cash advance on any of those three cards. So if you get caught short in Shaky Flats, Iowa, you can get cash in an emergency.

It's much better to use your plastic money in an emergency and to keep that emergency money fully invested. If you have to use your credit card for a cash advance, you can pay off your bill quickly with the money in your money fund. In the meantime, you won't have lost a day's worth of interest.

Tool 4: Why You Need a Retirement Plan—Today

Uncle Sam has given individuals at least three lovely ways to put money aside for retirement—tax shelters so flexible and attractive that with a little creative thinking, you can use them for other savings goals as well.

Deduct Now and Pay Taxes Later—You Win Both Ways. All allow you to deduct the money you contribute from your taxable income as you put it aside for the future. And all of these plans allow you to defer taxes on the income that your savings earn, as well as your principal, until you decide to withdraw your money.

Tax Shelter's Secret Weapon—Compounding. More important, your tax-deferred retirement plan takes the money that you would have normally paid in taxes and invests it to your benefit. That "compounding on a pretax basis," as it is called, can turn your investments into an earnings dynamo.

For example, if your money were earning only 10 percent a year in a money fund and you could defer your taxes, your money would quadruple in fourteen years. On the other hand, if you paid, say, 35 percent in state and federal taxes each year your money would only *double* in the same period—hardly better than keeping pace with inflation.

Naturally, Uncle Sam levies penalty taxes if you take money from most tax shelter accounts before retirement. But if you leave the money in for about seven years, the tax benefits can exceed the penalty. See Appendix 5 to find out your specific breakeven point. Of course, the lower the rate you get, the longer it takes to get ahead.

So think carefully about these three types of retirement plans:

- "Salary Reduction Accounts" (SARAs), known as 401(k) plans to the financial world
- Keogh plans for the self-employed
- Individual Retirement Accounts (IRAs) for nearly everybody and in addition to 401(k)s and Keoghs

You need at least one. For most salaried people SARAs are probably best, but unfortunately your employer has to offer this one to take advantage of it.

SARAs are new, but many employers, including most of the largest employers, now offer them to their employees. Check with your boss and see if your company has one or is planning to set one up soon.

Keogh plans are best suited for most self-employed people. If you're not self-employed and your employer doesn't offer a SARA (and even if they do and you can afford both plans), you should set up Individual Retirement Accounts (IRAs) for yourself and your spouse right away. Call a no-load mutual fund family today and have them send you the proper forms.

Tool 5: Trust Accounts for Your Children

Are you saving for your children's education? You aren't putting that money in a 5.5 percent passbook savings account, are you? Or is the money simply mixed with your own savings?

Because kids have little or no taxable income and you can give them money freely without paying any significant gift taxes, it makes sense to get as much as possible into their names and onto their tax returns.

It also makes sense to invest their savings relatively assertively, since it will have so long to compound its earnings to build for the future. After all, with no planning, you were going to keep it in your name and pay a quarter or a third of the income to the government, weren't you? Why not invest at least as much as you were going to pay in taxes in an assertive investment? Treat it as "mad money"—you were mad enough to consider giving it away to the government, weren't you?

You will need special trust accounts for your kids, established in a money market fund or other good investment. Any family of no-load mutual funds or any bank can establish these accounts for you under the Uniform Gifts to Minors Act of the state where you live. In most cases, you can give your children up to $10,000 without paying gift taxes. Then the income from the investments will belong to your kids. If a child's total income for a year is less than $3,200, he or she will only have to pay a very small tax on it.

Keep in mind, however, that you are giving this money to your children and that your gift is irrevocable. If your child decides to spend his or her college money on fast cars and loose living, well, that's the way it goes.

Tools You Don't Need

If you develop the above tool kit right away, your investment program will be off to a terrific start. The biggest block in your way right now may be conflicting advice from people who want to sell you investing "tools" that you don't need: things like stockbrokers' services, shares in mutual funds that charge a fee when you buy or sell them, and life insurance policies which are supposed to be "long-term investments."

Stockbrokers Are Often Just Salespeople

Face it, many stockbrokers are not investment advisers but carefully trained salespeople whose goal in life is to sell to you what their firms want to sell. Many will pay little attention to small investors and try to direct them into investments that earn the broker the highest commissions whether or not they are appropriate for those investors.

If your stockbroker recommends a "load" mutual fund, one that will pay him 5.5–8.5 percent of your money before you invest, listen to him. Make notes of what he recommends and then go and find a no-load fund that is similar and buy that. If you feel guilty you have not paid him for his advice, send him flowers; you will feel better and save a lot of money.

A long-term investment program needs to be flexible and free of unnecessary fees and charges. A full-service stockbroker with full-service charges every time you buy or sell just cuts too much into your return to make sense.

Avoid stockbrokers and learn how to manage your money yourself. You invested in this book—you are well on your way to independence.

You Bet Your Life, but Will You Be There to Win?

Similarly, most whole life insurance policies sold door-to-door as investments will waste your money. Your premiums for the first several years could simply pay the salesperson's commission.

All this means that your investment tool kit can be small and simple but must be chosen wisely. If you rely too much on "professional" advice you'll be helping professionals to get rich, not getting rich yourself.

Pack Up Your Tool Kit, Hop on Your Ship of Savings, and Sail On

Take the advice of this book, however, and you'll be on your way to wealth.

Your basic investment tool kit should simply consist of a low minimum-balance checking account, an account at a money market mutual fund that belongs to a larger family of funds, and the right kind of retirement and children's trust accounts. Just set up these tools, deposit regularly in the money market fund, and then use the tools I'll show you in the rest of this book. You can be rich. It just takes time.

3

Liberate the Lemons: Spring-Cleaning Your Financial House

People never cease to amaze me. "Oh, Bill," they say, "why are you talking to me about investing? Where could I find money to invest? I don't even have enough to live on. Even if I did, I couldn't afford to tie up my money. And I have no idea what I'll do when I'm forced to retire." Then I ask them a few questions and I find they have plenty of unproductive assets that could give them money to invest.

Where? They have a pile of money in their checking and savings accounts, a stack of savings bonds and old life insurance policies they don't understand, and a ton of stuff in the attic that they should have sold years ago. What these folks need—in fact, what almost everybody needs—is *asset liberation*. Liberate those lemons and put 'em to work.

Rethinking, Reworking, and Retooling

Asset liberation demands that you think carefully about the use of your major assets and see whether each is making the fullest contribution to your lifestyle. If an asset isn't performing the way you'd like, then it should be liquidated (turned back into investable cash) and redeployed for your benefit.

As we grow older, most of us grow wiser and have second thoughts about what we once thought were great ideas: a summer home (a great idea for the kids but now a nuisance to keep up without their help), the boat (which you now seem to use much less), or that membership in "the club" that now seems too far away. It may well be time to sell off some assets or cut some expenses and rechannel them into what you really want now.

Asset liberation means discarding old adages that say that you should never withdraw from your savings account or borrow against your life insurance except in a dire emergency and that you must keep every gift anyone has ever given you over the last thirty years for fear of offending the givers.

In the next few pages you are going to see those outmoded investment ideas in a whole new light. Those sacred passbook savings accounts and some of those old insurance policies are the easiest sources of money and your keys to a new liberated life.

Build Yourself a Balance Sheet

Sometimes just a couple of hours of clear thinking can change your life. I certainly hope you feel that way about the time you are spending reading this book. That's why I wrote this book—to change your life for the better.

Investing a couple of hours taking a close look at your financial situation —without someone like your stockbroker or insurance agent looking over your shoulder—can pay off handsomely.

Let's See Where You Stand

My father always loved to sit down with me and say, "Let's see where you stand." Then we would go over my liabilities (I had more liabilities than assets back in those days) and my savings, and Dad would give me some ideas on how to improve my situation—which sometimes meant a small loan or contribution from him—if I would save some money myself. If I saved a little, Dad would make it worth a lot.

Now it's time for *you* to invest a few hours to "see where you stand." The best part of taking inventory of your assets is that once you have done it, you may only have to redo it once in a long while. Why? Because you get a good "feel" for your own priorities.

You'll discover what is valuable to you and what isn't. Keep in mind that we're not talking only dollars and cents here—some assets, such as a home, silver services, and china knicknacks, have a sentimental value that you simply can't put a price on. Some expensive items in your budget—such as traveling and hobbies—may give you more pleasure than watching that money grow in your savings.

But most people spend first and ask questions later. Now is the time to start asking yourself about your spending habits and about what is really important to you. Even if you consider yourself a prudent saver, the answers you find could well surprise you.

Once you know where you can do some fine tuning (or even gross adjustments) to your finances, you will know exactly where you can squeeze the most cash out of your system with the least effort. More important, you will start developing better financial habits, and many of the improvements you make will be permanent improvements.

Striking a Good Balance

The first step is to take an inventory of your assets and liabilities. Accountants call this preparing a balance sheet, since both sides of a balance sheet balance. Assets minus liabilities equal net worth. It can be a surprising experience to take a look at You, Inc. and find out how much you are really worth.

Only when we have a full list of assets and liabilities can we see how we can improve our situation. So let's get down to work and take a look at strategies to find money to invest.

Figure 2 shows what the balance sheet for You, Inc. might look like. Let's start by listing your assets. The length of the list may surprise you.

Liquid assets:
1. Cash on hand
2. Bank accounts
    Checking
    Savings
    Money market accounts
3. Stocks and bonds
4. Savings bonds
5. Company thrift plan accounts
6. Money market mutual fund accounts
7. Other mutual fund accounts
8. Cash value of life insurance and annuities
9. Other liquid investments
    Prepaid real estate taxes
    IRAs, Keoghs, and SARA accounts

Other assets:

10. Home and other real estate
11. Automobiles
12. Other "big ticket" items (boat, personal computer, etc.)
    Appliances
    Furniture
    Jewelry, furs, etc.
    Hobby equipment
    Sporting equipment
    Collectibles

You, Inc. Balance Sheet

	1	2			1	2
1 ASSETS:			1 LIABILITIES : $			
2			2			
3 Liquid Assets:			3 Current Liabilities:			
4 Cash on Hand			4			
5 Bank Accts.			5 Current Bills Due			
6 Checking			6 Credit Card Bills			
7 Saving			7 Real Estate Taxes			
8 Money Market			8 Income Taxes			
9 Mutual Funds:			9 Installment Loans			
10 Money Market			10 Other Short-term			
11 Other			11 Loans			
12 IRA, etc. (if over 59½)			12			
13 Stock			13 Total Current			
14 Bonds			14 Liabilities			$
15 Savings Bonds			15			
16 Other:			16 Long-term Liabilities:			
17			17			
18 Total Liquid Assets:		$	18 Mortgages			
19			19 Home Improvement			
20 Other Assets:			20 Loans			
21			21 Auto Loans			
22 Retirement Plans			22 Education Loans			
23 1. IRA			23 Other Long-term			
24 2. SARA			24 Loans:			
25 3.			25			
26 Automobiles			26 Total Long-Term			
27 Personal Property			27 Liabilities			$
28 1. Jewelry			28			
29 2. Furs			29			
30 3. Sporting Equip.			30 NET WORTH			$
31 4. Boat, Motorcycle,			31			
32 Bicycles, Mopeds			32			
33 5. Furniture			33			
34 6. Collectibles			34			
35 7. Other			35			
36 Money Owed to You			36			
37 Interest in Business			37			
38 Tax Refund			38			
39 Other:			39			
40 Total Other :		$	40			
TOTAL ASSETS:		$				

Figure 2. Balance sheet for You, Inc.

13. Money owed to you by others
14. Any interest in a business
15. Vested interest in a company retirement plan
16. Senior citizen's retirement accounts
17. Tax refunds due
18. Other personal property

Are You Richer than You Thought?

Keep putting your balance sheet together until you are satisfied it is fairly complete. Neatness and precision don't necessarilly count here. Do the best you can and feel free to total it up once in a while to get a ballpark idea of how you are doing.

Once you have it in fairly good condition, you can start analyzing which strategies you can apply to improve your situation. I'll bet when you're done, though, you'll find you have far more assets than you had suspected.

Let's work our way systematically down the list of assets first:

1. "Cash on Hand" That Most Folks Don't Count

When you counted your cash on hand, did you include traveler's checks and foreign currency left from your last vacation? If you didn't, go back and do it. Then take your traveler's checks back to the bank for an immediate, investable refund.

Did you know that traveler's check companies make their money primarily by investing the cash you give them between the time you buy the checks and the time you use them? Why should you let them invest your money when you could be investing it yourself at a profit?

If you're worried about paying a 1 percent fee again the next time you need traveler's checks, don't. In the first place, investing the cash in a money fund for as little as a month will probably pay you an investment yield equal to the money you might lose in fees. Second, some banks will sell you traveler's checks without a fee. So cash in your unused checks immediately, and shop around the next time you need traveler's checks.

Cashing in foreign currency is a bit more difficult than cashing in traveler's checks because many banks pay an uncompetitive rate for foreign cash. Many, especially small banks, must function merely as brokers when you cash in Mexican pesos or Indian rupees. They pass your foreign cash to another, larger bank, which in turn sells it to someone who needs it. Shop for the best rate at two or three large banks, and you can eliminate the middleman.

One way to obtain a competitive rate is to call the main office of Deak-Perera, the largest independent foreign currency dealer, in New York toll-free at 800-221-5700. You'll learn what Deak is paying for the amount of currency you want to sell, and the location of the Deak office nearest you.

2. Accounts You Can Bank On

As you know from reading Chapter 2, most checking accounts are unnecessarily expensive. For example, NOW accounts pay only 5.25 percent while Super NOWs earn less than real money funds and charge more for services. Passbook saving yields are much too low and should be liberated immediately. Money Market Deposit Accounts average less than real money funds, and bank IRAs require you to tie up your money and deny you access to the stock market when you want to invest.

3. Are You Stuck on Your Stocks?

Take a look at your stock, bond, and mutual fund portfolio. About each investment you once purchased in a moment of optimism or plenty, ask yourself: Is this still doing what I wanted it to? Did it ever?

Everyone makes investments because they expect them to increase in value. And everyone—even the hottest hotshot investment professionals—is wrong some of the time. Smart investors sell their mistakes quickly. In fact, the tax laws almost require that you take your losses within six months or you lose many of the tax benefits.

Once the momentum of a stock market starts moving against you, it seems to take a miracle to turn it around in the right direction. Too many investors, on the other hand, hold onto their losers "waiting to break even"—and wind up selling after the stock has plunged 20, 30, or 50 percent. If you take your losses, you can start earning them back immediately. If you don't, you usually get hurt more and it's harder to get any significant breaks from the IRS.

Some folks confuse loyalty to their employers with investment strategies. I don't care how nice your boss is. If your own company's stock is declining in value, sell it. Sometimes the best-managed companies are bad investments. Someone else will buy your shares and the company will survive.

Unless you have a good investment reason for holding a stock you bought years ago, sell it off and get into an investment of your choice. Chapters 9–11 will help you choose the right investments.

Paper Gold. Do you have any old stock certificates that your father or grandfather left lying about for years uncounted? Have them checked out. If the company—or its successor—is still in business, you could have a bonanza on your hands.

Even if the company has gone down the tubes, there's a lively trade in antique stock certificates—particularly if the stock has a valuable signature, such as J. P. Morgan's or Henry Ford's.

If you want to check out the value of an antique stock certificate, send a photocopy (not the original) to: R. M. Smythe, Inc., 24 Broadway, New York, N.Y. 10004. Smythe's service will cost you $20, but they'll tell you whether the certificate has any current value or any collector's value.

4. Don't Lose with Savings Bonds

Don't be surprised if You, Inc. is also sitting on a pile of old U.S. savings bonds —a stack of ludicrously wasted assets.

Old savings bonds are the absolute dogs of the investment world: When inflation was running at 10 percent, the government was issuing savings bonds paying a miserly 6.5 percent. I'm surprised officials at the Treasury Department could sleep at night knowing that they were ripping off the widows and orphans of the country.

Many of the old bonds stopped earning interest when they matured; and if you don't turn 'em in, your money is earning nothing.

Uncle Sam Has a Conscience After All. Apparently someone at the Treasury repented, however, because as of November 1982 the yields of series EE and outstanding series E bonds (issued after October 1947) and savings notes ("Freedom Shares") become market-based if the bond is held for five years or longer after November 1982. And if market rates drop to very low levels, the bonds have a guaranteed minimum yield of 7.5 percent if held for five or more years.

The "market-based" rate structure seems carefully designed to confuse intelligent people who may receive savings bonds as gifts or in some sort of company "thrift program." So hang onto your hats as I explain how the government figures out the "market rate."

Every six months, the Treasury computes the average market yield during the previous half year on Treasury securities being traded in the wholesale money market that have approximately five years remaining to maturity. The savings bond rate is then set at 85 percent of this market average. At the end of five years, the average of the ten semiannual rates, compounded on a semiannual basis, determines a bond's five-year yield. Got that?

To further complicate matters, bonds held less than five years will earn interest on a predetermined, graduated scale that increases from 5.5 percent for bonds held one year to 7.5 percent for bonds held five years. After forty years, however, they earn no interest at all. The same is true for old series E bonds, so if you have some old, old bonds kicking around you should cash them in quickly.

Reporting of interest, for federal income tax purposes, may be deferred until EE bonds are cashed or reach final maturity. They are exempt from state and local income and personal property taxes, but they are generally subject to state estate and inheritance taxes.

So what's the bottom line on savings bonds? They still probably won't earn the equivalent of the average yield of money funds. Generally, you shouldn't bother with them. They are too illiquid, you don't get the full interest rates unless you hold them to maturity, and the rates aren't really competitive. I know it's considered patriotic to buy savings bonds, but it's equally patriotic to invest in a money fund which buys Treasury bills—and a whole lot more profitable.

If you or your loved ones have bonds that have been hanging around for a few years, on the other hand, it may be worthwhile to keep them until they qualify for the "market-based rate" after five years.

Since the rate calculation process is so complex, the only way to find out whether cashing in a bond that you've held for a few years makes sense is to ask a smart, friendly banker, who can evaluate the alternatives with special tables prepared by the U.S. Treasury Department.

5. Company Thrift Plan Accounts, Money Fund Accounts, and Other Mutual Fund Accounts

For company thrift plan accounts, you might want to reread section 3 above, but in general, if it's not paying at least as much as the average money fund, you should drop it like a live hand grenade. If your boss asks you why, tell him. If he's a good businessman, he should be glad to have someone with your good business sense on his staff. Maybe he'll even improve the company plan to make participating worthwhile.

As for money fund and mutual fund accounts, read the rest of this book before you evaluate them. Right now, simply list them as assets.

6. Get the Whole Benefit from Whole Life

If you've never considered your old life insurance policies a source of money to invest, you've made a big mistake. A whole life insurance policy allows you to borrow against it freely, and borrowing against old whole life policies is the easiest source of cheap money you will ever find. What's more, it's your money you are borrowing. If you have a policy issued before 1972 you're holding a gold mine of cheap money. If you bought it after that it's still a good source.

You see, in most cases, you can borrow against a pre-1972 whole life policy and pay only 4 percent interest! The interest rate on a whole life "policy loan" was written into the policy when the policy was written. If you borrow against an old whole life policy today you can make money even if you put the borrowed money into a lousy 5.5 percent passbook savings account. But you won't do that—you'll invest the money at money market yields or better.

If you borrow $20,000 at 4 percent and average a mere 10 percent annual return, you can make $1,200 new money a year without taking any significant risk. Further, it's one loan you should *never* pay off.

If you haven't already borrowed against a pre-1972 whole life insurance policy, you may be one of the few people left in the world who hasn't. According to the National Life Insurance Association, pre-1972 whole life insurance policy holders have borrowed more than $50 million against their policies. So why are you waiting?

If you own a policy written between 1972 and 1980, you can probably get a loan rate of between 6 and 8 percent, which is still an exceptionally good deal. Borrow immediately and invest the proceeds. (See Figure 3 for loans taken out on whole life policies since 1973.)

What About the Insurance? Borrowing against your whole life insurance policy can actually increase your insurance. If you talk with your agent you will probably find that you can use the money to buy even greater insurance coverage.

On the other hand, if you just borrowed the money out of the policy and put it into a savings account or a money fund, you could still end up with greater insurance. For example, if you had a $100,000 policy on which you borrowed $20,000 (what you can borrow depends on how much you have paid into the policy, not the face value) and you died the next day, the insurance company would pay your beneficiaries $80,000 and you would already have $20,000 in your savings *plus* whatever it had earned. That's more than $100,000.

Even better, the interest you pay to the insurance company is fully tax-deductible, and you could even use the money to invest in your IRA or SARA, deduct the principal and interest, and tax-defer all of the income until you withdraw it.

See what I mean? This is a loan you will never want to repay. Don't feel sorry for the insurance company either. I'm sure they negotiated their half of the deal harder than you did. Now they can live with it. I never felt I took advantage of my insurance company when I signed the contract; did you?

7. Other Liquid Assets

Prepaid Real Estate Taxes. If your bank requires you to include a monthly payment of your real estate taxes with your mortgage payment, it may be time to reopen that issue. If they will release you from that requirement, which may

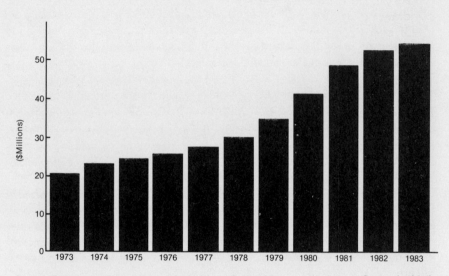

Figure 3. Loans taken out on whole life policies. (*Source:* American Council of Life Insurance)

be possible if you have made your mortgage payments dutifully for some time, then you can save that money yourself and invest it until it is due in an account which pays you—not the bank. Besides, as we will discuss later, this strategy may, in some cases, allow you to get the deduction for real estate taxes on your federal tax return a whole year sooner.

Is Today the Rainy Day You've Been Saving For? If you're over fifty-nine and a half, don't forget that your Individual Retirement Account or Keogh account should be listed on your balance sheet as a liquid asset. You can now withdraw money from your IRA or Keogh without penalty even if you haven't retired yet. You'll have to pay ordinary income taxes on the amount you withdraw, but that's true any time you take money from an IRA or Keogh.

Of course, if you're temporarily unemployed, you'll be in a lower tax bracket. While it's quite unlikely that you will face a lengthy bout of unemployment before you're ready to retire, it can happen. Tragically, it is people in their early sixties who are often the first to be fired and the last to be hired these days.

So, if you're over fifty-nine and a half and a financial emergency comes up, feel free to dip into your IRA or Keogh. If you get a job later on, you can start making contributions again, as long as that money is employment income. While you can't put in more than the maximum limits, you can contribute to your IRA or Keogh until you're seventy and a half.

If you're below the magic age when you can take distributions, you should realize that your money is not inaccessible and that, if worst comes to worst, you can get at your IRA or Keogh money if you really need it. To discourage people from doing so, the IRS imposes a 10 percent penalty on the amount of money you've withdrawn. You'll also have to pay ordinary income taxes on the amount you've withdrawn. To make matters worse, if you have your IRA or Keogh in a bank or thrift CD that hasn't matured, you'll have to pay the early withdrawal penalty as well.

There is one small loophole to this law, however, that you might want to take advantage of. Each year, you have sixty days—known as the rollover period—to decide what you want to do with your IRA or Keogh. During that period, you can use the money as you see fit—provided that you replace all of it by the end of sixty days. Of course, any interest you earn during those sixty days will be fully taxable. But in the event that you need a quick, short-term loan, you might consider taking advantage of the sixty-day rollover period.

So if you're above the magic age of fifty-nine and a half, draw on your IRA or Keogh when you need it. If you're below that age, do so only with caution. It is worth giving second thoughts to the penalties. That's why my favorite retirement account is a 401(k) plan, or SARA. In some forms of these plans, you can borrow from your account or make emergency withdrawals without penalty. I'll give you the details in Chapter 8.

8. Is It Time to Liberate Your Home?

Have your children grown and moved away? Is your house a burden rather than a joy? Are you wondering where you'll get the money to heat seven rooms which no one will use next year?

Well, if you're over fifty-five, that means it may be time to liberate that lovely home where you've spent so many delightful years. If you can bring yourself to part with it, let someone who needs an eight-room house buy yours. And let someone who's young enough to enjoy mowing the lawn and fixing the plumbing worry about those problems that have been piling up and graying your hair.

As we'll discuss in more detail in Chapter 7, by selling your home now you qualify for the best once-in-a-lifetime tax break Uncle Sam has ever offered. All the profits you make on your home will be absolutely *tax-free*, up to $125,000. Even if your state government taxes you, their tax will be at capital gains rates—generally a piddling 2 percent or so.

And if you dearly desire to hang onto the old place, Merrill Lynch and other stockbrokers have "equity access" programs which allow you to borrow back the equity you have built up in your home—at attractive rates.

It's not a bad idea to check this one out, since part of the process is getting an appraisal of your home and determining just how much equity you really have.

Another way of making your home more liquid is a "reverse mortgage," which enables you to sell your home for cash and lease it back for the rest of your life. Shop for one of these programs carefully—the broker can wind up taking a larger share of your equity than you'd like. But these programs illustrate the key point: There's no such thing as a frozen asset. You can liberate any real asset for a fuller, richer life.

9. Automobiles

One way to check out the value of your car is to ride down to your local used car lot and check out the trade-in or wholesale value of your car. They can look it up in the book for you; your car is worth maybe 80–90 percent of that figure. That's close enough for our purposes.

10. Check Your Home—Room by Room

You probably have more liquid assets than you realize, and far more invested in appliances, furniture, jewelry, hobby equipment, and other whatnots than you imagine. Fill out your balance sheet carefully. When listing liquid invest-ments, don't forget to include gold and silver coins and other items Aunt Martha may have given the family.

The first step is to identify all the assets. The next step is to figure out what each is worth and if it is actually salable. A good idea is to value personal property such as appliances at what you think it would bring if you sold it through a newspaper classified ad.

Go through your house room by room and add up the value of everything that could be advertised for $20 or more. Don't forget the attic, the cellar, the garage, and items that have been stored at friends' or relatives' houses. Keep detailed lists so you know exactly what you have.

If you aren't sure how to describe accurately what some of the items are, describe them in detail or take pictures of them. You'll need those lists when you try to liberate your unproductive assets by selling them. You'll also need the descriptions if you suffer a disaster and need to make an accurate insur-ance claim.

You Never Know What You Might Find. Stories of old masterpieces discovered in someone's attic are often simply figments of someone's imagina-tion, but we asked Sotheby's, the famous auction house, for some true stories. They supplied us with some real eye-openers.

One of their experts visited a small bungalow in the West Country of England to give advice on a painting. There he noticed a jar being used as a flower pot. The owner, who had no idea of its value and had occasionally left it outside her back door with a plant in it, was completely surprised to find that is was a rare Ming jar of considerable quality. It sold on July 15, 1980, for $690,855.

A man wondering whether his $20 gold piece had any real value put it in an envelope and mailed it to Sotheby's in New York. It turned out to be a very rare double eagle 1870 CC (the first year of the Carson City mint) which sold at auction for $10,000.

On a trip to Europe a Sotheby's expert noticed a bedside lamp: a red-and-white, pear-shaped vase topped with a large lampshade. The elderly couple who owned it had no idea of its value. It sold on December 16, 1980, for $672,000.

To help people find out what their items might be worth, Sotheby's (and probably other leading auction houses) will provide (Sotheby's does it *free*) a preliminary auction estimate on any property brought into the gallery. If you do not live near a gallery, a clear snapshot of each item normally will do. (Sotheby Parke Bernet, Inc. is located at 1334 York Avenue, New York, N.Y., 10021, phone (212) 472-3400. In Canada, Sotheby Parke Bernet (Canada), Inc. is at 156 Front Street West, Toronto, Ontario M5J 2L6, phone (416) 596-0300.)

Christie's Auction House also offers free oral appraisals, although if you want a written appraisal, say, for insurance purposes, you would have to pay a fee. The rate for a written appraisal fluctuates but is negotiable: It depends on the item being appraised and the services needed.

The odds that you will find a Rembrandt in your attic are slim, but who am I to say you won't? I love to be surprised.

Go West with the Best and Leave the Rest in the Chest. If you are planning a cross-country trip to the western part of the United States and have some Victorian antiques or old oak tables or chairs to sell, you might want to make some inquiries with antique dealers on your way. Items like these are very popular in the MidWest and West and command much higher prices (sometimes two or three times as much) there than on the east coast, where they are more commonly available. With a little planning you could make more than enough to pay for the trailer rental and maybe pay for your trip as well.

Are Your Tangible Assets Dead in the Water? According to research by the staff of a leading sailing magazine (which is never likely to print it), the average sailboat owner spends about twenty-two hours a year on his boat. Thus—including all the expenses of boat ownership—many ordinary, middle-class, amateur yachtsmen are paying $100 an hour or more for their time on the water. And I'm sure millions of owners of other expensive toys such as second homes, vacation condominiums, mink coats, hunting gear, and personal computers use them equally little.

Now, I believe in hobbies. Mine are collecting jazz, rock, folk, and blues recordings and building my wine cellar as an investment portfolio that I plan to destroy systematically with my best friends. The purpose of investing, after all, is to acquire the ability to do what gives you the most pleasure and financial security. So if you truly love owning a sailboat, then do it. If you truly love sailing, maybe you should rent one when you need it for those twenty-two hours a year.

Take an open-eyed look at each of your tangible assets such as boat, land, second home, and personal computer to decide whether each is worth holding onto. You may love these things too much to part with them. As I said, you could rent some of the finest boats in the world for a lot less than $100 an hour. A wise man once said, "A boat is a hole in the water into which you pour money."

Did your boat spend all last year tied to its mooring, developing rot, causing you headaches, and soaking up your cash? Liberate it.

Is the land you bought in Florida as retirement property worth less than you originally paid and is it too far away from anything for you to want to live there? If you were foolish enough to buy it, there is someone equally foolish to take it off your hands. Liberate it.

Is your personal computer gathering dust while manufacturers introduce new versions that provide twice the capacity at half the price? Unless it is something you really need, its value can go nowhere but down. Liberate it.

How to Liberate a Sleeping Asset. Remember two things when you try to get rid of one of these white elephants:

- First, you've got to find someone for whom your asset *isn't* a white elephant. That can be a tough job, but it's worthwhile.
- Second, you must price it so your buyer finds it worthwhile to deal with you rather than his friendly boat or real estate or personal computer dealer. (But don't cut the price so low that the transaction isn't worthwhile for you.)

It pays to advertise. A friend of mine ran a six-inch-long classified ad for his apartment sale when business forced him to move to another city. In the ad he listed everything for sale that he considered worth more than $12. He sold every single item he listed in the ad. But visitors to his sale made bids for less than 25 percent of the under-$12 items that he had not bothered to list.

The bottom lines:

- Nothing beats putting the specifics of your message where people genuinely interested in your item will be looking.
- There is no better way to get the full price you want for an item than having someone else in the room who came looking for the same thing.

If no one responds to your ads, try advertising somewhere else at a slightly lower price. Prices competitive with others in the newspaper may be too high to attract buyers. Many people deliberately offer their belongings at high prices in ads to see if they can locate a sucker who'll make them richer.

Also try rewriting your ad to convey the virtues of your white elephant more exquisitely. Include all the wonderful benefits it can give a buyer.

Patience pays off as well. Don't decide you have to take any offer that comes down the pike that day. Waiting may get the best price.

Stop Collecting Dust with Collectibles. Some items are too specialized for the typical classified section and too valuable to sell at a garage sale. To sell them, you need either a friend who's an expert or a reputable specialist appraiser or dealer.

Ask around. Almost everyone has a friend or a friend of a friend who's an antique buff. If you can't find one right away—or even if you can—a trip to the nearest flea market will no doubt be an enriching journey. I'm almost willing to say that your balance sheet can never be complete until you've visited a flea market: You'll not only get a better idea of the value of some items you already recognized as salable, you'll no doubt learn that some of your old "junk in the attic" might be precious to some people.

Does your attic contain souvenirs of an almost forgotten world's fair, early issues of *TV Guide,* or a dusty but original hula hoop? The flea market goers in your area may drool over them.

Get at least three bids. And if all seem too low, hold on a while longer or try the classified-ad route. Values for collectibles fluctuate even more than for other assets, and dealers who help you market them take a hefty cut. Collectibles are one investment you might as well hold, rather than sell, when the market is weak.

Organizing a Yard or Garage Sale. Though classified ads are great for selling cars and OK for selling sofas, they're usually terrible for selling used toys or books (unless the books fit a particular genre such as science fiction and can be sold in a magazine that caters to science fiction buffs).

A well-organized yard or garage sale can sell most of the items too small for a classified ad. And it's often easier to organize a yard sale than it is to haul all your excess assets to a flea market.

Here are tips on how to do it:

- Try to plan a sale jointly with neighbors. If you join forces you can offer more specific items in your advertising. The result: You will attract dozens more people than you could ever bring to your home alone.
- Place signs all over town. Ideally, start a week before the sale and check the day before to replace signs that kids have torn down. Some newspapers will provide free, professional-looking signs for yard sales that are also advertised in their pages.
- Be specific in newspaper advertising. An ad that says: "Yard Sale—21 Smith St., Pleasantville. Great assortment of quality merchandise" may draw some buyers. But an ad that says: "Yard Sale—21 Smith St., Pleasantville. High quality Victorian furniture, hunting and fishing gear, and used books (many science and science fiction)" will draw people seeking just what you have to offer and willing to pay your prices.
- Specify a rain date in all your announcements; in case of rain you will still capture most of the people who were originally interested.

You don't have to worry much about the sales taxes at a yard sale. No state really endeavors to collect taxes on such events, and some have special exemptions to their sales tax laws that make the typical yard sale tax-exempt. So with a well-structured yard sale and intelligent choice of which assets to sell, your family junk can make a real contribution to your investment program.

For Sentimental Reasons . . . Of course, many items mean far more to you than the value you can list on your balance sheet. Your favorite rocking chair isn't a potential source of money to invest, and by listing it on your balance sheet for $40 you aren't saying you'd sell it to the first person who offers you $50. But if you don't analyze the worth of everything you own, you'll never see how much you've got that you don't need.

11. "Neither a Borrower nor a Lender Be . . ."

Is your brother-in-law a deadbeat? Are you a soft touch for the guy at the next desk? Does your son still owe you money that financed a date he went out on three years ago?

Some loans you've made may be uncollectible, but all deserve at least some effort to recover your money. When people owe you money, collecting can be the easiest way of finding money to invest. You might find that, if they can't pay in cash, they can contribute some items to your next garage sale. And if you *can't* collect, at least making the effort will discourage people from asking to borrow again.

The key principle is: Don't dismiss any asset as a lost cause until you have tried to turn it into investable cash.

12. Minding Your Own Business

Do you own your own business? Did your no-good brother-in-law talk you into investing in his? Do you still own part of a family business?

Whatever your ownership in a business, it's time to take a close look at that ownership in terms of how good an investment it is or has been and just how liquid your investment is.

Would You Do It Again? When you are looking at your business as an investment, you want to look at it from several viewpoints: Does it pay you a better salary than if you worked for someone else? Would you even consider working for someone else? Does it give you a return over and above what you pay yourself and your family members who work with you? Has the value of the business increased over the years—so that you would invest in your business before choosing other investments? What other financial and psychological benefits do you get from the business—are they worth the hard work and long hours?

I looked at my business—newsletter publishing, public speaking, book authorship, conference presentation, and managing a data base on money market mutual funds and related statistics. From an investment viewpoint, it's a mixed blessing. Most years it has provided me with a comfortable living, but it has occasionally driven me to working very long hours, traveling constantly, and worrying about the company's finances, management, and editorial quality. It has provided me with an exciting lifestyle, however, and given me a chance to do good and do well at the same time. But it has given me a lot of sleepless nights.

But as an investment, it has paid off handsomely. I work hard and live well, both of which I love. The value of my company has grown, and we have had some very attractive offers for parts of our business. So far, we have decided not to sell off any of our businesses, but it is good to know what they could be worth to someone else. Considering that I started with nothing, the return has been astronomical.

What Is Your Business Worth to Someone Else? This is a highly speculative question but one which you should be discussing with your advisers. It is a useful subject to keep on the agenda when you talk with your accountants and lawyers. It would be good to know what you would do if you were to become incapacitated or pass on to that great shopping center in the sky.

By the way, speaking of advisers, I highly recommend that you seriously consider an informal board of advisers, regardless of how big your business is. They can help you by asking the "dumb" questions that no one else will have the guts to ask you, like "Why are you doing what you are doing?" Experienced businessmen in your field and related fields are usually pleased to be asked to advise you. And most will be pleased to do it for a chance to share a good bottle of wine or scotch and maybe a nice dinner with you.

Who are good candidates for a board of advisers? Major suppliers, fellow businessmen you meet at professional or trade group meetings, retired executives in your field (talk with the Small Business Administration's Service Corps of Retired Executives—SCORE) and others. What can you expect from them? Fresh perspectives and ideas, identification of trends in your business, contacts with more active consultants, prospective buyers for your business, and friendship. I have a board of advisers to keep me on my toes, and it has been a truly rewarding experience: a pain in the tush sometimes, and a revelation others.

Could You Do It Again? If you have a business that is salable, and you have a talent for starting businesses, maybe you should consider starting and selling businesses for a living. Let me tell you, that can be a whole lot more profitable than running the businesses and a whole lot more stimulating. I have a good friend who started along that route with a lot of stamina and a little seed money. She chose a home-cleaning franchise and after less than one year has three franchises. She plans to buy franchises from people who are not good managers, build them up, and then sell them to someone with less stamina and more money. She'll make it.

13. If the Vest Fits, Wear It—It's Tailored for You

Just what is a vested interest in a company thrift or retirement plan? It's the money that the big bosses (the ones with the vests) have decided is yours to keep regardless of how long you stay with the company. It's the part that you can roll over into your IRA or the next company's retirement plan. It's yours.

Some company plans will say, for example, "We will match up to X percent of your contribution to the thrift plan each year and if you leave you will have a vested interest in any monies that have been in the plan for at least three years."

This is your money. Although you will wish to continue to keep it tax-sheltered, you will probably also want to take charge of investing it yourself.

14. Liberate Your IRA

Let's have some straight talk about Individual Retirement Accounts. An IRA is not an investment—it is a *shelter* over an investment. The most popular choices are bank or thrift CDs or MMDAs and mutual funds. Most people choose bank or thrift CDs because they are the most widely publicized. Nearly all knowledgeable investment advisers recommend no-load mutual funds.

You are permitted to have as many IRAs as you want (although your total yearly contribution to all your IRAs may not exceed $2,000 in earned income) and to change trustees of your IRA as frequently as you wish. If your money is in a bank MMDA and you decide that you would rather have it in a money market mutual fund, you are free to change trustees. Just call up the money fund of your choice and they will help you fill out the forms to move your money, or withdraw the money yourself—you have sixty days to reinvest it. As long as you put it back into an approved IRA, the IRS doesn't care (unless of course you are trying to contribute more than the prescribed limits).

The only problem you will have is if your bank charges an early withdrawal penalty of their own invention. Only banks (and some load mutual funds) charge early withdrawal penalties; money funds and no-load mutual funds do not.

So why should you keep your money in a load mutual fund or a bank account where it costs more to invest or where your money is tied up in a low-yielding account? No reason? Then liberate it as soon as you finish reading this book.

15. Tax Refunds Due—Don't Forget 'Em

A lot of us seem to get a refund check from the IRS each spring—that means that we are overwithholding our withholding taxes so we won't have any taxes to pay on April 15. *That's dumb.* It means you are using the U.S. government as a noninterest-bearing savings account. Why don't you *under*pay a bit and invest the money to your benefit? Talk to your personnel manager about adjusting your withholding—or skip over to Chapter 6, where I give all the details.

16. What Else You Got?

You probably have other assets we have not discussed—down payments on a home or condo, utility deposits you may get back if you ask, or the last month's rent on your apartment. Don't forget to list them.

How About Your Kids' Assets? List assets that legally belong to your children on a separate list just so you won't forget they exist. Those assets aren't yours—if they were, you'd have to pay taxes on any income they generate.

Remember, you are responsible for setting good examples for your children and that includes teaching them to manage their money. If your list of their assets includes passbook savings accounts, old savings bonds, and checks from the grandparents that you've had in a drawer since the kids' last birthdays, you will want to teach them today's financial management common sense, not yesterday's.

It never fails to amaze me that people will take great pains to manage their own money well and then turn around and tell their kids to put their savings in a passbook savings account. Shame on you. There are money funds paying twice the interest and with no minimum investment requirements.

Considering how long much of the kids' money will be in the account, you are a fool not to get a fair return. With little or no taxes to be paid and lots of time to compound the returns, a little forethought can make a big difference when they need the money.

Grandparents are even worse than parents. They give kids U.S. savings bonds, souvenir coins chosen for aesthetic rather than investment reasons, and old "heirlooms" with no practical value. Parents' instincts are usually to drop these gifts into a safe deposit box or a corner of the attic with some vague hope that they will someday be nice to look at.

Why not encourage the grandparents to help the kids build a brighter future? Children remember loving attention and the wisdom of their grandparents much longer than frivolous gifts. Money fund accounts rather than pass-book savings or savings bonds (which today might not even be patriotic the way Congress seems to take the money and spend it) and collectible coins can be both aesthetically satisfying and good investments.

You're Rich (More or Less)! Now What Do You Do?

Now that you know your assets, it's time to go back and sort through them for money to invest—and for money you can use to eliminate some of the onerous liabilities you've listed on the other side of the page.

Current liabilities:

1. Credit card bills
2. Real estate taxes due
3. Income taxes due
4. Installment loans and other short-term loans

Long-term liabilities:

5. Mortgages
6. Other long-term debt

1. Credit Card Bills

These are the easy debts to remember. The daily mail tells you just how they are mounting. The important things you must do to help yourself are as follows:

- Make sure you know just when you must pay the bills to avoid late charges
- Make sure you know how much interest you are paying on the balances.

That second item will become important, since very often the first and best investments you can make are paying off loans. Why invest at 10 percent if you can save 20 percent on the same amount, improve your credit, and still have access to the money if you need it?

2. Real Estate Taxes Due

Don't forget that you may have already paid some of these with your mortgage payments. Pay them like all bills when they are due, not a day sooner unless it looks as if your community is not going to get the bills out before the end of the year and you might lose a tax deduction this year—then pay the bill early.

3. Income Taxes Due

Don't forget to estimate how much you will have to pay in income taxes and make sure you will have enough money on hand to pay the difference. Also, you must make sure that you have prepaid at least 80 percent of your federal income taxes before tax time or a penalty could be assessed.

4. Installment Loans and Other Short-Term Loans

These loans and obligations occasionally need to be reviewed and, if necessary, consolidated so you can handle them. They are often expensive money, and by using some of your investable money you can reduce them and save a lot in interest costs as well as make the payments more liveable.

You also need to list the longer-term headaches—those that are due in over one year, as follows. (Now we are getting to the biggies, which we will discuss in much more detail in the next chapter.)

5. Mortgages

The most important things to know about your mortgage are the following:

1. How is the rate calculated? Is it a fixed rate, which means that your monthly payment will probably not change, or is it a variable rate? If it is variable, on what basis does it vary? What is the rate tied to? How is it tied? For example, it could be two percentage points above the FHA mortgage rate or FHLBB mortgage prime rate.

2. Is there a prepayment penalty? If you wanted to make a voluntary "reduction of principal" additional monthly payment or prepay the mortgage and refinance it at a lower rate, could you do it without penalties? You signed the mortgage; you should make sure that you understand the terms. You should have done that before you signed the mortgage. You may have known the terms but forgot. This, incidentally, is why you need a good lawyer to review any contracts you sign. Mine did, and we cut out a lot of requirements that were negotiable—we negotiated and we won.

3. Is the mortgage assumable? Can someone else assume responsibility for your 5 percent mortgage without having to refinance the mortgage at a higher rate? If so, you can get a much better price for your house, since that provision in the mortgage will save the buyer a ton of money in the future.

6. Other Long-Term Debt

As with all loans, you should study the terms of the contract, the interest rates being charged, the prepayment penalties, and any restrictions on how you can repay the loans.

Very often, it is advantageous to invest some of the money you are finding to pay off loans—the ones with the highest interest rates first. Of course, you should *never* pay off loans that have interest rates below Donoghue's Money Fund Average.

Donoghue's Rule for Savers

This is very important. *If you use money you have found to invest to pay off loans to save money, continue to make the payments you were making before —only this time pay yourself.* Maintaining the discipline of setting aside money each week to invest is crucial to building your investments.

What's Your Net Worth?

If you take your total liabilities, which you have just listed, and subtract them from your total assets, you will have some idea of just how much you are worth. Let's hope the figure is positive.

Now we have to think about improving your condition by using some of the money you have found to invest either to earn more money or to reduce your interest expenses.

Your First Steps

Quickly take a few basic steps in liberating your assets. Do you have excess cash on hand or money stuck in passbook savings accounts? Invest it immediately! Some people have four or five bank accounts—a practice that's just not smart if they accept rotten (or zero) interest rates for the dubious privilege of holding several passbooks. If you want to maintain one account for savings, another for paying taxes, and a third as a place to accumulate vacation money, keep all three accounts in money market mutual funds.

Next, evaluate the money on deposit at a company thrift plan. Most thrift plans offer better deals than banks. They were even a good deal in the dark days before money market funds. Some plans—Section 401(k) Salary Reduction Accounts (SARAs) and plans where companies match employee contributions—are great deals. But, of course, not all companies offer them.

Finally, evaluate the amount in your checking account or accounts. How long will it take you to spend the amount you have there? If the answer is more than a week or two, you've got too much money asleep in the bank.

Now Invest That Cash—Quickly

All those sleepy assets you're awakening will provide cash—but don't forget that the cash you're liberating can disappear the way most of the other cash you've acquired over the past few decades has disappeared. Just as important as discovering hidden assets is putting that money to work quickly, before you get a chance to spend it.

So whenever you liberate a white elephant, be sure to deposit the cash in your money market account immediately. And if you write checks on your money market account for some ordinary expenses, it's a good idea to find another, more permanent investment for much of your newly liberated money as quickly as possible. Chapters 9–11 will discuss some additional investments far better than the musty locales where your wealth had been hidden until you liberated it.

Liberating Lemons—The First Key to Finding Money to Invest

Remember, a stock or a piece of land or a savings bond or a boat or an old bookcase doesn't know you own it. It won't be hurt or upset if you sell it.

So *don't stay with an investment that's not making money for you.* And don't keep *anything* valuable if it's useless to you. The government will not fall if you sell off your old bonds. The banking system won't collapse if you move your money from your savings account. And Aunt Matilda won't roll over in her grave again if you sell the silverware that has been sitting in the attic since 1963.

It's time to liberate those "lemon" assets and put the money into real investments. Your assets should be making you rich, not offering shelter to homeless spiders. Get them moving!

4

Cutting Down Your Major Expenses

Every two weeks when my paycheck used to come in, I would get a warm comfortable feeling. I always thought I would have nearly enough to spend and a significant amount left over to invest.

But then I'd get just four or five big bills: my mortgage payment, a couple of loan payments, a credit card bill, an insurance bill or two, and perhaps a heating oil or medical bill. Usually none seemed enormous by itself. All were for "necessities." But suddenly I'd realize that I was going to end the month deeper in debt than I began it.

My paycheck was big enough to support an investment program. My mistake was thinking that because mortgage bills and such were inevitable, I had to just grin and bear the pain they caused. And that somehow I could count on modest spending habits to leave something "left over" after "necessities" had been purchased.

Actually, big expenses offer the best opportunities for cuts. If I'd trimmed my big expenses, I could have started investing right away. Cut $50 from a $500-a-month mortgage bill, for example, and you'll have $600 a year to invest. Do you think big cuts are impossible? Well, look carefully at the expense cuts I offer in this chapter.

With major expenses, you'll find that the bigger they are, the harder, or "lower," you can make them fall.

Renovating Your Mortgage Loan

Look at your monthly mortgage statement. Are you paying into an "escrow" account to cover your property tax bill? If so, the bank is keeping money you should be investing. Not only that, but the bank is probably paying the money to the town on your behalf at the wrong time. So you're paying extra income taxes and losing much more investment income than you might think.

Banks traditionally require borrowers to maintain escrow accounts for a good reason: If a borrower ignores his tax bill, defaults on his mortgage, and then runs off to Tierra del Fuego, the town will take the house for nonpayment of taxes before the bank can touch it. The bank will be left with absolutely nothing.

In reality, you're not going to run off without paying your taxes. And if you've been doing business at the same bank for a couple of years, the banker knows it. For you, the escrow account is a piece of nonsense. It probably pays you no interest whatsoever. The only people who are worse money managers than the people who run escrow accounts at banks are the people who send out the tax bills for town governments. Generally, local tax bills are due twice a year. The people at the bank send the town your money as soon as they get the bills. But the people at town hall are often a few months behind on their billing, so you really have no idea when your tax money will actually go out.

If you were handling the payments yourself, you'd know:

- First, to pay the tax bill on time. Your bank could use the unpaid bill to force you to accelerate payments on a low interest rate mortgage—some have. Your town will hit you with a late penalty as well.
- Second, to be sure to bring your tax payments up to date by the end of every year in which you expect a substantial income tax liability (and that means *every* year, for most people). Property tax payments are fully tax-deductible for the year *in which they are paid.* So you should pay them at the end of the year when they are due even if the folks in town hall are so disorganized that they won't send out the bill till the following January. Why should you have to wait to take a deduction just because the town assessors are disorganized?

The people handling your escrow account won't care about these concerns at all. If you've paid your mortgage promptly for the last couple of years, go down to the bank and ask them to stop billing you for escrow payments. Most banks will do that these days. Then take your escrow money and invest it until you have to pay your taxes. And if they won't let you, it may be worthwhile to refinance your mortgage with a bank that will.

The Joys of Refinancing—Sometimes

What interest rate are you paying on your mortgage? Are you one of those poor souls who bought a house when mortgage rates hovered near 18 percent?

Whenever interest rates for new mortgages fall 2.25 points or more below the rate on your mortgage, you should consider refinancing. Beware—the fees you incur can sometimes eat up all the money you save. But refinancing savings can be dramatic.

For example, if you had a $75,000 mortgage at 18 percent, you'd pay almost $13,500 a year in interest. If you took out a new 12 percent mortgage for the same amount, however, you'd pay only $9,000 a year. That's a savings of $4,500 a year—$375 a month!

Unfortunately, you're dealing with banks, and banks just love to slash your savings with fees. If you're refinancing a mortgage, you'll pay for processing, points, title searches, appraisals, credit reports, and other services. Your old mortgage may also require a prepayment fee. And don't forget that, while interest is fully tax-deductible, many of these fees are not.

So look closely at the costs involved. Lots of people have saved $100 a month or more. But if refinancing would reduce your monthly payment by less than $60, it may not be worth the bother. Just wait to see if interest rates will fall farther, and keep on writing off your interest on your taxes. See Chapter 6 for all the details.

Adjustable Rates Will Turn Against You

What about adjustable rate mortgages? Banks over the past few years have turned to promoting these deals—generally giving borrowers lower monthly payments at first in exchange for allowing payments to rise if interest rates rise in the future.

In principle, adjustable rate mortgages aren't a bad idea. Banks hate taking risks almost as much as they hate to pay you more than 5 percent interest on your money. By accepting an adjustable rate you can take some of the interest rate gamble. And if you're lucky, you'll receive a better deal in exchange.

Unfortunately, adjustable rate mortgages usually tempt borrowers most when they're most risky. Adjustable mortgage rates usually move with short-term loan rates rather than long-term rates, and short-term rates rise and fall far more than long-term rates. The adjustable rate mortgage looks best when short-term rates are farthest below long-term rates. That's when lenders promote it most aggressively, too. But at these times it's likely that adjustments will go in only one direction—up.

A good adjustable rate mortgage has a cap on how fast interest rates can rise and how high they can go. Compare several adjustable rate mortgages before you take one out, and ask yourself what would happen to you if short-term interest rates rose to 20 percent and long-term rates to 18 percent. It's happened before, and it can happen again.

Avoid adjustable rate mortgages if you're refinancing. You can afford to wait and see whether fixed rate mortgages will fall farther. If you're buying a home, on the other hand, you may find no better deal than an adjustable rate mortgage. Take one, but only *very* carefully.

How to Save Thousands in Interest—Without Refinancing

If you're one of those people who just won't get much benefit from refinancing, then you should look into another way of saving a bundle on your mortgage: adding voluntary prepayments of principal. It's a perfectly legal way of making fantastic savings over the course of your mortgage—if you can afford it.

Richard Band, editor of *Personal Finance,* came up with this one, and it's a beauty. Here's how it works.

Most mortgages take advantage of the miracle of interest compounding, which allows most investments to grow at a fantastic rate. But a mortgage is a miracle for your mortgage company—not you.

For example, a thirty-year mortgage for $75,000 at 13 percent works out to monthly payments of $829.65. Over the balance of that loan, you'll shell out $223,674 in interest—almost three times the amount of the loan.

But most mortgages have buried inside the fine print an allowance for you to make voluntary prepayments of principal. In some cases the prepayment can be as little as $1 per month. If you're not sure if your mortgage does have such a clause, drag out a copy and read it carefully.

You might not be very excited about paying more on your mortgage. But if you pay just $25 extra per month on your mortgage, you'll save $59,372 over the course of your mortgage and shorten your term to twenty-three years and four months. If you pay as much as $100 per month, you'll save $119,252 over the course of your mortgage. Of course, if you can prepay more, the savings will be even more dramatic.

Best of all, you won't really decrease your interest deductions by that much in the first few years of your mortgage when you really need it. The big rewards come later in the mortgage, when the compounding effect takes off. So if you can afford an extra $25–$100 per month on your mortgage, it will really pay off over the long haul.

Is It Time to Move?

If your mortgage (or your rent) is eating too much of your income, maybe you should move rather than refinance. Your home involves all sorts of costs: property taxes, transportation, and heating are only the most obvious. Your auto and homeowner's insurance rates are based on the neighborhood where you live. Some people incur the extra costs of sending their kids to private schools because they feel public schools in their districts are inadequate.

If you refinance, you'll have to pay many of the expenses of selling your house anyway. And sometimes you can escape from a high-interest mortgage more cheaply when you sell your house than if you simply refinance.

A house or condominium is, of course, the biggest and most difficult purchase most of us ever make. But it's worthwhile: If you haven't bought one yet, you should try. The interest payments on your mortgage will be fully tax-deductible while your rent payments aren't. The house is itself a good investment. And the tax savings provide a significant addition to your investable cash.

If you bought a few years ago and have decided you made a mistake, you're in luck. Unless you bought a termite nest, you can almost certainly sell your home at a profit. Roll the profit into a new home and pay no tax whatsoever. Or, if you're over fifty-five, pocket the whole profit (up to $125,000) tax-free. That'll give you plenty of opportunity to do your home buying right this time around.

All in all, if you've considered your mortgage or rent payments untouchable for money to invest, you've been making a big mistake.

Escaping the Debt Traps

Some folks spend 10 percent of their incomes repaying credit card debts, installment loans, and accompanying interest. What a waste!

Unless inflation is very high (it isn't as I write this), repay early all except very low interest debts and debts that involve early repayment penalties. Make repayments your first step in your program of "paying yourself first." After all, earning 8 to 12 percent on your investments won't do you much good if you're paying 12 to 20 percent on your debts.

Not all debt is bad all the time. When you think about reducing loan payments, you should think first about inflation. Why? Because inflation eats away at the value of dollars, and when inflation is high you can pay for your goods with cheaper dollars later. It actually makes sense to increase your debt if you can do it at interest rates lower than the inflation rate.

Some debts at reasonable interest rates make sense even when inflation is low. Mortgages and some other secured loans often carry modest interest rates, for example. They're great if the alternative is paying rent.

Your first objective, however, should be to get rid of high interest debt if inflation is low—or if both inflation and interest rates are high at the same time. Credit card debt, finance company loans, and retailers' "easy payment plans" are the worst deals, though any kind of loan can involve excruciating interest rates if it was taken out at the wrong time.

The Rule of 78s: When the Early Bird Lays an Egg

Loans differ in repayment provisions. With credit card loans, many mortgages, and some personal loans, you can repay early and save the remaining interest. But on some types of loans, the interest saving is a lot less than you'd expect. The fine print in some loan agreements contains the innocuous-sounding "rule of 78s" (sometimes known as the "sum of the digits," because the sum of the digits 1 through 12 equals 78) and makes paying off early a very bad idea. If your debts involve the "rule of 78s," you're best off simply repaying as your bank bills you, and putting your "pay yourself first" cash into your money fund account.

Suppose, for example, you've taken out a $1,500 student loan at an annual rate of 9 percent. You have five years to pay your debt. Your monthly payments are $31.14. The interest due over the five-year period is $368.40. You want to pay off your loan on your thirtieth payment, or in one-half the time you'd agreed to. If you agreed to abide by the rule of 78s, you'll save only $93.

The details of how the rule of 78s works are complex and best left to bankers. (After all, if this thing were comprehensible, people wouldn't stand for it, would they?) Just remember that when the rule of 78s is applied, you wind up paying a much higher net interest rate than was listed in the loan agreement. If you take out a $10,000, fifteen-year loan at 18 percent and pay it off after one year, for example, you actually pay 23.87 percent interest on the money you borrowed.

If you think this method of computing interest is unfair, you're not alone: Several states think it's unfair too and have either prohibited or restricted its use. But if you are offered a loan covered by the rule of 78s, the best you can do is read your loan agreement carefully before you sign. Make sure that when you pay off debts to cut your expenses, you don't pay off debts covered by the rule of 78s.

Coolly Cut Credit Card Costs

Credit cards are a wonderful convenience. But are you paying for that convenience when you don't have to? Or are you using it too much? If one of your major expenditures is credit card bills, including interest on many of your purchases, look closely at how you use your card and you may make significant savings.

Some credit card problems can originate in statehouses, not with consumers' financial houses. Have you ever received two or three letters in a month urging you to apply for a credit card with a New York bank? Well, in my home state of Massachusetts, you get one month to pay your bill before the interest rate charges start to pile up, and the interest rate can't exceed 18 percent. That's a good deal, because I get to use my money for a full month before I pay for what I've bought.

But most of the New York banks have located their credit card operations in states with virtually no limits on what they can charge. And in addition, the New York banks are a lot more "sophisticated" about including promotional circulars for trashy merchandise in your credit card bill. That means they send you more circulars than your neighborhood bank probably does, and they design them so they're harder to ignore. One bank even sets up its return envelope so you can't use it until you've read, torn off, and thrown away this month's promotion for clocks, totebags, or whatever.

Mail order financial services may be a good deal some day—it certainly costs the New York banks less to mail me a circular than it costs my local bank to have an officer talk to me. The banks could use those savings to give me better services. But for now the enormous banks seem dedicated to the proposition that big shot New York bankers need not provide value for their customers' money. Study their brochures carefully before you do business with them.

Careful Credit Card Shopping Is Smart

But don't give up on your credit card entirely. I make as many of my major purchases as possible with my cards. Why? The bill doesn't come due for at least a month (often two months, if the store is slow at sending the charge slip to the credit card company). That means I can keep the money to invest for an extra month or two. It's like getting a 2 percent discount on everything I buy.

But it works only if I manage to pay my full credit card bill every month. If I didn't, I'd get billed for interest charges on everything.

That's the key point. Pay your bill in full every month, and most credit cards are a good deal. But if you fail to pay up regularly, or if carrying a credit card encourages you to buy junk you don't need, then your cards can be key reasons why you're staying poor.

So if you've got a good credit card deal from your bank, you aren't buying a hoard of unnecessary junk, and you manage to pay your bill on time almost every month, then fine. Your credit card is a valuable financial tool.

If your credit card bills are pinching your budget with unnecessary purchases or interest payments, however, then it's time to cut back. The first step is to make sure you're dealing with the right kind of bank. Then eliminate credit card buying that's unnecessary. And learn to pay your whole bill every time it comes due.

Insure Yourself—But Don't Cheat Yourself

I once knew an insurance agent who said, "There are two ways I can guarantee a seat by myself on an airplane. One is to wear a dark suit, sunglasses, and read the Bible aloud when I sit down. The other is to tell people I'm an insurance agent."

Most people would rather be stuck in Podunk, Arkansas, for the annual winter wheat festival than sit down and look at their insurance coverage. That's probably because, deep down inside, they don't know how much coverage they really need. So they buy a ton and try to forget about it. And some insurance agents aren't much help—they'll try to sell you additional insurance coverage even if you've already got enough insurance to cover an intercontinental airline.

But if you've got more coverage than you need, then you've got money to invest. It may take some digging, but you could find a gold mine in overstuffed insurance policies. So take a deep breath, bring out your insurance papers, and take a good look.

Begin by looking at what kind of life insurance you've got. In the last chapter I showed you what a good deal you can get borrowing against whole life insurance policies. But that doesn't mean I think all whole life policies are a good idea. I also pointed out that borrowing against a whole life policy was in fact a form of borrowing your own money. And the best way to buy insurance is not to give the insurance company a lot of money so it will give you some back; it is to give the insurance company as little money as possible in the first place. When you're looking for money to invest, nothing beats keeping in your own pocket money that you might otherwise be paying to a life insurance company.

Agents of the Money Market Revolution

Life insurance comes in a wide variety of forms, from "term" to "universal life." Term insurance simply gives you a certain amount of protection for a given period of time. Think of term insurance as a bet with the insurance company. If the term expires and you don't, then the money you spent on the premium is gone. If you expire within the period of time specified in the policy, then your survivors get the amount of coverage you bought—often many times more than what you invested. Your survivors get a great rate of return, as long as you don't. Since your odds of dying increase as you get older, term insurance gets more expensive as you get on in years.

Whole life insurance, on the other hand, gives you the protection of term and also builds up a cash value over the period of the insurance contract—generally 20 years or so. In its most basic form—which, for convenience, we'll simply call whole life insurance—the company guarantees you a specific rate on the cash value, or equity portion, as well as a certain amount of term protection. As the cash value grows, the term protection diminishes.

Until recently, the old advice of "buy term and invest the rest" was probably the best rule of thumb. Quite simply, the returns on whole life insurance were most competitive with passbook savings accounts—and you should know by now what a loser a passbook savings account could be. Furthermore, the fees you had to pay for whole life—sales commissions and withdrawal and administrative fees—ate away at the measly return you got. So if you simply bought the far cheaper term insurance and did some prudent investing in the money market, you made a smart move back then.

But the money market revolution hit the insurance industry as well as the banking industry—and, I'm proud to say, changed insurance for the better. People took a look at the low returns on whole life policies and the high money market yields, cashed in their insurance policies, and left the insurance industry out in left field.

New Policies—And New Complications

In order to compete, the insurance industry has come out with a dazzling array of products that can give you term insurance protection and competitive rates on the cash value of your premium. Known as "universal life," "variable life," and a slew of other names, these types of policies can be a good deal— sometimes. But you've got to shop carefully before you invest.

The insurance industry—possibly the largest financial industry in the world —is almost completely unregulated at the federal level. Unlike nearly every other type of financial industry, there are no federal watchdogs peering over the insurance industry's shoulder to make sure they operate prudently and in your interest. Instead, the insurance industry is governed by numerous state regulations, all different and most confusing. So to get the good deals out there, you've got to be a smart, patient shopper.

But before you even start shopping, it makes sense to take a hard look at what you want from insurance—how much you need, what type you need, and whether the benefits are worth the price. With all varieties of whole life, you must be particularly careful. Whole life insurance is not only protection for you and your loved ones but also an investment. And if you're buying any other type of insurance than term, you've got to make sure that your policy stands up as an investment and as an insurance policy.

Know What You Really Need

Life insurance is essential for most people. You want to protect your loved ones in case anything terrible—such as death or disability—happens to you.

And even if you don't want to provide for someone else's welfare, you probably don't want to burden other people with the expenses of your funeral. But whatever type of insurance you buy—from low-cost term insurance, which simply gives your family death benefits, to the many varieties of whole life—you should check to make sure you're not buying more than you need.

So first you've got to figure out how much life insurance you *really* need. The first rule to remember about life insurance is that you should buy enough to *maintain* your loved ones' lifestyle, not improve it. For example, if you bought your life insurance with the idea that you wanted to buy a bungalow in the Berkshires, then you probably bought a lot more than you needed.

If your spouse has a career and can maintain his or her lifestyle without you, then you'd be better off investing at least part of your life insurance money. Besides, reducing your life insurance might also reduce the possibility of premeditiated homicide (or suicide, for that matter) during some dark winter of discontent.

Naturally, if you're approaching middle age, you'll probably want to assure your spouse's comfort throughout his or her life. But if you are a childless couple of 35 or younger, sit down with your spouse and ask him or her how long your insurance benefits should last. It's not really an enjoyable topic of discussion, but you might be surprised at the answers you get—in this age of the working couple, it's important to many people to know that they could live independently if they had to. And, of course, many young couples would rather use their money for their enjoyment now, rather than after their lover's demise.

If you have children, of course, the picture will change. You'll want to insure that your offspring do not suffer unnecessarily in the event of your untimely departure into the hereafter. You'll probably also want to make sure that your children can go to college. But even with children, there are some other factors to consider.

First of all, what is the state of your Social Security account? If you've contributed enough to Social Security, your family will receive payments until your youngest child is 16. Your children will also receive a lesser payment until age 18 (or 19 if still in high school). The sums involved can be considerable —as much as $14,000 per year. The Social Security office can't give you an exact figure for "survivor benefits," but they can give you an estimate. For example, in 1983 the monthly average payment for a widow with two children was $1,393.

Secondly, how much can your spouse be reasonably expected to provide for your children's welfare? If your spouse is working now and you have children, it's a safe bet that he or she will want to continue working after you're gone.

To summarize, then, you should develop an insurance worksheet. Here's a checklist of items to consider:

1. How long do I want insurance coverage to last for my family?
2. What other sources of income will they have in the event of my death? (Be sure to include your spouse's income, Social Security benefits, and any investments you have made.)
3. How much do I want to put away for my children's education?

All these are questions to ask when you're looking for insurance protection. If you're looking for an insurance investment, then you have many more questions to ask.

Many universal and variable life insurance products offer you a variety of options for the equity portion of the premium, from variable interest rates to mutual fund switching. The ones that offer mutual fund switching can be particularly good deals—sometimes.

For policies with variable interest rates, you must make sure that you get a truly competitive rate—at least equal to Donoghue's Money Fund average —once all the sales commissions and other fees have been taken into account. To do this, you need to sit down with an insurance agent—preferably several agents—and question them closely on the fees and commissions involved.

With insurance policies that allow mutual fund switching or any other type of investment, you must do the same. You must also be sure that the policy allows free switching and that the funds the company offers have good performance records. You must also make sure that the policy offers funds and other investments that you want. If you want to follow the SLYC system, the policy must offer an aggressive growth fund and a money fund.

With any type of whole life policy, you must also be sure that you can afford the steep annual premiums and that paying the premium won't put too much of a cramp in your other savings plans. If you feel that you can do better without a whole life policy, then by all means do so.

Don't rush into any insurance product without checking all your options carefully. Insurance agents are fine people, but they're salespeople as well. Don't allow yourself to be pressured into a policy, and don't take out the premium on the first visit. A good agent will allow you to shop around, take your time, and ask all the questions you want.

If you'd like an independent analysis, the National Insurance Consumer Organization (NICO) will provide one for $20. See Appendixes 1 and 2 for all the details.

The Rest of Your Insurance Bill

Review other kinds of insurance as carefully as life insurance—though you may find fewer opportunities for quick savings.

Review each of your major kinds of insurance at least every year or two, generally when the policy comes up for renewal.

Automatically Check Your Auto Insurance

Ask an agent from another insurance company how much your auto insurance would cost if you bought it through him. And make sure you aren't buying more coverage than you need.

Regulations vary enormously from state to state, but your state probably requires a minimum amount of coverage to make sure you can pay at least some of the cost if you hurt someone else or damage some property in an accident. You may want to buy some additional liability insurance so if someone sues you for $100,000 you'll be protected. You'll also want to spend a few dollars to cover damage that could be done to your car by an uninsured motorist and perhaps medical costs incurred by someone riding in your car.

But other optional coverages are generally unlikely ever to return to you what you put in. Insuring any kind of risk that you could survive without insurance is simply an investment. If you insure against window breakage or the possibility that you'll need to be towed, you're simply investing your money in a bet that those unfortunate events will occur. If your car never has an accident, you lose.

Think about optional coverages clearly: Recognize that if the insurance company didn't charge you more than it paid out, it couldn't survive.

"Towing insurance" is a particularly bad deal. For only a few dollars a year, you can join the American Automobile Association (AAA), whose emergency road service will help you for nothing or for a modest cost wherever you drive in the United States. You can probably find a nearby office listed under "AAA" in the white pages of the nearest big-city telephone directory.

If your car is new and valuable, you'll probably want some fire, theft, and collision insurance. But take large deductibles to keep your rates down.

Simply put, most optional coverages are a lousy bet. Think of the money you're spending on them today as part of your investment pool. And decide to move most of it into other, more lucrative investments.

Don't Forget Discounts

Once you've chosen the right amount of insurance, make sure you're paying the right price for it. Insurance companies offer a bewildering array of discounts in various states. Ask if you're entitled to any of these:

- Discounts for people who don't commute in their cars
- Discounts for people who drive less than 6,500 miles a year

- Discounts for nondrinkers and nonsmokers
- Discounts for drivers over sixty-five
- Discounts for people who pay their bills in full once a year
- Discounts for driving a car whose bumpers meet collision-resistance standards
- Discounts for parking in a garage rather than on the street

And check to see if your union or professional organization offers a group auto insurance policy at substantial savings.

Insure Your Children the Right Way

Insurance rates for young drivers are outrageous. Be sure to:

- Have your child take driver education courses, which lower your insurance rates
- Seek a "good student" discount for your young driver
- Obtain a special discount if he or she attends college more than 100 miles from home and doesn't drive there
- Insure your child under your name even if one car is "his" or "hers"

Don't have your child apply for insurance on his or her own. However awful the rates you pay for a young person driving on your policy, they're generally much worse for a young person who is listed as the owner of a car.

The Lowest Priced Company Isn't Necessarily the Cheapest

It's important that you don't pay for insurance you don't need and that you take all the discounts you're entitled to. But be careful before switching to a low-cost company. Ask why their costs are so low. If it's because they only handle "careful drivers," ask whether they will drop you the first time you scrape someone else's fender.

There *are* good mail-order deals on auto insurance. But when you're shopping around, it may be a good idea to concentrate on companies and agencies recommended by friends. After all, what you're buying is help in time of need. If the company isn't set up to help you, what good is their low price?

Protecting Your Home

Homeowner's or renter's insurance seems a good deal compared to life, auto, and health insurance. Broad policies insure your home against everything but war, earthquake, flood, and a few other catastrophes. It makes sense for most people to get them.

But be sure you shop around for homeowner's insurance too. And be sure you take a significant deductible to cut your rates.

Don't Take Everything the Doctor Orders

When I was growing up, Momma called a doctor whenever she thought we needed one and paid him whatever he charged. Of course, in those days what he charged was about $8 . . . for a house call.

Today you probably pay $50 for a five-minute visit with the man in his office and a test or two conducted by a nurse. Then you go and fill a prescription or two and pay another $35.

Now, if your employer gives you medical insurance that will pay whatever your doctor charges, then these costs may not bother you. But if you're like most folks, it's time to consider whether the attitude that was good enough for Momma is a bit too generous for you.

Nowadays, there's a surplus of dentists and of many types of doctors. Many dentists and doctors charge less than what some call the "reasonable and customary rate."

Don't go to the cheapest doctor around, but when you ask a friend to recommend a doctor, don't be afraid to ask, "How much does he charge?"

The New Opportunity in Health Care

Another alternative is to join a "health maintenance organization." Many people don't seem to understand the savings an HMO can bring them. For a flat fee that's about the same as you or your employer now pay for ordinary medical insurance, HMOs will cover all your medical expenses except for per-visit and per-prescription charges that can be as low as a dollar or two.

HMOs do it by putting their doctors on salary. You get regular checkups, too. Naturally, there are good and bad HMOs just as there are good and bad pediatricians and good and bad hospitals. But if there's an HMO in your area, you're missing a good opportunity to liberate money if you don't check it out.

Drugs Needn't Be Downers

In buying drugs, the choices are far more clear-cut than in choosing doctors. Most over-the-counter remedies are compounded of well-defined ingredients which everyone in the industry understands. Aspirin is aspirin, and vitamin C is vitamin C. Small drug companies and drug store chains have produced lower-priced versions of most well-known over-the-counter drugs, and they'll usually work just as well. If you have any doubts, ask your pharmacist or your doctor, whomever you trust more.

The pharmacist can also provide generic versions of many prescription drugs if your doctor's prescription so permits. Since most doctors aren't subject to the financial constraints of ordinary mortals, they tend to prescribe the big drug companies' versions of most drugs on the off chance that a difference may exist in the way the big companies' and the small companies' drugs work.

Many doctors, however, will help you if you ask them to prescribe a generic version of the drug you need.

A Little Energy Will Cut Energy Bills

You've heard plenty of public-spirited lectures about cutting energy consumption. You've even turned down your thermostat and caulked a few windows. But did you know that many contractors will *guarantee* that energy saving improvements they make in your home will pay for themselves within two years? Here are two checklists of energy-saving ideas. The first contains simple steps which an eighty-five-year-old grandmother could do herself:

1. Caulk areas where drafts enter the house. A caulking "gun" and caulk can be purchased for a few dollars in any hardware store, or you can use "rope caulk"—a claylike material that you can simply push into drafty spaces.
2. Wrap hot water pipes and heating ducts with insulation.
3. Place an "insulating blanket" over your hot-water heater.
4. Change your furnace air filter regularly.
5. Place plastic "storm windows" over regular windows that aren't thick enough to keep out the winter.
6. Cover or otherwise insulate basement windows.
7. Place heat reflectors behind baseboard or room-sized radiators. (Aluminum foil makes a useful reflector.)
8. Install a "water miser" shower head to reduce hot water bills. (You may want to call a plumber for this if your old shower head can't be removed easily. Be sure to install the new one securely, as you can be injured if it falls off.)

The following projects are major do-it-yourself jobs. Having a professional do them rather than continuing to put off doing them yourself can be one of your best investments:

1. Insulate your attic.
2. Insulate the stairway that leads to your attic.

3. Insulate along the "sill"—the horizontal timber or block where the main construction of your house joins the foundation.
4. Install new storm windows.

Don't forget that if you live in an area where air conditioning costs are as high as heating costs, many of these same measures will reduce your air conditioning bills.

Your first step in saving energy should be to arrange for an energy audit. In most areas the local gas or electric utility can set up an energy audit for $10 or so. Watch for a notice mailed with your utility bills or call your utility to see if it offer audits. Generally state regulators more or less force utilities to provide this service. The auditors will gladly point out which jobs you can easily do yourself and which a contractor could do better. They can also recommend a contractor, though their recommendation may be no more reliable—indeed, may be less reliable—than your next-door neighbor's.

Any improvement which will pay for itself in two or three years is a fine investment—one well worth borrowing to make. That's because your return on your investment will not only be immediate savings but will also include increased value for your house. You also get a nice tax credit for your efforts, which I'll explain in Chapter 6.

Ask contractors what savings they'll guarantee. Guarantees should be taken with a grain of salt: When it comes time to judge whether savings have met projections, the contractor's formula will determine your savings.

But even if it takes four years to get back the money you spent improving your house rather than the two or three the contractor promised, you'll still have achieved a nice profit.

The Right Time to Buy

We all try to buy items on sale, but do you think you could save more money if you knew *when* items would go on sale? Okay, here's a list of sales that typically seem to take place in each month of the year, according to Sylvia Porter:

- *January*—A big month for sales. Shop for appliances, art supplies, bicycles, blankets, books, dishes, dresses, furniture, furs, glassware, handbags, high fidelity gear, housewares, infants' wear, linens, lingerie, men's shirts, men's winter wear, quilts, refrigerators, rugs, shoes, sportswear, towels, toys, water heaters.
- *February*—Air conditioners, art supplies, bedding, bicycles, cars, curtains, furniture, women's hats, housewares, lamps, men's shirts, high fidelity gear, rugs, silverware, toys.

- *March*—Spring clothes, hosiery, laundry appliances, skates, ski equipment.
- *April*—Women's coats, hats, infants' wear, ranges, mens' and boys' suits.
- *May*—Blankets, handbags, linens, lingerie, sportswear, tablecloths, televisions, tires.
- *June*—Building materials, frozen foods, televisions.
- *July*—Appliances, bathing suits, children's clothing, colognes, fuel oil, handbags, lingerie, men's shirts, rugs, shoes.
- *August*—Air conditioners, bathing suits, bedding, camping equipment, new cars, coats, drapes, furniture, furs, hardware, lamps, paints, rugs, school clothes and supplies, tires, towels.
- *September*—Batteries and mufflers, bicycles, new cars, china, furniture, gardening equipment, hardware, lamps, paints.
- *October*—Bicycles, china, fishing equipment, hosiery, school supplies.
- *November*—Blankets, used cars, children's clothing, coats, quilts, ranges, suits, water heaters.
- *December*—Blankets, used cars, women's coats, quilts, shoes.

Is All This Enough to Help You Find Money to Invest?

There's plenty of money in your paycheck to start you on the road to smart investing. I hope this chapter has shown that you just have to seek it in the right way.

If we haven't given you enough tips here, turn to the next chapter. I'll show you how to develop a cash plan that will guarantee you success.

5

Cash Planning: Your Way
to a Better Life

There is no way you are going to get rich or live like a rich person strictly by being lucky. There just never really were people like John Beresford Tipton, the millionaire on the sixties TV show—called "The Millionaire," of course—who sent out his butler every week to present some unsuspecting citizen with a check for $1 million.

You Can Budget a Failure, but You Have to Plan Success

Even those "lucky" people who win at the lotteries had the presence of mind to be in "the right place at the right time"—usually after being in the right place at the *wrong* time hundreds of times. It takes a plan—even if you're playing the lottery.

For example, I worked as a consultant to the Small Business Administration (SBA) in the early seventies. My assignments usually involved a small business which had an SBA-guaranteed loan and was far behind in its loan payments. I was its last chance before SBA foreclosed. Sometimes I could help, sometimes I couldn't.

I remember my first assignment. Fresh from Temple University's MBA program, I visited my client at his place of business. "I'm from the government and I'm here to help you," I introduced myself, hoping to strike terror in his heart. He just blinked at me.

Since that tactic didn't work, I continued, "The first thing we have to do is put together some cash flow projections." I said that because part of my job was to keep the clients in business until I could figure out how to help them out of their problem. No response.

I had a feeling that this was going to be a tougher job than I thought. "I'd like to see your financial records," I said, exasperated.

Without saying a word, he handed me a year's worth of unopened mail! I opened the letter on top. It was from the Philadelphia Electric Company, telling him that his electricity was going to be cut off that day. He had not paid them in three months, and he was in the *ice cream* business. That was my first exposure to truly liquid assets.

I was able to stave off failure for him for a while, but it was an impossible situation. He had himself boxed into a corner—too high costs, not enough sales, and he was too deep in debt to get out. He eventually declared bankruptcy, which was a smart decision since it gave him a new chance to start again—a lot wiser.

Cash Is the Name of the Game

Obviously, the ice cream dealer didn't have a plan for managing his cash flow. He didn't know how to generate cash when he needed it or even how to know when he didn't have enough money. He just bounced checks.

Since you have to pay your bills with cash, and cash is the only thing you can use to invest, what you need to do is to plan your cash flows—to develop your own CASHPLAN.

Actually, developing a CASHPLAN today is a fairly easy thing because, between your bank statement, your charge card statements, and your checkbook, you have most of what you need to get started.

Planning the Ways and Means

Congress has the right idea. The Ways and Means Committee is a very important part of the congressional process. They hammer out all the details of all the fiscal bills that wend their way through Congress. Your own ways and means committee can be an important part of your family's planning process.

The best way to get your family to stick to a CASHPLAN is to get the whole family into the planning process. How do you expect your kids to learn how to manage their financial lives if you don't set a good example? How do you expect your spouse to survive after you are gone if you don't teach him or her how the family's finances work?

There is nothing sadder than the thought of your spouse throwing your hard-earned family assets on the "mercy" of your local stockbroker, accountant, or life insurance agent. You shouldn't leave your family unprepared for managing the family finances. After all, running a family is much like running a small business.

There are other good reasons for letting the whole family in on the business: (1) If it's not their plan, how can they be expected to live with it? (2) If the plan doesn't keep on schedule, you'll know about it fast because someone will complain. After all, if you have a hard time keeping to a CASHPLAN, then you probably need a little guidance and encouragement. Who would be better for that than members of your own family?

Developing a Family "Business Plan"

Probably the reason so few families are prepared to manage their finances and so few family leaders are willing to teach them is that most heads of the household don't know where to start.

Let me give you some insight into making some sense of your finances so you can put together at least the basics of your family CASHPLAN.

Get yourself some accounting spreadsheet worksheets at your local stationer, or, if you have a home computer, this might be a good time to check out one of the leading spreadsheet programs. Which brings me to my next topic.

Would All This Be More Fun with a Computer?

A computer spreadsheet program could tell you immediately how much your savings will increase in a year—and in ten years—if you cut $10 from your restaurant CASHPLAN, for example. Nowadays, half the world is trying to sell you a home computer to help with your CASHPLAN. So should you buy one to make you a better CASHPLANner?

In a word, no. The computer won't let you CASHPLAN much better than you could with a plain old pad of paper.

I'm no fan of the home budgeting programs that stores sell for $19.95 and up. They try to ask you the same kinds of questions that I will ask you here. Not only that, they are stupidly inflexible: I tried one which assumed I was setting up the CASHPLAN in January, and I couldn't persuade it that I was starting in May.

Only one guy I know feels he's really saved a lot of money with a home budgeting program. He's done it by setting up his bank account so he can't write checks except on his computer. Every time he writes a check he has to enter twelve different codes to tell the computer how the check should be classified. It certainly discourages check-writing, but there are easier ways to save money.

On the other hand, if you already have a computer or if you want to buy one because you think it will be a great toy, you're right to believe it can help you manage your finances, as long as you don't expect miracles. My point is that you should understand how your CASHPLAN works and not expect a machine to do the work for you. A program after all is only as good as its programmer. It's fairly easy to set up a CASHPLAN on a spreadsheet program (VisiCalc, Perfect Calc, MultiPlan, SuperCalc, etc.). Spreadsheets cost a bit more than some home budgeting programs, but they'll help you do any kind of financial calculation you could ever want. If you do try to budget for your household on a computer, setting up the CASHPLAN with a spreadsheet program is probably the way to go.

If you don't have a computer, you should try to see if there is one available to you, either at work, your local library, or at a nearby public school. If you can't get your hands on a computer, try some "user-friendly woodware"—in other words, a pencil.

At any rate, set up your worksheet. Page 1 will be for your income. Page 2 will be for your fixed expenses. Page 3 will be for your discretionary expenses. Page 4 will be to put it all together.

Getting Down to It

This is serious business. Put aside a few evenings or rainy Sunday afternoons and find a place to work that's comfortable for you.

I love to work in my loft office with my Walkman loaded with my favorite music. It may sound a bit confusing, but it seems to shut out the rest of the world and allows me to concentrate on my work. I'm writing this to the strains of some tapes of old rock and roll goodies I love. Jazz also works well for me. Of course, whatever method works for me may well drive you nuts—and vice versa. Most important is to make your workplace comfortable.

The First Step: Defining the Means

What are your means? Where does your cash come from, or where could it come from? You have to start by listing your sources of cash flow first before you can start planning how to stimulate them to contribute more.

Salaries: The Wages of Win

The obvious sources of the means to live well are your salaries. Think of your salary and that of your spouse (a more and more common situation today) as the sales of your family "company." Like any kind of sales, they need some analysis for hidden opportunities for improvement.

Start with your gross salaries before deductions, not your paycheck, in doing your close review of your income. In looking at your paychecks, consider some of the following:

Are you withholding too much in taxes? Should you adjust your withholding to reflect the taxes you will save from your contribution to the IRA or 401(k) program (details are in Chapter 8) you are planning? Have you adjusted your withholding to reflect the tax shelter of the mortgage interest on your new home? If not, you're losing a great deal of cash flow that could be working for you now—not a year from now.

Do you really need some of the insurance that you are paying for through deductions from your paycheck? Can you buy it cheaper somewhere else? Make a note to have your insurance agent check it out. Does your spouse have identical coverage, making it unnecessary for you to pay for the same coverage? If so, you could get a substantial insurance rebate from your spouse's employer—without losing a bit of coverage.

Are you overwithholding on FICA because you changed jobs during the year? Employers are required to start withholding fresh when you start your new job, but the most they can base their withholding on in any one year is $37,000. If you've been earning, say, $40,000 for the first ten months of the year and then jump to a job that pays $45,000, you should make sure that you're not overpaying your FICA. You can get it back when you file your tax returns—but why wait? Keep in mind that while you probably can't stop FICA withholding you can claim additional exemptions and reduce your withholding taxes by visiting your personnel department. You can increase your take-home pay next week.

Are you taking advantage of your employer's thrift plans, which can be some of the best investments around for many people? If not, skip over to Chapter 8, read about employee thrift plans, and then talk to the manager of your company's plan. Chances are you'll want to contribute more to the plan and deduct more on your tax return. Check it out.

Are you due for a raise? Should you be talking with the boss about it now? Could you be making more by "jobhopping"? Sometimes that's the only way to get a really big raise if you are growing professionally faster than your job.

Could you be borrowing from your 401(k) program or your company credit union more cheaply than from your bank or thrift institution or even your credit card balances? (I'll tell you about the 401(k) program—a type of company retirement plan—in Chapter 8.)

A careful review of your paycheck with either your company's personnel department, your boss, or the office manager is always a good idea. It may alert you to some benefits the company has that you have overlooked or some deductions that may no longer be necessary.

You should get a fiscal checkup every six months or so just as you should get a physical checkup. Your finances change rapidly, and every penny you can find is more money to invest.

What Other Income Do You Have?

Now you can get around to listing any other income you may have coming to you—income from a rental property, regular payments from Daddy's trust (you lucky son-of-a-gun!), inheritances, income from an annuity, retirement plan, Social Security, or whatever you might have.

List 'em all. Then look at each carefully to see how you can increase your cash flow, free up money to invest, or reallocate your cash resources to more productive and hard-working cash generators.

Drain Dollars Out of Your Savings Accounts

This is also a good time to drain the cash out of those low-interest passbook savings accounts. I know you have them. We all do. If you're working on a checklist of "to do's," put withdrawing your passbook savings accounts and getting them into a modern savings program high on the list.

If you need some reassurance, let me quickly explode some of the myths that keep people in passbook accounts. Ready?

Myth 1—"I may need the money in an emergency." Anything you need in an emergency can be charged on a major credit card. What will you need? Airline tickets? Hospital bills? Hotel bills? Think about it. If you need it, you can probably charge it.

Myth 2—"I don't want to pay more taxes. If I earn more, I will have to pay higher taxes." But you will still have more money for *you* after you pay taxes. Would you rather the bank pay taxes on their earnings on *your* money? Last year they earned over $14 billion on folks like you.

Myth 3—"I don't want to tie up my money." Are you smoking some funny cigarettes? When you get to Chapters 9 and 10, I am going to recommend only investments that can be liquidated into your checking account in one business day. Running out of excuses? Sorry to be a bit repetitive, but you and I both know you needed it.

Interrogating Your Investment Income

Are you *in* the know with your *in*vestments? Are you even *in*terested in your *in*terest? You bet you are. While reading Chapter 3, you probably had some second thoughts about your investments and your assets. You will have a lot more to think about when you read the rest of this book.

I am not trying to get you to invest differently yet. I am talking about your cash flow. And sometimes your investments are a fine source of cash flow.

What have your savings and investments done for you lately? That's what they are there for. To help you. The purpose of investing is to live better. That doesn't mean that you can't spend your investment income. Just because you elected an "automatic reinvestment of interest and dividends program" when you set up your investment or savings account doesn't mean that's right for you all of the time.

Sometimes you need to use your savings on a temporary basis. If you have set up a systematic savings program so you are committed to building up your cash resources, then you should not be afraid to draw upon it once in a while.

Let's face it—when you are getting married, moving, sending the kids to college or private school, buying the kids their first car, rewarding your hard work with a special vacation or trip, replacing the old TV with one of those new stereo TVs or a video cassette recorder, you might think about tapping your investment money.

Recognize the Rainy Day You Have Been Saving For

For example, suppose you're between jobs. There's no shame in that. I got fired from three jobs before I found out that I was my own best employer. In times like that, you will remember that this is the rainy day you started saving for in the first place.

When times are hard or temporary demands on you are heavier than usual, you might want to start taking the interest or dividends as an income supplement. You might even want to set up a check-a-month plan from your savings for a year or so until you "bridge the gap."

Are you beginning to see the difference between income and cash flow? A dividend reinvestment program is a good long-term idea. The only problem is that you are generating taxable income which only increases your taxes without giving you any cash flow with which to pay the taxes. If you can afford to forego the income and pay the taxes, do it. But if you need the cash, don't be embarrassed to say so.

Fixing Up the Fixed Expenses

Now we are getting into the guts of your CASHPLAN. Once you have analyzed your cash inflows and listed each on your CASHPLAN worksheet's page 1, let's move on to page 2, your fixed obligations.

Here it will be useful to get together your checkbook, your bank statements, and your credit card statements. They will serve as a pretty good checklist unless, of course, you pay a lot of your bills in cash or by money order, in which case you may have a problem unless you save your receipts.

I am constantly amazed when we get a payment for a subscription order to my newsletter, *MONEYLETTER,* paid for by cash or money order. I wonder what those people use for proof of payment when tax time comes around. I guess they are used to money orders, but that subscription, like any other form of investment advice, is tax-deductible for investors and savers.

The point is, if you don't pay by check or credit card, you won't be able to justify your deductions when tax time comes around—and deductions can be a big source of money to invest.

Start out by making a list of fixed expenses. Include your rent or mortgage payments, car loan payments, insurance payments, and so on. The checks and credit card statements you've gathered will remind you of other fixed costs. For items you pay annually (car or life insurance, perhaps), make a note of which month they come due. Analyze each closely as you list them.

If you're a page skipper, you should skip back to Chapter 4, where I tell you how to reduce your major expenses. Right now we're more concerned with getting an overall picture of your cash flow and asking the right questions about all of your expenses.

Rent. When does your lease come up for renewal? What will the rent increase be? Can you negotiate a no-penalty exit clause so you could move if you wanted without paying a penalty? Most landlords will do that after the first year if you ask.

Also, if you have a good deal of money tied up in security deposits and the other large up-front expenses that landlords love to hit you with, you should ask your state housing authority if the landlord is obligated to pay you interest. If so, make sure it's written in your lease. It adds up—and it's some compensation for having all that money out of your reach for so long.

If you can't do anything about your rent right now, then simply write down your monthly payment on your liabilities sheet and move on to your next expense.

Mortgage. If you haven't already looked at Chapter 4, go back to the section on how to reduce your mortgage. You can save thousands with fairly small mortgage prepayments. If you've already started to do so, fine. If not, you should consider it.

Keep in mind, however, that if you're earning more on your investments than your mortgage rate, you should probably keep your mortgage as it is—no matter how many little notes your bank has sent you offering seemingly attractive early-payment options. A cheap mortgage is golden, and don't let anyone talk you out of it unless you're absolutely desperate to own your home outright. And don't feel sorry for the bank—they knew the job was dangerous when they took it.

Car Payments. Should I be refinancing my car through my credit union at lower rates? Should I get a cheaper car? Is the old gas guzzler ready to be traded in? Should I get a nicer used car and avoid the horrible depreciation a new car suffers in the first year? These are all questions you should think about when you look at your car payments.

Once again, look at the rate on the loan. If you can invest the money at a higher return, don't repay it any sooner than you have to. If you can't invest the money at a higher return, then simply write it down as an outflow and pay it off as soon as you can.

Car Insurance. Do I need all this insurance? Should I get higher deductibles? Forget collision insurance on the clunker? Should I move to the suburbs to save money on the theft insurance? Do I save anything if I let them take the monthly payment directly out of my checking account each month? If they will take one-twelfth of the annual fee each month, why not let the money earn money for me in the meantime and save the cost of the checks and the late charges?

Life Insurance. Am I overdoing it? Can I use the cash value of my whole life insurance policy for other investments or to buy more insurance coverage? How much do I really need?

I'll bet you haven't reviewed your insurance coverage in years. While you are looking at everything, this is a good time to call in your agent for a review. Tell him or her you are doing it to save money. My independent insurance agent is brilliant at finding me the cheapest insurance in the land if I tell him what I want. If I let him sell me something without really looking at it carefully, it's usually not what I need.

Other Insurance. Do you have household insurance? Has it been updated to cover any valuables you have acquired—a coin or stamp collection, paintings, a valuable camera? Do you have pictures of your valuables or receipts for them in case everything gets wiped out? If so, do you keep them somewhere other than in your house?

Most important, are you paying for insurance you already get free at work? Or worse, insurance which you can't remember why you bought? Better check that first.

Property Taxes. These seem to come once or twice a year. Two important things to remember are:

1. Property taxes paid by individuals are deductible on your federal income tax return *in the year they are actually paid.* Some municipalities are slow in billing the property taxes and send out the bills too late to be paid in the current year, so you end up paying them in the next year and not getting the tax deduction for yet another year. Try to prepay taxes if you can if your municipality is a slow biller.
2. If your bank or mortgage company is paying the taxes for you, see if

you can talk them out of that scam. While they might say it's convenient for you, you're losing out on some money to invest.

If you have paid your mortgage on a timely basis each month, your bank may be willing to waive that requirement. Don't ask a clerk or teller about it, however. Find a bank officer—you need someone who has the authority to authorize the exception to their policy. Of course, you should avoid such practices in a new mortgage.

Some banks refuse to pay your taxes—with your money—until they are billed for them. That will cost you a deduction this year, and that's money out of *your* pocket for their stubbornness. Don't let it happen.

If you want some support in fighting your bank, write me. I love to expose practices like this in my column. If your newspaper doesn't carry my column, tell them to call me and I'll see if my syndicator will let me give them that column *free.*

Other Direct Taxes. If you are required to pay state or local taxes that are not deducted directly from your paycheck, don't forget to put some money aside to pay them as well. A regular "pay yourself first" check to your money fund account might be a good idea if you need the discipline to save for these kind of taxes.

Cable TV. *I love it.* But it can be addicting. Just keep in mind that you pay for all of the services you pick up. If you watch PBS's "Nightly Business Report" or CNN's "MoneyLine" or "It's Your Money" or ESPN's "Business News," you might find that you can justify deducting part of your cable bills as investment information. But don't overdo it, and check with your tax consultant before you do. But I think these shows are every bit as important to my investment strategies as the newsletters I read. Perhaps the IRS will think so too.

You may find that the movies you want to see are running on more than one pay-TV service. You might want to consider rotating from HBO to the Movie Channel to Cinemax to Preview or whatever your choices are every three months or so. With a little planning you can save a bit of money. You might also wait for some sales to lock in your channel choices.

Another thought is to let your children pay for a special channel they want, the Disney Channel for example, rather than use the same money in their allowance for movies. It's a whole lot cheaper, and it's a lot more likely that they'll watch it regularly instead of forgetting about it. With any luck at all, they'll find that having spending money is more fun than watching TV all the time.

Tuition. Don't forget to plan for your tuition payments if you are going to night school, college, or trade school. If you invest some of your money to attend one of the many investment seminars, the tuition, travel, and other expenses you incur are tax-deductible and a lot of fun as well.

I still learn a lot from listening to my fellow speakers. Howard Ruff's National Conventions each spring in San Diego and Orlando are excellent values—a lot of excellent speakers at low cost. The granddaddy of them all, the National Committee for Monetary Reform (NCMR), is also a lot of fun. Each fall, you get a chance to meet and listen to every major investment adviser in the country—and take a tax-deductible trip to New Orleans as well.

Public Transportation. If you commute to work, you have to provide for the nondeductible costs of commuting. Taking a look at what public transportation costs you a year in money and in time might make you take a more realistic look at car pools or alternative ways to get to work.

While this is a basic out-of-pocket expense, some insurance companies offer a discount on your auto insurance if you show them a year's worth of prepaid rapid transit passes. The discount is usually small—say, 10 percent —but it's worth it if you or your spouse use public transportation regularly.

Pledged Donations. Let's not forget our obligations to support favorite charities and churches. This is a lovely and usually unchallenged deduction on your tax returns, but we usually don't keep close track of our contributions. All you need to do to correct this situation is to ask for receipts.

You might think about taking those old books that are simply gathering dust and occupying space in the cellar or attic and giving them to your local library. Get them to give you a written receipt for your tax-deductible contribution. That's really a good idea for freeing up money to invest. You get more shelf space and a tax deduction as well.

While we're at it, I'd like to put in a good word for Goodwill Industries. You could certainly take some of those old clothes that are jamming up your closets and turn them to good use. Give them to Goodwill and let some folks have them who need them more than you. If you get a receipt, you'll get a tax deduction for it as well. Folks who do good can do well, too.

Loan Payments and Credit Card Payments. Now we're getting into some really productive territory. These can be some of the most expensive and seductive ways to borrow money. It's so nice not to have to ask someone for an overdraft on your checking account, a credit card loan, or an easy-credit draft. We all intend to pay them off before they cost us much, but we all let these expensive loans build up.

When they are carrying 18–22 percent interest rates as many of these do, it may be time to raid your savings a bit—especially if you are one of those folks with the passbook savings accounts—and pay off these loans. After all, a 22 percent return each year from the interest you save looks much better than the 10 percent or so you are earning on your money fund account.

Take a good look at the balances you are building up in your checking accounts and you will get a pretty clear picture of what the rainy day you were saving for looks like. You can always get the cash back in an emergency—especially if you show a track record of repaying these loans. A good credit record that shows you are the kind of person who repays his or her loans will allow you to borrow at much cheaper rates in the future.

Borrowing money is nothing to be ashamed of. Not knowing how to borrow is. Save your credit card for emergencies: You can nearly always get a better rate for personal loans at your bank or credit union.

Child Support/Alimony. It's a sad commentary on today's world that real life pressures, challenges, and temptations cause many of today's marriages to fail. The facts of life today are that financial responsibilities do not stop when a relationship ends. Often child support and alimony payments are a very necessary part of your financial CASHPLAN. I consider the support I provide for my children a sacred obligation which has loomed very heavy at times in my career but always came out of the first dollars I earned.

If these are part of your expenses, they are important responsibilities. Just remember, alimony is deductible for the payor and taxable to the payee; child support is not deductible to the payor nor is it taxable to the payee.

Tallying Up Your Fixed Expenses. These and other fixed commitments you have to face every month or once a year are an important part of your CASHPLAN because if you can't handle them you have a whole lot worse problems to deal with. You are probably a good candidate for credit counseling, consolidation loans, and maybe even personal bankruptcy. Don't be bashful to ask for help if you need it—that's what credit counselors are for. It's better that you seek them out than have the courts appoint one for you.

Now you have to tally up your fixed commitments. With some luck, they are not more than your net income, which is your income after taxes and other deductions.

Now for the Tough Stuff to Budget—Your Living Expenses

Now come the toughest expenses to control. Sift through your canceled checks, your credit card statements, and your bank statement, and, for the

Page 1   CASHPLAN

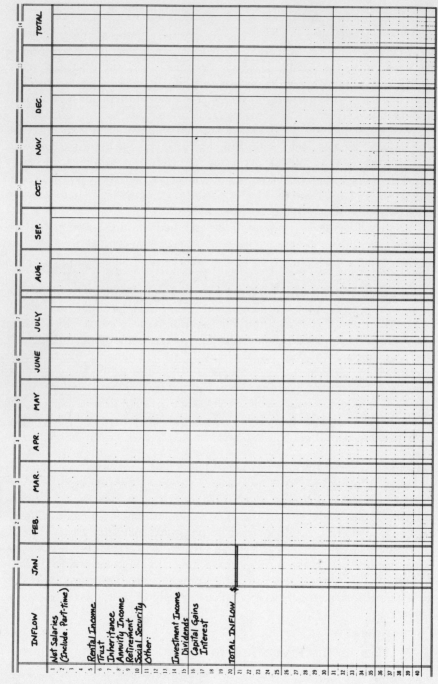

Figure 4. CASHPLAN.

Page 2 CASHPLAN

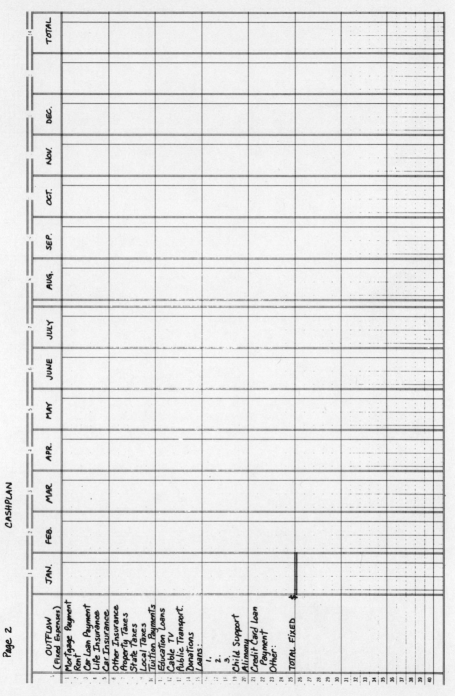

Figure 4 *(continued)*.

Page 3   CASH PLAN

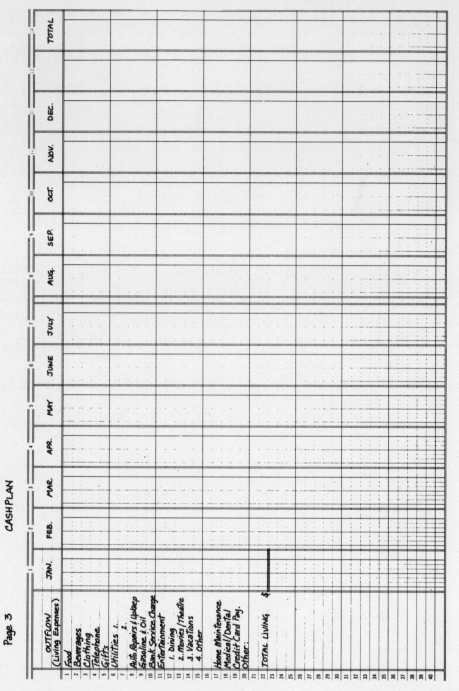

Figure 4 *(continued)*.

Page 4

CASH PLAN

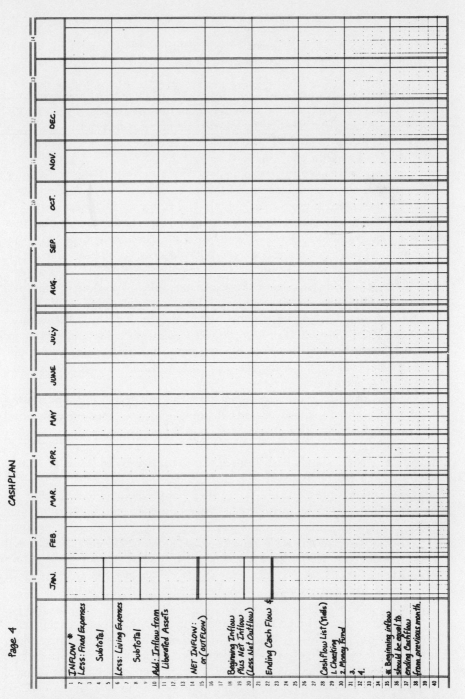

Figure 4 *(continued)*.

items you pay in cash, your memory, and figure out how much you've been spending each month for the following items.

Bank Service Charges and Lost Interest. While you're looking at your bank statements, this is a good time to look at how much you are paying for banking services. This can add up quickly. After all, if it is only, say, $20 a month, that works out to $240 a year. At only 10 percent interest, that's worth another $24 a year to you.

But, you say, I have to have a bank account, don't I? (Refer to Chapter 2 for a more complete discussion of this point if you need to.) The answer is No! It may seem to be convenient, but it is not absolutely necessary.

Consider this: Most consumer money funds offer checking, and about five offer no-minimum free checking services, so you don't have to pay for your checks—and you'll get interest on your daily balances. If you keep an average account balance of only $1,000, at 10 percent that is worth $100 a year plus the $240 you would save on checking in our example. That's like earning $340 a year, or 34 percent, on the money you use to pay your bills.

Of course, unless you keep rather large balances you would not want to deposit a lot of checks in your money fund account since the fund is likely to put a fourteen-to-thirty day hold on the deposited checks. But you could arrange with your employer to have your pay electronically deposited in your money fund account.

Getting cash is easy too. Supermarkets will cash your checks. Some money funds offer cash through automated teller machines. So you could work it out to operate without a bank checking account if you wanted to.

Food Is a Necessity—But Enormous Grocery Bills Aren't. At the supermarket checkout you can save more than you imagine. Most people cut out coupons, but many end up never using them. Why not? Most likely they just aren't keeping close track of their grocery budget and don't realize how much coupons and other economizing strategies can do to keep it in line.

Why not set your grocery budget $4 a week below the amount you have been spending and plan to save that much per week by clipping coupons for products you would have bought anyway? If you live in an area where some stores offer double-coupon days, you can go for even more savings. Why not try for a cut of $7 a week?

Generic and store-brand canned goods, paper products, and soaps and detergents can save you even more than coupons. The quality of these items is often as good as that of nationally advertised brands. Who eats advertising, anyway? Most important, all cost 10–60 percent less than the name brands. Try these attractive lower-priced products and be sure to keep track of which ones you like.

You can save dramatically on your food shopping if you follow these rules:

- Shop at a regular time and on a regular day each week. Then it's easier to keep track of your spending, and you're much more likely to remember to bring the coupons you've clipped.
- Read grocery store ads regularly. Which stores offer double coupons, and when? Is there a "food warehouse store" near you—a store which offers a limited selection of brands with little decor, and prices noticeably lower than ordinary supermarkets? If so, plan to visit it at least once a month.
- Never cut out a coupon for a product you wouldn't want without the coupon. At best, you'll accumulate paper you don't need. At worst, you'll wind up buying a lot of unnecessary junk (which is exactly what the manufacturers have in mind when they produce the coupons).
- Keep your coupons in one place. A "coupon-minder" wallet, available for $3.95 or so, will help you to sort and store your coupons. It can be a good investment.
- Always compare the cost of the product you're buying with the coupon and the cost of competing products without coupons. Sometimes manufacturers raise prices, and then spend some of the money that the price increase brings on coupons.

A woman I know bought four jars of a brand of instant coffee she didn't really like, just because she had four twenty-five-cent coupons and the store was offering "double coupon days." Unfortunately, when I looked at the jars and calculated the cost per ounce, she was paying more than she would have paid for the brand she actually preferred.

Using all your skills, how much do you think you can cut your *weekly* food budget? You can add four times that amount to your *monthly* "pay yourself first" commitment.

Clothing. With the emergence of national chains of discount clothing stores offering "brand names for less," it pays to shop frequently. I buy all of my dress shirts at one of these stores and save probably 50–60 percent on shirts. I also get a better selection of designer shirts since very few stores carry anything with any style in larger sizes. (I stopped being a small person a long time ago —I think it was in the third grade.)

It's also wise for men and women to watch for ads for "Hong Kong" custom suits or the like. You can get some very nice buys and suits that are made to fit you. Usually ordering two or more suits at the same time can save you even more. If you are an "odd" size like me, this may be the only way to get suits that fit properly. Incidentally, my tailor says to buy two pairs of pants with men's suits. Since the pants wear out first, you can double the life of your suits.

Gasoline. Shop around for gas stations that offer self-service pumps and save a few cents a gallon. If you drive a lot, you can save a lot. A person who buys, say, twenty gallons of gas a week to commute can save over $40 a year and another $40 if he or she pays in cash instead of charging the gas. A small savings, but every little bit helps.

Car pools can help you save gas. If there are four of you at work who are driving from the same general area, you could save three quarters of your expenses by car pooling. If you are in the twenty-gallon-a-week club, paying $1.10 a gallon, that means you spend over $1,100 a year on gas. Car pooling would save you nearly $850 a year on gas alone.

Auto Repairs. This is a sticky one. Car repairs always seem to crop up just at the wrong time. Of course, car pooling can greatly reduce the wear and tear on your car, and preventive maintenance—such as changing the oil regularly —can make your car last much longer.

Birthday and Christmas Gifts. With a little planning, this is one area where you can save a lot of money. But if you wait until Christmas, it's gonna cost you.

What I do is keep constantly on the lookout for just the "right" gift for my family and friends—all year round. I pride myself on giving just the right thing to my special friends and family. You can never seem to find that right gift when you need it, but if you are constantly on the lookout you can bring a lot of joy to your friends and family.

One idea we use at the office might be a useful gift idea for you. Instead of giving meaningless gifts to our business associates and employees—fruit-cakes, smoked pheasants, appointment books, and the like—we give American Express "Be My Guest" certificates. These handy little items, available to American Express cardholders, can be prepared in any amount you wish— we normally use $25 denominations—and are redeemable at the restaurant of the recipient's choice.

I find that most folks save them to take their favorite people to dinner and we get the nicest notes from our friends about the lovely dinner experience they had on us. From our viewpoint, the cost is fixed and we only have to pay when they actually use the certificates.

Other friends we know decide on a gift, like cutlery, that a large number of their friends will want, and they buy in bulk from a manufacturer. Amazing how clever people can be when they put their heads together.

Don't forget post-Christmas sales. Late December and early January are great times to buy Christmas cards and other items in bulk.

Telephone. Have you looked closely at the new long distance telephone services? If you are running a long distance telephone bill of over $35 a month or find yourself making a lot of long distance calls from telephone booths, you should consider MCI, SPRINT, or one of the other services.

Granted, it is a hassle once in a while to remember your access number and billing code for the new long-distance carriers, but once you get it down, the thought that you are saving 40 percent or more over Ma Bell's rates makes it all worthwhile.

It may be just the thing to encourage you to renew an old acquaintance, call your kids at college, get them to call you more often, or say "Hi" to Mom more frequently. If it works, it's worth it. And the services are getting better every day.

Are your children the main source of your phone bills? If so, you might let your kids pay their own telephone bills and learn what a telephone costs.

Are you still renting a telephone? Do you really need all of those extensions? Should you go out and buy your own telephones? Some of the stores have telephones so cheap that you could afford to keep a spare or two around the house. Some cost less than a few months' rental. Besides, when was the last time your had a problem with your telephone?

Other Utilities (Gas, Oil, Electricity). Did you turn out the lights and adjust the thermostat when your left the house today? When you went on your vacation? These bills can really mount up.

Have your asked your utility company for advice on conserving energy and reducing your heating and lighting bills? Sometimes they can do an energy efficiency audit and show you how a little well-placed insulation can cut your bills significantly. It's certainly worth a try—and you can get a tax break for certain energy-saving measures.

You would really be amazed at what storm windows or insulating plastic over the windows in winter can do for your heating bills. Not heating a few seldom-used rooms can save a bit as well.

Have you talked with the utility company about a budget plan where they take a fixed amount out of your checkbook each month? This type of program helps people with massive winter heating bills, and sometimes the utility company will give you a discount for allowing them to simplify their billing process.

Restaurants. I dearly love dining out. I love to see what excellent goodies chefs can whip up and I like to try things like prime rib and rack of lamb that I could never cook as well at home. But have you looked at the prices lately? A fine meal and a bottle of wine could blow your entire CASHPLAN!

There are some ways to have the best of both worlds—fine dining at

CASHPLAN prices. For example, call up some of the leading restaurants and ask them if there are any local dining coupon books around your area. These promotional books for a very small price can save you hundreds of dollars on "twofer" prices (two dinners for the price of one). Also, if you have a dining or entertainment card, you might call them. These companies all have some special deals for you. That's their job.

One of my favorite evenings out, since I love the fruit of the vine, is to go to one of my favorite wine bars with a charming friend. Frequently they have wine by the glass—a full four- or five-ounce glass—or, what I really love, two-ounce tasters. It's cheaper than a full meal in a good restaurant and a nice way to spend the evening. And in some states and at some restaurants you may be permitted or even encouraged to bring in your own wine at no charge or for a small corkage charge. This is a good way to enjoy your own wine cellar while enjoying the pleasure of someone else's cooking. Check your state laws and your favorite restaurants.

Why not enjoy that great wine you found for $3 instead of an unknown wine on the wine list for $30? Don't be bashful. It's your evening and your palate that must be pleased.

Movies/Entertainment. Thank God for cable TV and video cassette recorders! Some of the world's greatest entertainment can be at your disposal when you want it. All the movies you were too busy to see or which were too expensive to see are on your own TV. Just remember, as I noted earlier, you pay for all the services you pick up.

Of course, the plethora of new smaller multiscreen movie theaters and dollar matinees all over make seeing the new movies much more attractive. In my hometown we have Cinema One through One Hundred to choose from —everything from *Jaws 14* through *Rocky 8* is showing.

Vacations. If you are willing to be a little flexible on where and when you spend your vacation, you can have a lot of fun and go some exciting places. How? Talk with your travel agent.

Travel agents are paid by the airlines and the hotels; you won't have to pay any more by going through them. In fact, considering the attractiveness of many of the travel packages, you can save a lot of money using a travel agent. Good agents are worth their weight in gold.

You should also look into some of the low-cost airlines that have flourished since airline deregulation. While you generally don't get much in the way of "frills," you can save a lot of money by bringing your own food and reading material. After all, getting there is only the start of a vacation.

Finally, planned charters by church groups, alumni associations, and other nonprofit groups can save you vast amounts of money on vacations, particularly if you're going abroad. Many of these charters don't require that you stay with the group once you land—all you have to do is make sure that you're at the airport when the plane takes off.

Home Maintenance. If you have a bent for doing repairs yourself, good "fix-it-yourself" books can save you a mint. With plumbers and carpenters pulling down between $12 and $30 per hour, it could well be worth investing in some tools and instructions.

Before you start tearing down walls and pouring foundations, however, you should make a frank analysis of your abilities or you'll wind up causing more damage than improvements. For example, I had a friend who, encouraged at his success in home handiwork, built a fireplace and chimney in his living room. The next night, a world-class thunderstorm struck the area and flattened his chimney—as well as his new car, which was parked beside it.

The moral of the story is that minor repairs and housework are a good place to save. If you must undertake major work, give someone else a hand on their house first and see how it's done. Or shell out the money to have the job done right.

Medical/Dental. Most people don't want to scrimp on medical or dental expenses—and rightly so. A filling that's gone bad can cost you plenty if you have to get a root canal, and there's nothing more disheartening than hearing a doctor say "Oops!" when he or she is handling vital parts of your anatomy.

But that doesn't mean that you should pay any outrageous fee your doctor quotes you, either. The cost of medical or dental work is not necessarily indicative of its quality. You should shop around for a doctor whose fees seem reasonable (and within your insurance limits) and with whom you feel comfortable. You don't have to go to the Mayo Clinic to get good medical or dental work done.

Incidentally, you can get good deals on minor dental work, such as teeth cleaning, by going to a dental school for the work. The students are watched carefully by highly qualified dentists, and they do fine jobs—often for as little as $5 a visit.

Finally, should you fall ill and need a prescription, make sure to ask the doctor if a generic brand of medicine wouldn't cure your ills. Generic drugs are absolutely the same thing as name-brand ones—but they cost a whole lot less.

Putting the Puzzle Together

Now its time to put your family CASHPLAN together. You have all of the basic information on your family's cash flow.

Your worksheet should now be complete. Enter your gross income for each month, deduct the withholding taxes, and calculate the bottom line on page 1. Now total page 2, which lists your other fixed or required payments. When you're finished with page 2, total page 3 for your variable expenses.

All finished? Now deduct the totals on pages 2 and 3 from the total on page 1. That will give you the total addition to (or deduction from) your liquid cash resources each month. Some months, especially when you have high annual payments for auto and life insurance and maybe tuition, you will have negative cash flows. In others—hopefully most of them—you will have positive cash flows.

It's time to call a family meeting to discuss the CASHPLAN. You have most of the information you need and a list of items to be discussed on a yellow pad. You're ready to go.

Reason should prevail. Maybe it would be wise to discuss the CASHPLAN with your spouse first and get his or her input, make a list of the issues you want to discuss, and decide whose job it will be to be the devil's advocate who will question all of the assumptions and argue against the majority to make sure you have thought of everything.

It's a good idea to assign some of the items to be researched to various members of the family. That way everyone gets some experience having to be responsible for something. You might assign your daughter to check out the telephone companies, your son to check with the utility company about conservation suggestions, yourself to review your loan situations and the mortgage, and perhaps your spouse can check out the insurance situation.

Make it a family affair. That way everyone learns something new. And don't forget to discuss how you want to invest or spend your savings. That should be a group effort as well. Remember, some will want to spend their share and some will want to save and invest for a bigger long-term goal. Both will learn in the process.

So! Where Do You Cut?

The first thing to do is to put priorities on each category of spending. Number the categories in order of importance to you, using 1 as the most important and 5 as the least important.

Don't get upset if your list shows a lot of 1s and not many 5s. Obviously some expenses, such as food, gasoline, and property taxes, will get 1s. Some people find money to invest by ignoring their property tax bills, but I sure don't want you telling some court that you started doing that because Bill Donoghue told you to.

In addition, some "frivolous" expenses, such as restaurants, movies, and vacations, may also get top priority. I spend a lot on tapes and records because

I love music. When I made out my CASHPLAN, I didn't cut down on music. If you love something, then keep it. If you don't, you'll cheat.

But do you find that you're spending more than you like on low-priority items? For example, *do you spend $30 per week on lunches* at work? If you brought your lunch a few times a week, you could still eat well and save $10–$30. In the course of a year, that's $520–$1,560.

I found, for example, that entertaining at home is more fun (and far cheaper) than going out to a restaurant with friends. So instead of blowing $100 at a fine restaurant every two weeks, I invite friends over and cook the meal myself. Not only have I improved my skill as a cook and wine steward, but my friends invite me over to their houses in return.

As a CASHPLAN-cutting incentive, don't forget how we showed in Chapter 1 that monthly savings of only $40 can add up to as much as $1 million over thirty years, if it's invested properly and if the market is with you.

Now You're Ready to Roll

Now that you've formulated your CASHPLAN, make every effort to stick with it. Don't be discouraged if you slide off track every once in a while—that's perfectly normal. Just make sure you don't slide too fast or too far.

If you find yourself unable to keep to the CASHPLAN, then you've simply made some unrealistic assumptions on your planning. Go back over the CASHPLAN with your family and see if you can isolate the trouble spots.

Make a habit of going over your CASHPLAN at least every six months. Your finances can change rapidly, and you should take any shifts in your income or outflow into account. Remember, a CASHPLAN is not a static, do-it-once-and-forget-about-it item. It must be reviewed, and reviewed carefully, as often as possible.

Once you've gotten your CASHPLAN under way, however, you'll find that there's a lot more money kicking around in your pocket than you ever thought. Your family business will be all the better once you've figured out your ways and means—and you'll have more money to invest.

6

"Brilliant Deductions, Sherlock," or Getting Out from Under a Tax

By now you might think—and rightly so—that you're getting pretty smart about how to handle your finances. You've gotten a handle on setting your own investment goals, you've figured out your net worth, and you've decided to redeploy some or all of your lazier assets. You've even developed a CASH-PLAN to squeeze all the money you can out of your cash flow.

But if you're like most people, you're probably paying more than you should in taxes. And that could wipe out much of the gains you've made so far.

To Fund or Refund, That Is the Question

Did you get a tax refund last year? Then you already know where to find more money to invest. Get your tax withholding in order and invest that money you've been lending tax-free to the government.

Did you take the short form tax shortcut last year? Then you probably missed taking advantage of a lot of legitimate deductions and wasted money you could have found to invest. In either case, this is the time to resolve to get your tax planning in order.

Make your resolutions now—your new year starts today. I'm going to show you how you can cut your tax bill and start getting your tax cuts back in your next paycheck.

Turning the Tables on the Tax Man

Let's start with those of you who had a tax refund last year. *Are you nuts?* You're lending money interest-free to the government every time you do that.

Would the government do that for you? No way.

Fantasize with me a bit. Let's see how the IRS would react if we tried to sell them that same line of malarkey.

You walk into the IRS office on April 15 and ask to talk to your IRS representative. "Listen," you say, "I'm a little short this month. How about an interest-free loan so I can pay my taxes?"

An icy mask descends upon the IRS examiner's face. "You are aware, of course, that nonpayment of taxes is a federal offense and you could be jailed for nonpayment?"

"Well, yes," you say, "but I'm going to pay my taxes. I just thought that if you had a little extra cash you might just lend it to me for a month. I'll pay you back in May and we'll be square."

The IRS man looks at you like someone about to squash an annoying insect. "The IRS does not give loans, sir," he replies.

"Well, look," you offer, "how about if I pay you next month? You won't have to lend me any money. I'll just give you an IOU."

The IRS man takes a deep breath. "That will cost you 5 percent of your tax bill each month if you fail to file your return. If you file and do not pay on time, you'll be charged ½ of 1 percent of your unpaid taxes each month, up to but not exceeding 25 percent of your tax bill. Incidentally, that's on top of the regular interest we charge you for being late. If you fail to file and fail to pay, of course, you'll incur both penalties. And by the way, the ½ percent a month interest penalty is not deductible."

"Gee winnikers, what a rotten thing to do," you say. "All I wanted was an interest-free loan." The IRS man smiles coldly.

Now, of course, you can generally get a filing extension if you need it, but you'll still have to pay 100 percent of your taxes by April 15 or incur the penalties. In any event, you're certainly not going to get the IRS to lend you money interest-free. So why are you giving the IRS an interest-free loan by overpaying your taxes?

A Refund Is Fun for a Day, Invested Cash Is a Blessing All Year

Some people like to get a tax refund at the end of the year. It makes them feel temporarily wealthy. Other people use it as a sort of forced savings account. But if you do get a tax refund at the end of the year, you're losing out on more money than you save.

Suppose, for example, that you get $1,200 back from the IRS at the end of the year. If you'd invested $100 a month during the course of the year at 10 percent simple interest, you would have had more than $1,260 by the time you got your tax refund.

If $60 extra money to invest doesn't sound good to you, then you should think about what you could have done with that $1,200 during the course of the year. You could have started an Individual Retirement Account. You could have reaped some handsome returns in the stock market or the money market. You could have had money to invest. And you could have done any of those things a whole year sooner than you could if you loaned it to the government interest-free.

"OK," you say, "I have sinned. How do I correct my wicked ways?"

Withhold on Your Withholding

Actually, it's a very simple procedure. Walk down to your personnel department and ask for IRS form W-4, which sets the amount of income tax to be withheld from your weekly paycheck. You probably filled out this form when you were first hired, and, if you're like just about everyone else, you've probably never dealt with it since. (See Figure 5.)

You're allowed to take one withholding exemption for every $1,000 worth of exemptions and deductions you have each year. Bear in mind, however, you need exemptions and deductions over and above the exemptions for each of us the IRS has already built into your withholding. For example, everyone should take an exemption for themselves, as well as one for each dependent, normally a nonemployed spouse and/or children. Other common exemptions are for people who are blind or over sixty-five.

But you can take an exemption on your W-4 for any other deduction that you plan to take this year, provided that your deductions are over the amount already built in by the IRS. You can find out how much is built in on the W-4 worksheet. For example, supposing you bought a house this year, and your wallet feels emptier than a barrel full of holes. A substantial amount of your monthly mortgage payment is interest. Interest is tax-deductible, and the deductions you take from your withholding for your mortgage interest could make a big difference.

Getting Some Help to Pay for Your House

Let's say that you took out a $60,000, thirty-year mortgage at 13 percent. Your monthly payments would be $663.72 each month. Over the course of one year, your interest would be $7,789.02.

At any rate, that's $7,789.02 worth of tax deductions. Instead of paying at your ordinary tax rate, you should subtract $3,400 from $7,789. That makes $4,389 worth of extra deductions. You should trot down immediately to your personnel office and take another four deductions. You'll start getting more money in your weekly paycheck—and the IRS won't come breaking down your door in the middle of the night and carting you off to the big house for tax evasion, either.

Table 1—For Figuring Your Withholding Allowances For Estimated Tax Credits and Income Averaging (Line E)

Estimated Salaries and Wages from All sources	Single Employees		Head of Household Employees		Married Employees (When Spouse not Employed)		Married Employees (When Both Spouses are Employed)	
	(A)	(B)	(A)	(B)	(A)	(B)	(A)	(B)
Under $15,000	$ 90	$150	$ 30	$150	$ 50	$120	$ 0	$120
15,000-25,000	120	250	0	250	70	170	310	170
25,001-35,000	190	300	0	300	130	250	800	220
35,001-45,000	250	370	0	370	170	320	1,500	250
45,001-55,000	690	370	0	370	230	340	2,210	330
55,001-65,000	1,470	370	220	370	310	370	3,020	330
Over 65,000	2,460	370	920	370	680	370	3,400	370

Worksheet to Figure Your Withholding Allowances to be Entered on Line 4 of Form W-4

A Personal allowances .... ▶ **A**

B Special withholding allowance (not to exceed 1 allowance—see instructions on page 1) .... ▶ **B**

C Allowances for dependents .... ▶ **C**

If you are not claiming any deductions or credits, skip lines D and E.

D Allowances for estimated deductions:

  1 Enter the total amount of your estimated itemized deductions, alimony payments, qualified retirement contributions including IRA and Keogh (H.R. 10) plans, deduction for a married couple when both work, business losses including net operating loss carryovers, moving expenses, employee business expenses, penalty on early withdrawal of savings, and charitable contributions for nonitemizers for the year .... ▶ **1** $

  2 If you do not plan to itemize deductions, enter $500 on line D2. If you plan to itemize, find your total estimated salaries and wages amount in the left column of the table below. (Include salaries and wages of both spouses.) Read across to the right and find the amount from the column that applies to you. Enter that amount on line D2. .... ▶ **2** $

Estimated salaries and wages from all sources:	Single and Head of Household Employees (only one job)	Married Employees (one spouse working and one job only)	Employees with more than one job or Married Employees with both spouses working [1]	
Under $15,000	. . $2,800 . .	. . . . $3,900 . .	. . . . 40%	
15,000-35,000	. . 2,800 . .	. . . . 3,900 . .	. . . . 23%	of estimated salaries and wages
35,001-50,000	. . 8% } of estimated salaries and wages	. . 3,900 . .	. . . . 20%	
Over $50,000	. . 10% }	. . 7% } of estimated salaries and wages	. . . . 18% }	

  3 Subtract line D2 from line D1 (But not less than zero) .... ▶ **3** $

  4 Divide the amount on line D3 by $1,000 (increase any fraction to the next whole number). Enter here . . . ▶ **D**

E Allowances for tax credits and income averaging: use Table 1 above for figuring withholding allowances

  1 Enter tax credits, excess social security tax withheld, and tax reduction from income averaging $

  2 Enter the column (A) amount from Table 1 for your salary range and filing status (single, etc.). However, enter 0 if you claim 1 or more allowances on line D4 .... $

  3 Subtract line 2 from line 1 (If zero or less, do not complete lines 4 and 5) ...... $

  4 Find the column (B) amount from Table 1 for your salary range and filing status .... $

  5 Divide line 3 by line 4. Increase any fraction to the next whole number. This is the maximum number of withholding allowances for tax credits and income averaging. Enter here .... ▶ **E**

Example: A taxpayer who expects to file a Federal income tax return as a single person estimates annual wages of $12,000 and tax credits of $650. The $12,000 falls in the wage bracket of under $15,000. The value in column (A) is 90. Subtracting this from the estimated credits of 650 leaves 560. The value in column (B) is 150. Dividing 560 by 150 gives 3.7. Since any fraction is increased to the next whole number, show 4 on line E.

F Total (add lines A through E). Enter total here and on line 4 of Form W-4 .... ▶ **F**

[1] If you earn 10% or less of your total wages from other jobs or one spouse earns 10% or less of the couple's combined total wages, you can use the "Single and Head of Household Employees (only one job)" or "Married Employees (one spouse working and one job only)" table, whichever is appropriate.

You can take a $1,000 exemption for every $1,000 worth of deductions over $3,400. If you go overboard and claim more than fourteen deductions, your employer is obligated to send in your W-4 so the IRS can check up on you. Of course, if you have fourteen legitimate exemptions, take them. Otherwise, fourteen should be just about enough for anybody. Be happy with your newly increased cash flow.

If you really want money to invest, however, don't go off and blow your raise on a new dinner. Pay yourself what you would have paid the IRS and put the money into your investment kitty. Pay yourself first, remember?

Just One More Question about This Withholding Business

At this point, you may be asking yourself, "Just what can I deduct from my taxes—and claim on my W-4?" Not to dodge the question, but anything you can deduct from your income taxes you can probably legitimately claim on your W-4.

What can you deduct from your taxes? I thought you'd never ask. Let's take a brief walk through the state of Taxes and see if we can find the capital—you know, Dollars, Taxes.

How to Find an Investment on Your Return

First of all, you should understand how the IRS figures your income taxes. You start with your gross income, or the amount of income before the tax man steps in with his greedy paws. So start by figuring out your total income—that is, any money you've gotten from wages, salaries, tips, interest and dividends, alimony, pensions, rents, annuities, and what not. You also have to report any money you've made illegally. If you don't, it's a criminal offense.

Then you start adjusting your income to see how much is taxable. You do this by claiming certain specified deductions and exemptions, such as those for business expenses and your IRA and Keogh contributions. What remains is your adjusted gross income.

Once you've figured out your adjusted gross income, you can take other deductions, such as medical and dental expenses, to get your taxable income as low as possible. So no matter what your gross salary, the most important factor is your taxable income—that is, the amount of money you're actually taxed on.

Naturally, you want to adjust your income downward as much as possible. The less taxable income you have, the less taxes you pay. Start with the obvious: Take the exemptions that apply to you, such as those for yourself, your spouse, your dependents, and any others, such as those for the blind and senior citizens.

Now it's time to figure out ways to make your taxable income even smaller. You start by figuring out your adjusted gross income.

Adjusting Your Gross Income

Now, your adjusted gross income is your total income minus certain IRS-approved deductions. Here they are, blow by blow. Look them over carefully: They may help you get big tax breaks later on.

Moving Expenses. If you've moved and the distance between the new job location and your former home is more than thirty-five miles from your old job and former home, you can take some of your moving expenses off your taxes. You've got to work at least thirty-nine weeks of the next twelve months to qualify for this one.

Specifically, you can deduct the cost of traveling to your new home, moving your furniture, house-hunting trips, and disposing of your old home and buying a new one.

Suppose, for example, that you move from New York city to some place quieter—like a condo above a gong factory in Chicago. You spent $2,000 on house-hunting trips to Chicago, another $3,000 in moving expenses, and $5,000 in getting your old house sold and your new house bought. All of the above expenses are deductible—within certain limitations.

The IRS has kindly provided a chart that spells out the limitations for moving expenses. (See Figure 6.)

IRA and Keogh Contributions. Any contributions you make to an IRA or Keogh (or 401(k)) plan are tax-deductible in the current year. For example, suppose you made $20,000 during the year and you contributed $2,000 to your IRA before April 15 the next year. You can deduct the $2,000 from your gross income.

While many people seem disappointed that they can't take their IRA contribution as a credit from the amount they owe in taxes, an IRA contribution isn't a bad deduction. A single individual who earned $20,000 in 1984, for example, would have paid $731 less in taxes by contributing $2,000 to an IRA. And by reducing your adjusted gross income, your IRA contribution can open the door for itemizing your deductions.

Incidentally, you can make a contribution to your IRA for the previous year right up until the April 15 deadline for filing your taxes. For example, suppose you were making out your tax return for 1984 in March of 1985. You can still make a contribution to your 1984 IRA. In fact, you can file your tax return in March, claim your deduction, and not write a check to your IRA custodian until April 15.

Moving Expense Dollar Limits

Type of Expense	Marital Status	Dollar Limits	
		Form 3903	Form 3903F
Household goods and personal effects (line 1, Form 3903 or 3903F)	Not applicable	No limit	No limit
Travel expenses (line 2, Form 3903 or 3903F)	Not applicable	No limit	No limit
Househunting and temporary living expenses (lines 3 and 4, Form 3903 or 3903F)	Single	$1,500	$4,500
	Married filing jointly—		
	1) Spouses shared same new home at end of tax year	$1,500	$4,500
	2) Both spouses began work at new job locations but lived apart at end of tax year	$3,000 (limited to $1,500 each)	$9,000 (limited to $4,500 each)
	Married filing separately—		
	1) Both spouses began work at new job locations and lived together at end of tax year	$750 each	$2,250 each
	2) One working spouse	$1,500	$4,500
	3) Both spouses began work at new job locations but lived apart at end of tax year	$1,500 each	$4,500 each
Househunting and temporary living expenses; and expenses of selling and buying home (lines 3, 4, 7, and 8, Form 3903 or 3903F)	Single	$3,000	$6,000
	Married filing jointly—		
	1) Spouses shared same new home at end of tax year	$3,000	$6,000
	2) Both spouses began work at new job locations but lived apart at end of tax year	$6,000 (limited to $3,000 each)	$12,000 (limited to $6,000 each)
	Married filing separately—		
	1) Both spouses began work at new job locations and lived together at end of tax year	$1,500 each	$3,000 each
	2) One working spouse	$3,000	$6,000
	3) Both spouses began work at new job locations but lived apart at end of tax year	$3,000 each	$6,000 each

Figure 6. IRS publication 521 (rev. November 1983). Note that the limitations differ for moves outside the country, which is what the notation about Form 3903F refers to. If you do decide to claim moving deductions, it also wouldn't hurt to call up your local IRS office and ask for IRS publication 521—it's free for the asking. (*Source:* Internal Revenue Service)

It's not a bad idea to make your contribution to your 1985 IRA at the same time to tax-defer the earnings longer. Don't forget to add two exemptions for it on your current withholding certificate (if you haven't already claimed those exemptions). That way you get that tax benefit in your next paycheck.

Alimony. Alimony payments are deductible from your gross income. If you *receive* alimony, however, you'll have to count it as income.

There is one blessing to this last item, however: Alimony is counted as earned income, which means that you can use up to $2,000 worth of your alimony payments to contribute to an IRA. So if you feel out in the cold, it's some comfort that you can use your alimony payments to plan for your retirement.

A tax deduction generated by a marriage gone sour may seem like cold comfort, but at least you'll be able to make up for a bit of your lost income. Take your deduction and try not to think too hard about it.

Child support, on the other hand, is not deductible any more than it was when you were married. And, of course, it's tax-free to the spouse who receives it.

Deduction for a Married Couple When Both Work. If you and your spouse both work, you can get a nice deduction (up to $3,000) for your labors. Write down both of your gross incomes, making sure to deduct your IRA contributions and business expenses from your gross income. Now take the smaller income and deduct 10 percent of it from the gross income on your joint return.

For example, suppose Joe and Mary Bing were filing jointly. Joe made $20,000 per year, and Mary made $35,000. Joe contributed $1,000 to his IRA, while Mary was able to come up with $2,000. Their adjusted gross salary for computing their deduction for their labors was $19,000 for Joe and $33,000 for Mary.

Ten percent of Joe's adjusted salary, the smaller one, was $1,900. Joe and Mary can deduct $1,900 from their gross income. It's a nice break for couples who both work and find that their tax bracket when filing jointly is much higher than it would be if they were still single.

Penalty for Early Withdrawal of Savings. Did you buy a certificate of deposit and have to take your money out before it matured? If you did, then you've understood the real meaning of that ubiquitous phrase on bank ads, "Substantial penalty for early withdrawal."

You do have some minor comfort, however: Whatever you lost trying to get your own money back is deductible from your gross income. You won't get back all you lost, because the deduction only reduces the amount of income you're taxed on, but every deduction helps.

Employee Business Expenses. When you go on business trips, are you compensated for all your travel expenses, such as the costs of transportation, meals, and lodging?

The laws say that you can deduct the unreimbursed costs of business from your gross income. If you have the receipts for them, total them up and deduct them from your gross income. Remember that if your employer reimbursed you for your expenses, they are not deductible. Of course, the expenses must be "ordinary and necessary," which means that you can't deduct, say, the costs of sending a carload of gorillas to your competition's trade show booth.

Disability Income Exclusion. If you had to retire before retirement age because you were permanently disabled, you can exclude part of your disability income from your gross salary. The rules governing disability income are rather complex, however, and you should consult with the IRS or a tax consultant to figure out your best options.

Figuring Your Adjusted Gross Income

If you subtract the deductions above from your gross income, you'll have what the IRS considers your adjusted gross income. Your next step is to try to get that figure lower by itemizing your deductions. The deductions below are the real gold mines, because they lower your total taxable income. So keep careful track of them as you read them, and make a note to yourself whenever you see something you can use.

Itemizing Your Way to Investment Cash

In order to make itemizing worthwhile, there is a minimum your itemized deductions have to total.

How much? According to the IRS, if you're married and filing jointly, you must have at least $3,400* worth of itemized deductions to make itemizing

*As provided for in the Economic Recovery Tax Act of 1981, the federal government announced that in 1985 it will institute the first automatic adjustment of the income tax for inflation. In 1985 all income tax exemptions, tax brackets, and the standard deduction will be increased by 4.1 percent. This adjustment, or indexing, will help to minimize "bracket creep"—the situation where tax rates keep increasing but people's incomes merely stay even with the inflation rate. So, in 1985 the $1,000-a-person exemption will be increased by 4.1 percent, to $1,040. Tax brackets will also be widened by 4.1 percent, allowing more income to be taxed at the lower rate. As for the standard deduction, the single taxpayer, for example, will see his deduction raised from $2,300 to $2,390.

worthwhile. If you're filing as a single person or as the head of a household, you must have $2,300 in deductions to itemize. If you're married and filing separately, you should have at least $1,700 worth of deductions.

Now, these hurdles may seem formidable, but the truth is that, if you keep good records of your expenses, you'll probably find you have no trouble exceeding them.

As you read through the deductible items listed later in this chapter, make note of the ones that pertain to you. Whenever possible, pay for these items by check or get a receipt. The advantage of this is twofold: First, you'll be amazed at the deductible expenses you incur during the course of the year. Second, if the IRS calls you in and asks for an accounting, you'll be able to prove your deductions.

Don't Be Afraid to Take What's Coming to You

If you're terrified by the thought of an audit, you shouldn't be. In the first place, if you act in good faith—that is, if you don't deliberately try to cheat—you probably don't have much to worry about. Now, of course, if you claim your seventeen cats as dependents, you'll probably get what's coming to you.

But the IRS is more concerned with massive abuses—such as phony tax shelters and outright tax evasion—so they probably won't nickel-and-dime you for every little deduction you take. But keep good records, just in case.

The way most people get audited is the same way people get tapped for jury duty—by sheer dumb luck. You see, every three years the IRS taps 50,000 people on a random basis, both to strike fear in the hearts of tax-payers and to get a reasonably objective idea of what taxpayers are doing in general.

Interest Expenses. If you're like most red-blooded Americans, you're probably deep in debt. But there is one minor consolation to being up to your eyes in hock: All the money you pay in interest is generally tax-deductible.

The interest on personal loans, for example, is fully tax-deductible. If you have an auto loan, a college education loan, or a personal loan of any nature, you can deduct your interest payments from your taxable income. You may also deduct credit card interest, separately stated finance charges, installment plan interest, and revolving charge account interest. If you own a privately held business, you can also deduct the interest payments on business loans.

Mortgage interest, thank God, is also tax-deductible, as are most "points" you pay when you're buying a house. This is a wonderful tax break for all homeowners. In fact, homeowners are just about the only people who have enough interest deductions to make interest deductions worthwhile. Inciden-tally, if you decide to pay off your mortgage early and get hit with a mortgage prepayment penalty, you can usually deduct that from your taxable interest as well.

You can even deduct the interest (and the principal in this case) on a loan you take out to invest in a tax-qualified savings or retirement plan, such as an IRA or Keogh plan.

And Now for the Bad News on Interest. Of course, there are interest expenses that you *can't* deduct. For example, if you sell your house, you can't deduct the "points" you may have to pay to the bank or to your real estate agent. You also can't deduct the interest on money you borrowed to carry single-premium life insurance or to buy tax-free securities.

The IRS also considers service charges, such as the type the bank sticks you with for just about everything imaginable, as personal nondeductible expenses, and you should look at them the same way you do at other annoyances in life, like parking tickets and long-distance telephone surcharges. Incidentally, other charges the bank will hit you with, such as credit investigation fees and loan fees, are also nondeductible.

As long as we're at it, the IRS says you can't deduct the penalties it levies for delinquent taxpayers or late filers. So pay promptly and avoid the hassle.

Medical and Dental Expenses. Are you sick of taxes? Me, too. But you probably won't be able to deduct any expenses associated with that type of illness from your taxes.

If you do come down with a bona fide illness, however, you can deduct your medical costs from your taxes—at least, the part of your medical expenses that aren't paid for by your medical insurance. The IRS defines medical expenses as payments you make for the diagnosis, treatment, or prevention of disease.

For example, suppose you wake up on the wrong side of bed and fall two stories into the hedges below. You can deduct the cost of the ambulance ride, the diagnosis and treatment costs that aren't covered by your insurance, the cost of your medications, as well as the costs of the premiums themselves, as long as you pay for the premiums out of your own pocket. If you fall down an open manhole, you might be able to deduct the cover charge.

Now, as with all deductible items, there are a few catches to medical deductions. In the first place, your medical deductions have to be *more* than 5 percent of your adjusted gross income.

For example, if your adjusted gross income was $20,000 during the year, 5 percent of that is $1,000. If you don't have at least $1,000 worth of medical deductions, you won't be able to claim them.

The 5 percent limit has another meaning in IRS-ese: You must deduct 5 percent of your adjusted gross income from your medical deductions. So if the person in the above example had $1,800 worth of medical deductions, he or she would be able to deduct only $800. In layman's language, you have to be a pretty sick cookie to get a large medical deduction.

In the case of deductions for medicines, you'll have to meet the 5 percent rule above. You can deduct the cost of all prescription medicines for treatment of illness. If you take birth control pills, you can deduct them, and, if you can get a prescription for Laetril, you can deduct that as well. Don't get too carried away, however: Nonprescription items like toiletries, toothpaste, and cosmetics are not deductible, nor is bottled water.

Of course, fees paid to doctors are entirely deductible, as are dentist's bills. So if little Bucky needs braces, you can probably deduct that from your taxes as well.

Uncle Sam also allows you to claim deductions for medical treatments that are somewhat controversial. For example, if you visit a chiropractor, you can deduct those fees from your taxes. You can also deduct acupuncture treatments from your taxes, as well as any fees from Christian Science practitioners.

If you take other treatments not listed above, you should consult with the IRS or your tax adviser as to whether they're deductible. Witch doctors probably aren't deductible except, perhaps, as entertainment.

The government also permits you (quite rightly) to deduct alcohol and drug dependency treatments, as well as psychoanalysis, from your tax bills. Any legal operation costs are also deductible, as are laboratory fees for the same. Incidentally, you can claim face-lifts and other cosmetic surgery, as well as electrolysis by a qualified practitioner.

You can also deduct a certain amount of improvements to your home that you make because of illness or disability minus the amount of capital improvement involved. For example, suppose you install a wheelchair ramp in your home and it costs you $2,000. According to an appraiser, this increases the value of your home by $1,000. You can deduct the remaining $1,000 as a medical expense.

Finally, any expenditures you need to make because of your illness or infirmity are also deductible. This includes the costs of wheelchairs, Braille books and magazines, as well as the cost of any transportation you need to get medical treatment.

What If My Insurance Pays It All? If your insurance pays for all of your medical and dental expenses, then you can't deduct them. But if you pay for your health insurance yourself, then you can deduct that amount from your taxes. Include it with your other medical deductions which are also subject to the 5 percent test. If your boss pays for your medical insurance, however, you can't take his payments off your taxes.

Of course, in many cases health insurance doesn't cover all medical expenses; whatever you get hit with once the insurance company has made its payment you can deduct.

State and Local Taxes. I live in Massachusetts, which people here call "Taxachussets" because of the high state and local taxes. Now, there's not much you can do about state and local taxes, except deduct them from your federal taxes. You can deduct state and local income taxes, real estate taxes, sales taxes, and personal property taxes. If you need to figure out your state sales taxes, you don't need to keep records of every candy bar you bought in the past year: The IRS has guidelines you can use to figure out this expense. For those of you who can discipline yourselves to keep good records, your actual sales tax payments will nearly always exceed the tables.

Don't forget that larger tax items, such as the sales taxes on purchasing a car, airplane, or boat and those incurred when you buy building materials for fixing up your home are deductible in addition to the estimated sales tax allowances.

Charitable Contributions. If you do good by donating to charities, you can deduct your contributions from your adjusted gross income. Keep any checks or receipts that you get from your favorite local charity.

If you got receipts for the clothes, toys, or other things you donated when you decided to clean out your attic, you can deduct their market value as well.

Casualty and Theft Losses. If someone stole your car or if your house got hit by lightning, you can deduct your uninsured casualty loss on your taxes, provided your loss was worth at least $100. But your total casualty deduction must be at least 10 percent of your adjusted gross income. In addition, you must subtract $100 from each loss when you figure your deduction.

Here again, good record keeping is important. For example, suppose someone took a $6,000 diamond ring from your house. In many cases, homeowner's insurance has a $500 or so limit on jewelry, cash, and other valuables. So you got a $500 payment. Big deal. But you can claim a $5,400 loss from your taxable income, provided that amount is more than 10 percent of your adjusted gross income.

Miscellaneous Deductions. Now, there's a whole slew of other odd deductions that you can take. While it would take the better part of this book to explain them all in detail, here are some of the more salient ones:

- *A deduction that's due:* If you belong to a union or to some other support group for your profession, you can deduct the dues from your taxes.

- *Get smart and pay less taxes:* If you pursue employment-related education, you can deduct the cost of your education from your taxes. According to the IRS, you can deduct the costs of tuition, books, lab fees, and other expenses you incur while getting your education.

Now, this doesn't mean that little Jimmy can deduct his college tuition from his taxes: Your deductible educational expenses are only valid if they are required by your employer or if they maintain or improve skills required in doing your present work.

Making Smart Investing Tax-Deductible. Most expenses that you incur in the course of intelligent investing are tax-deductible. For example, if you subscribe to an investment newsletter like Donoghue's *MONEYLETTER,* or if you pay for investment advice, you can deduct these charges from your taxes. Keep in mind, however, that the IRS has clamped down on taking deductions for home computers used in investing.

Is That All There Is? In a word, no. These are the most common deductions available. Other deductions may be open to you, and you should check them out. (See Figure 7 for the itemized deductions schedule.)

Tax Credits

But there is one other class of tax break that's available to you, and that's called a tax credit. A tax credit is the best type of tax break around, because you get to deduct the amount of the credit directly from your taxes. For example, suppose you owed $1,500 in taxes and had a $500 tax credit. Your taxes would be reduced by $500, making your tax payment $1,000.

Because tax credits are such a good deal, there are precious few of them. The most common tax credits are for home energy credits, child care, and business expenditures.

Save on Heating Bills and Taxes, Too. Here in Massachussetts, it gets so cold that we hop into the icebox to thaw out. It gets so cold that we also spend inordinate amounts on heating bills.

Now, Congress doesn't mind people paying a fortune in heating bills, but they do get upset about our country's dependence on foreign energy sources —such as oil, for instance. So, as an incentive for everyone to conserve energy, they created energy tax credits.

Essentially, you get two different types of tax credits for saving energy. The first type of tax credit is for measures you take to conserve energy in the home, such as insulating your attic or installing storm windows. The other type is for

SCHEDULES A&B (Form 1040) Department of the Treasury Internal Revenue Service (0)	**Schedule A—Itemized Deductions** (Schedule B is on back) ▶ Attach to Form 1040. ▶ See Instructions for Schedules A and B (Form 1040).		OMB No. 1545-0074 19**83** 07
Name(s) as shown on Form 1040			Your social security number

Medical and Dental Expenses (Do not include expenses reimbursed or paid by others.) *(See page 18 of Instructions.)*	1 Medicines and drugs	1		
	2 Write 1% of Form 1040, line 33	2		
	3 Subtract line 2 from line 1. If line 2 is more than line 1, write zero . .	3		
	4 Other medical and dental expenses:			
	a Doctors, dentists, nurses, hospitals, insurance premiums you paid for medical and dental care, etc.	4a		
	b Transportation	4b		
	c Other (list—include hearing aids, dentures, eyeglasses, etc.) ▶			
		4c		
	5 Add lines 3 through 4c	5		
	6 Multiply amount on Form 1040, line 33, by 5% (.05) . .	6		
	7 Subtract line 6 from line 5. If line 6 is more than line 5, write zero . . . . ▶	7		
Taxes *(See page 19 of Instructions.)*	8 State and local income	8		
	9 Real estate	9		
	10 a General sales (see sales tax tables)	10a		
	b General sales on motor vehicles	10b		
	11 Other (list—include personal property) ▶	11		
	12 Add lines 8 through 11. Write your answer here . . . . ▶	12		
Interest Expense *(See page 20 of Instructions.)*	13 a Home mortgage interest paid to financial institutions	13a		
	b Home mortgage interest paid to individuals (show that person's name and address) ▶	13b		
	14 Credit cards and charge accounts	14		
	15 Other (list) ▶	15		
	16 Add lines 13a through 15. Write your answer here . . . . ▶	16		
Contributions *(See page 20 of Instructions.)*	17 a Cash contributions. (If you gave $3,000 or more to any one organization, report those contributions on line 17b.)	17a		
	b Cash contributions totaling $3,000 or more to any one organization. (Show to whom you gave and how much you gave.) ▶	17b		
	18 Other than cash (attach required statement)	18		
	19 Carryover from prior year	19		
	20 Add lines 17a through 19. Write your answer here . . . . ▶	20		
Casualty and Theft Losses	21 Total casualty or theft loss(es) (attach Form 4684) (see page 20 of Instructions). . . . . . ▶	21		
Miscellaneous Deductions *(See page 21 of Instructions.)*	22 Union and professional dues	22		
	23 Tax return preparation fee	23		
	24 Other (list) ▶	24		
	25 Add lines 22 through 24. Write your answer here. . . . . ▶	25		
Summary of Itemized Deductions *(See page 21 of Instructions.)*	26 Add lines 7, 12, 16, 20, 21, and 25	26		
	27 If you checked Form 1040 { Filing Status box 2 or 5, write $3,400 Filing Status box 1 or 4, write $2,300 Filing Status box 3, write $1,700 }	27		
	28 Subtract line 27 from line 26. Write your answer here and on Form 1040, line 34a. (If line 27 is more than line 26, see the Instructions for line 28 on page 21.). . . . . ▶	28		

For Paperwork Reduction Act Notice, see Form 1040 Instructions.   Schedule A (Form 1040) 1983

Figure 7. IRS schedule A—itemized deductions (Form 1040). (*Source:* Internal Revenue Service)

installing an energy system that relies on a renewable energy source, such as solar, wind, or geothermal energy.

The credit you get for energy conservation steps is equal to 15 percent of the first $2,000 you spend. For example, suppose you decide to reinsulate your house and the bill comes to $2,500. You can deduct 15 percent of $2,000, or $300, from your tax bill. If your tax bill is less than $300, you can carry forward the credit to next year's taxes.

This credit applies to most expenses you incur to conserve energy, such as storm or thermal windows, exterior weatherstripping, insulation, and certain energy-saving improvements on your furnace, like electronic ignition systems that replace pilot lights. Heat pumps, wood stoves, and new exterior siding, however, don't count.

The improvements you make must be designed to last at least three years, so you probably won't get credit for tacking plastic over your windows. Also, you must claim the credit in the year in which you make your repairs.

You can also get a tax break if you decide to replace all or part of your present energy system with one that runs entirely or in part from geothermal, wind, or solar power. The credit is 40 percent of the first $10,000 you spend, or a maximum of $4,000.

For example, suppose you live on Mt. St. Helens and decide you want to heat your house by means of a hot air vent from the basement. It costs you $10,000 to dig the hole and keep out the lava. You'll be able to deduct $4,000 directly from your taxes.

Keep in mind that the IRS has a fairly strict definition of renewable energy sources, so check with them before you take a credit for putting Bowser on a treadmill. Incidentally, you can't claim a swimming pool as a solar collector, so don't try it.

A Helping Hand for Working Parents. If both you and your spouse work, you can get a tax credit for any child care you need to enable you to continue working. The tax credit is equal to up to 20–30 percent of the expenses you incur, depending on your income level.

To take this deduction, the IRS requires that both spouses be working. There are two exceptions to this rule, however: if one spouse is a full-time student for five months during the year, or if one spouse is physically or mentally unable to care for himself or herself, then the IRS considers that spouse to be working.

All expenses you use to calculate your credit must be for the well-being and protection of the child and must allow you to work. For example, if you employ a full-time sitter while you are working, or if you send your child to a day-care center, you may use those expenses as a basis for figuring your credit.

Giving Credit to Business Expenditures. You can get tax breaks for capital business expenses—such as personal computers (PCs), copier machines, and other "ordinary and necessary" business expenses. For example, if you are a freelance writer and you use your PC as a word processor, your PC is an ordinary and necessary expense, just as a typewriter would be. If you need to buy a copier for your business, you can also get a tax credit for the copier.

You can get three different types of tax breaks for a business computer. One type is a one-time investment tax credit of 8 percent of the cost of the business equipment. You can deduct your investment tax credit directly from your tax bill.

For example, suppose you bought a HAL 2001 for $5,000 and used it for your aerospace research business. Eight percent of $5,000 is $400. If you owed $1,500 in taxes, your investment tax credit would reduce your tax bill to $1,100.

As an extra bonus, if you elect to take a tax credit, you can also depreciate your business equipment over five years under the Accelerated Cost Recovery System (ACRS). Under ACRS, you can depreciate 15 percent of the cost of the computer during the first year, 22 percent during the second year, and 21 percent for the next three years.

Keep in mind that a personal computer must be used for business to qualify for a tax credit and that only the business portion may be deducted. Congress and the IRS have been concerned that some people buy computers and claim the cost as a business expense when, in fact, they are using it to play Zorp or erase NASA's data files. To put an end to such frivolous deductions, the Budget Deficit Reduction Act of 1984 says that you must use your PC at least 50 percent of the time for business purposes during the first year of use to qualify for the investment tax credit and for the ACRS method of depreciation.

If you don't meet the 50 percent test during the first year, you'll lose the credit and have to settle for straight-line depreciation. If you don't meet the 50 percent test in subsequent years, you'll have to refund the tax credit and any excess ACRS depreciation will be added to your gross income.

In order to prove that you've used your PC for business purposes, you must keep a detailed log that documents your business use of your computer. If you don't have a log that documents the time, date, and reason for use of your computer, your tax credits could be disallowed and you could get hit with IRS fines for negligence.

How to Make a Good Year Better

If this year you make 40 percent more than the average of the past four years' taxable income plus a bit, you may find that Uncle Sam has a nice tax break for you—income averaging.

Before you wallow through four years of back income tax files, however, you should make sure you're eligible to income average. Uncle Sam doesn't like to be too generous with tax breaks like this one.

As its name implies, income averaging allows you to pay taxes on your average taxable income over a four-year period. If you want to figure out whether income averaging is worthwhile for you, the Internal Revenue Service recommends that you:

1. Find your average yearly taxable income from the past three years, not including this year's taxable income.
2. Multiply the above total by 1.40.

If your taxable income this year is greater than the figure you get by following the steps above, it will probably benefit you to income average. For example, suppose you had an average of $20,000 a year in taxable income for the past three years. $20,000 times 1.40 is $28,000. So, if you earned more than $28,000 this year, you would want to try income averaging.

Using the above formula will only give you a rough idea of whether or not you earned a high enough income to make income averaging worthwhile. The actual calculations involved with income averaging are fairly complex. After all, this is the IRS. For the excruciatingly complete details, consult the IRS publication entitled, surprisingly enough, *Income Averaging.* It's free at your local IRS office.

If you can't remember where you kept your tax records for the past few years, or if Fido used them for his own unspeakable purposes while they were stored in the basement, now—before the year-end rush—is the time to get duplicate copies. The IRS will want $5 per return in advance (you knew that was coming).

A Caveat about Taxes

Tax laws change frequently, as do tax rates and IRS rulings. This chapter is intended to show you the deductions, exemptions, and credits that are available to you. Keep in mind, however, that while the tax rules I've talked about are accurate to the best of my (and my accountant's) knowledge, I'm not a prophet, nor was I meant to be. Congress can change any of the above rulings at any time.

So before you make any moves to reduce your taxes, check to make sure that you're not working with unavoidably dated information. One of the best ways to check the tax breaks available to you is to write to the IRS for their list of free publications. You can also check in the appendix of this book for a list of IRS publications. While the IRS's writing tends to be a tad on the obtuse side, these publications are essential for anyone interested in paying less taxes—and all the publications are free. I've included some important addresses in the back of this book for your convenience.

You should also consider a reputable tax preparer, particularly if you feel that you have a goodly amount of deductions. The fees that tax preparers charge are generally reasonable, and they're also tax-deductible.

Less Taxes Mean More Money to Invest

Looking at tax laws, deductions and credits may not be your idea of a good time. I know it isn't mine. But it pays to keep an eye on deductible expenses all the time. The more deductions you can get, the less taxes you pay. And the less taxes you pay, the more money you have to invest.

So the time you spend slaving over your tax return can be well worth the effort—and there's a special feeling you get when you know that part of your investment kitty comes courtesy of the IRS. Now let's see how to avoid taxes on the earnings of your investments, so you can keep even more of your money from the tax man.

7

Deep in the Heart of Taxes: A Primer on How to Keep Your Investment Returns

> What's the difference between
> a taxidermist and the tax man?
> The taxidermist only takes the skin.
> —*Mark Twain*

The whole purpose of investing is to increase and enjoy your wealth. If you wind up paying most of your gains to the Internal Revenue Service, you've missed the point entirely. But you can turn the Internal Revenue Service into your own Individual Revenue Source—if you know how to do it.

How to Avoid Taxes Without Evading Them

Tax evasion is the willful failure to report income and gains and pay the taxes you owe on them. If you practice tax evasion, you can save a lot of money —and you can also do a lot of time in the big house free of charge. Obviously, evading taxes is simply a form of high-stakes gambling—with several years of your life as the stakes.

When most tax evaders are brought to justice, it turns out that it was taxes on their investment profits that they failed to report. I suspect that they just failed to plan for the tax consequences of their investment success —and couldn't bear to enrich Uncle Sam with part of their hard-earned winnings.

Tax avoidance, on the other hand, is arranging your investments so you owe little or no tax on your gains. There is absolutely nothing illegal about tax avoidance. If you don't believe me, listen to what former federal judge Learned Hand had to say about tax avoidance:

"Over and over again courts have said that there is nothing sinister in so arranging one's affairs as to keep taxes as low as possible. Everybody does so, rich or poor; and all do right, for nobody owes any public duty to pay more tax than the law demands; taxes are enforced exactions, not voluntary contributions."

What's Taxable and What's Not Makes a Big Difference

Knowing who gets what share of each kind of investment income can make paying the tax man a whole lot more palatable—because it lets you *plan* to keep your payments small. So don't chicken out now. Read the following tax primer slowly. (Don't be afraid to read this chapter a few times, if you must. It's *your money* the IRS is taking.)

This chapter will help you understand how the government treats several different kinds of income—and it will point out several kinds of cash flow which are virtually tax exempt because the government doesn't classify them as income. More important, it will tell you how to earn the right kinds of income to minimize your taxes and maximize your investible cash.

I'll show you how to keep the tax man from your door and, I hope, earn you a whole lot more money on your investments—your share of your investments, that is.

Six Kinds of Investment "Income"—and Two Kinds That Aren't Income at All

1. Ordinary Income: The Easiest to Earn and the Most Heavily Taxed. The sad truth is that nothing is taxed at a higher rate than ordinary income: wages, salaries, stock and mutual fund dividends, and interest from your bank accounts, certificates of deposit, or bonds. All of these types of income are considered ordinary income and qualify for precious few tax breaks.

On wages, salaries, and self-employment income, you can't even invest the tax money for a while—you must pay taxes as the income comes in. Your employer must withhold money from every paycheck. If you are self-employed you must pay taxes every quarter. To make sure you don't neglect any of your obligations, the government requires you to give your social security number to almost anyone who might pay you ordinary income and demands that they report what they've paid to the IRS.

Unfortunately, ordinary investment income seems to be the kind of income that most people seek. Now, every investor needs income-producing investments such as money market mutual funds at some time. Despite this fact, I recommend money funds for two distinct purposes: as a highly liquid parking lot for your cash between other investments and as a place for your short-term savings.

You see, putting your money in an income investment is best considered a defensive position, something you do with your money because interest rates are unusually high and the easy-to-earn yields are tempting or because you personally are unusually averse to risk—or simply because you're waiting for a better opportunity in another market. With a money fund, you'll always be able to seek greener pastures quickly—and you'll earn a fair money market rate of interest while you're waiting for new opportunities.

The other purpose of a money fund is for saving money that you know you'll be needing sometime in the future (you don't know exactly when) and you just want to put it aside and forget it, as many savers wish to do. For example, if you're saving for a house or some other personal goal and want easy liquidity and no risk, then a money fund is your best choice.

If you do put money in income investments for the long haul, however, you'll want to find ways to make that income something other than ordinary. We'll give you some suggestions in this chapter and the next.

2. Income from Tax-free Investments: It Isn't Always Risk-free. The federal and state governments made a deal a long time ago: The state governments would not tax interest on the U.S. government's Treasury bills and the federal government would not tax interest on municipal and state governments' borrowings.

In addition, the federal government made a special ruling that permitted mutual funds which put money in investments exempt from federal taxes to pass through this tax exemption to their investors. This has made tax-free mutual funds very attractive investments for people in high tax brackets.

Moreover, some states (including California, Massachusetts, and New York) exempt mutual funds which invest exclusively in state and municipal securities issued within their state from state taxes as well. Double tax-free income and double tax-free short-term money market mutual funds are very attractive investments. In New York City you can even buy *triple* tax-free mutual funds—funds whose income is exempt from federal, state, and city income taxes.

But beware. Most tax-free securities aren't the safe, simple income investments that money market mutual funds are because most tax-free securities are issued for longer periods than money market securities. Interest-bearing long-term securities can produce capital losses when interest rates rise and their prices fall (though they can also produce capital gains when interest rates decline and prices rise).

For example, when you or your mutual fund buy a long-term tax-exempt bond, the issuer guarantees a fixed amount of income per year—if you buy a $10,000, 12 percent bond due in the year 2000, for instance, you know you'll receive $100 every month until the year 2000, when the issuer pays off the bond.

If interest rates go down between the time you buy the bond and the time you sell it, however, other investors will be willing to pay you more than $10,000 for your bond. If interest rates fall to 8 percent, for example, new bonds due in the year 2000 would be paying only $80 per year and your old 12 percent bond, paying $100 per year, would be worth more.

Suppose, however, that rates rise to 14 percent. Now investors can get $1,400 a year from a new $10,000 bond. They won't touch your $100-a-month bond except at a greatly reduced price.

This isn't an unusual event, either. If you'd bought tax-free bonds in the spring of 1983, for example, their value would have declined more than 5 percent over the next year—wiping out the majority of the interest income you would have received.

I remember a wonderful gentleman who called in on a radio talk show in Miami. "I bought a tax-free investment that yields 10 percent. Did I do the right thing?" he asked.

"If you are in the 50 percent tax bracket at the federal level, that is the same as a taxable investment that yields 20 percent. But if interest rates rise, the market value of your investment could decline. Can you hold it to maturity?" I replied.

"It's a twenty-year bond, and I'm eighty. I hope so," was his optimistic answer. If he simply needed the income from the tax-free investment, he probably was doing fine. But if he ever might need his principal back, he was taking a big risk.

Tax-free bonds also involve credit risk, which means that some issuers may not be able to pay back the loan you've made them. If you invest your life savings in a tax-free bond and the issuer goes under, well, you're sunk.

It's happened before—most notably with the Washington Public Power Supply System (WPPSS) bonds (or WHOOPS bonds, as they came to be known). When the issuer defaulted on several bonds, many people nearing retirement were left with near-worthless pieces of paper for their life savings. That's a tragedy you should avoid.

You can minimize your risk with these bonds by buying insured municipal bonds. The insurer guarantees the principal and the timely payment of interest on them. While they generally give you a lower yield, the peace of mind may be worth the smaller return.

Another way is to diversify by creating your own portfolio of several different high-quality issuers. That way, if one goes bust, you'll still have money left on which to retire. But unless you know how to pick and choose among the enormous amounts of tax-free securities available (some 1.2 million at this writing), your best bet would be a diversified, professionally managed mutual fund.

If you want a tax-free investment that entails much less risk, you should take a look at tax-free and double tax-free money funds which invest exclusively in short-term state and local government securities. Tax-free money funds, like regular money market funds, keep a constant price per share of $1 —which means that there is very little risk to your investment money with these funds. (See Table 6 for a list of the double and triple tax-exempt money funds.)

But tax-free funds pay lower dividends—often dividends so much lower that these funds aren't worthwhile for anyone but the highest bracket taxpayer. Are tax-free investments for you? That depends on your tax bracket and, for the high-yielding investments in long-term issues, on your willingness to accept risk.

Do you know your tax bracket? If not, shame on you. Figure out what your taxable income will be this year and check the tax table in this book for your highest tax bracket. That is what you will pay on the next dollar you earn. That's your federal tax bracket for 1984. You might want to call the IRS and ask if the tax rate has increased or decreased since last year. Now add in your state and local income taxes, if any. That's your overall tax bracket. Pretty high, huh? But is it high enough to make tax-free investments worthwhile?

It's easy to find out, because the calculation is simple. You have to compare the yield you can get on a tax-free investment with the after-tax yield you could get from a directly comparable taxable investment. First, simply calculate how much of every ordinary income dollar the government lets you keep for yourself. That's just $1 minus your tax bracket. (If you're in the 40 percent bracket, for instance, $1 − $.40 = $.60.)

Next, multiply that figure by the yield you can get from fully taxable investments comparable to the tax-free investment you are considering. If the tax-free investment involves the risk of long-term bond investing, be sure to compare its yield to the yield of an investment in taxable long-term bonds. (If a taxable investment were yielding 12 percent, for example, the investor in the 40 percent bracket would have to find a comparable tax-free investment yielding at least 7.2 percent, since $12 \times .6 = 7.2$.) Generally, tax-free investments make sense for people in the 50 percent bracket and sometimes for those in as low as the 42 percent bracket. Double and triple tax-free investments sometimes make sense for people in even lower brackets. (See Table 7 for a comparison of taxable and tax-free yields.)

But wait! Even if you are in those high brackets, don't tie up all your money in tax-free investments yet—unless you're so rich you don't care about opportunities to make more money elsewhere. Whatever your tax bracket, tax-free investments can never make you as rich as capital gains, tax deferrals, and other careful strategies to conserve and expand your wealth. So be sure to take a close look at the next few chapters before you sink all your hard-earned cash into tax-free investments.

Table 6   Money Funds Specifically Designed to Be Double and Triple Tax-exempt

Name of Fund	Type of Fund	Tax-exempt Status	Minimum Investment
Benham California Tax-Free Trust Benham Management Corp. 755 Page Mill Road Palo Alto, CA 94304 (800) 227-8380 (US) (800) 982-6150 (CA)	General purpose	Double	$1,000
Municipal Fund for California Investors Provident Inst. Management Corp. Suite 204, Webster Bldg. Concord Plaza, 3411 Silverside Road Wilmington, DE 19810 (800) 221-8120 (US) (212) 323-7712 (NY)	Sold by Shearson Brokers	Triple	$5,000
Municipal Fund for New York Investors Provident Institute Management Corp. Suite 204, Webster Bldg. Concord Plaza, 3411 Silverside Road Wilmington, DE 19810 (800) 221-8120 (US) (212) 323-7712 (NY)	Sold by Shearson Brokers	Triple	$5,000
Reserve N.Y. Tax-Exempt Trust/N.Y. Reserve N.Y. Tax-Exempt Trust/Reserve N.Y. Reserve Management Co. 810 Seventh Avenue New York, NY 10019 (800) 223-5547 (US) (212) 977-9880 (NY)	General purpose General purpose	Triple Triple	$1,000 $1,000

Fidelity MassFree Fund Fidelity Investments 82 Devonshire Street Boston, MA 02106 (800) 343-6324 (US) (617) 523-1919 (MA)	General purpose	Triple	$2,500
Massachusetts Tax-Free Money Fund The Boston Co. One Boston Place Boston, MA 02106 (800) 343-6324 (US) (617) 956-9740 (MA)	General purpose	Double	$1,000

Source: Donoghue's Mutual Funds Almanac (15th ed.).

Table 7   Tax-Free Equivalent Table (%)

Tax-exempt Yields (%)	1984 Tax Bracket						
	34%	38%	42%	45%	48%	49%	50%
4.00	6.06	6.45	6.90	7.27	7.69	7.84	8.00
4.50	6.82	7.26	7.76	8.18	8.65	8.82	9.00
5.00	7.58	8.06	8.62	9.09	9.62	9.80	10.00
5.50	8.33	8.87	9.48	10.00	10.58	10.78	11.00
6.00	9.09	9.68	10.34	10.91	11.54	11.76	12.00
6.50	9.85	10.48	11.21	11.82	12.50	12.75	13.00
7.00	10.61	11.29	12.07	12.73	13.46	13.73	14.00
7.50	11.36	12.10	12.93	13.64	14.42	14.71	15.00
8.00	12.12	12.90	13.79	14.55	15.38	15.69	16.00
8.50	12.88	13.71	14.66	15.45	16.35	16.67	17.00
9.00	13.64	14.52	15.52	16.36	17.31	17.65	18.00
9.50	14.39	15.32	16.38	17.27	18.27	18.63	19.00
10.00	15.15	16.13	17.24	18.18	19.23	19.61	20.00
10.50	15.91	16.94	18.10	19.09	20.19	20.59	21.00
11.00	16.67	17.74	18.97	20.00	21.15	21.57	22.00
11.50	17.42	18.55	19.83	20.91	22.12	22.55	23.00
12.00	18.18	19.35	20.69	21.82	23.08	23.53	24.00

Note: Net amount subject to federal income tax after deductions and exemptions.
Source: Donoghue's Mutual Funds Almanac (15th ed.).

3. Capital Gains Can Be Exciting, and They Improve with Age. When you buy stocks, shares of mutual funds that invest in them, or even real estate or gold, you are making a capital investment. If you achieve a profit by selling a capital investment you have owned less than six months, it is taxed as ordinary income. But the government wants to encourage people to make long-term capital investments, so if you hold your stocks or mutual fund shares for at least six months, the profit you make is taxed at 40 percent of the rate for ordinary income. (For example, people in the 40 percent tax bracket pay only 16 percent on long-term capital gains.)

If you were in the 40 percent tax bracket, bought a stock today at $100 a share, earned $10 in dividends and sold the stock in five months at $200 a share, you would pay $4 in taxes on the dividends and $40 in taxes on the gain, leaving you with a $66 per share profit. If you had waited and sold one month later, you would still pay $4 in taxes on the dividends but only $16 in taxes on the gain, leaving you with a $90 per share profit.

There are two morals to this story:

First, the taxation of long-term capital gains is so advantageous that even the most modest investing success can make you significantly richer than you could ever become by buying income securities—whether taxable or tax-free.

Second, when you are successful in the market you should hold onto the stocks or mutual funds you've bought for a full six months, if you possibly can. Remember, you can stand a 15–35 percent or so decline in value while waiting for long-term treatment and *still* come out ahead of where you would have been if you'd sold early.

You can even get capital gains treatment on part of your profits from investing in fixed income investments like bonds. If the price of a bond rises —which usually happens when interest rates decline—you can sell at a profit and the profit is taxed as a capital gain. (See Table 8 for long-term capital gain breakeven.)

There's one other way to get income which the government will let you count as a capital gain. Many successful mutual funds pay "long-term capital gains distributions" once a year—distributions from their past stock market profits. If you invest in one of these funds and receive a long-term capital gains distribution, it's taxable to you as a long-term gain, even if you bought the mutual fund shares the day before the distribution was declared (although you must hold onto your shares at least six months to qualify).

You should keep in mind that you get this special tax treatment because you are taking a certain amount of risk. The value of your capital investment could decline, and you could lose money instead. But even losses on this type of investment have favored tax treatment, which I'll explain later on.

A final point: Capital gains taxes demonstrate more than any other kind of income one crucial aspect of investing and taxes: the importance of good record keeping. The government requires you to know how much you paid for stocks, bonds, and mutual fund shares as well as when you bought and sold them.

Sometimes stockbrokers or mutual fund managers don't keep your records readily available for previous years. So it may be up to you to prove when you bought your investments. If your records are a mess, you'll either wind up paying more taxes than necessary or you'll pay less than you should and live in fear of an IRS audit.

4. Money You Can Put Away Now and Pay Taxes on Later. It is technically called "deferred income." But more realistically it is called "everyman's and everywoman's tax shelter." Deferred income is money which you can put aside and often (if it is tax-qualified, as is an Individual Retirement Account) deduct from your tax return. You need not pay any taxes on the investment income that this money earns until you decide to withdraw it. Deferred income means *big* tax savings *now.*

There are three wonderfully generous income-deferral plans for average people: IRAs (Individual Retirement Accounts), Keoghs (for the self-employed), and SARAs or Salary Reduction Plans (technically known as 401(k)s). If you're an employee of a company offering a SARA or 401(k) plan,

Table 8   Long-Term Capital Gain Breakeven

Tax Bracket	$100 Short-Term Capital Gain			Under Long-Term Capital Gain Tax a $100 Profit Can Decline to			A Percentage Decline of:*
	Before-Tax Profit	Tax	After-Tax Profit	Before-Tax Profit	Tax	After-Tax Profit	
20%	$100	$20.00	$80.00	$86.96	$ 6.96	$80.00	13.04
22	100	22.00	78.00	85.53	7.53	78.00	14.47
23	100	23.00	77.00	84.80	7.80	77.00	15.20
24	100	24.00	76.00	84.07	8.07	76.00	15.93
25	100	25.00	75.00	83.33	8.33	75.00	16.67
26	100	26.00	74.00	82.59	8.59	74.00	17.41
28	100	28.00	72.00	81.08	9.08	72.00	18.99
30	100	30.00	70.00	79.55	9.55	70.00	20.45
32	100	32.00	68.00	77.98	9.98	68.00	22.02
33	100	33.00	67.00	77.19	10.19	67.00	22.81
34	100	34.00	66.00	76.39	10.39	66.00	23.61
35	100	35.00	65.00	75.58	10.58	65.00	24.42
38	100	38.00	62.00	73.11	11.11	62.00	26.89
42	100	42.00	58.00	69.71	11.71	58.00	30.29
45	100	45.00	55.00	67.07	12.07	55.00	32.93
48	100	48.00	52.00	64.36	12.36	52.00	35.64
49	100	49.00	51.00	63.43	12.43	51.00	36.57
50	100	50.00	50.00	62.50	12.50	50.00	37.50

*The percentage decline may be used with any dollar amount of profit. To figure the long-term term before-tax profit needed to breakeven:

Before-tax profit (short-term) $\times$ percentage decline (i.e., figure in last column that corresponds to your tax bracket) = X

Before-tax profit (short-term) $- X$ = before-tax profit (long-term)

This is the figure your long-term profit can decline to before taxes.
To check the above figure:

Before-tax profit (long-term) $-$ (40%) (your tax bracket) = after-tax profit (long-term)

which should equal your short-term after-tax profit.

take advantage of that plan first, then set up an IRA if you can afford one and finally set up a Keogh plan to shelter the self-employment income you make knitting tiny sweaters to sell at your local flea market on Sundays.

Many annuity and insurance plans also defer taxes on the income they accumulate for you, though they don't let you deduct the money you put into them from your tax return. Deferring taxes on income is so important—and potentially so lucrative—that I devote the whole of Chapter 8 to this wonderful subject. I want to be sure you understand why tax deferred retirement accounts are important for much more than just retirement.

5. The Big Exclusion: When Mother's House Becomes a Mother Lode. Perhaps the biggest single tax break you'll ever get is the special break given homeowners over fifty-five who sell their home. If you sell your home at a profit—and most people make big profits when they sell their houses these days—you get a one-time tax exclusion. You pay absolutely no taxes on your capital gain up to $125,000.

This is a big reason why many retirees should sell their big houses after the children have grown up and moved out and reinvest in a condominium or simply rent. You get the size home you really need and are willing to maintain *and* you get a substantial tax-free addition to your money to invest.

6. Low-Tax Income for Your Kids: How to Start a "Familiar" Tax Shelter. We all know that kids are just about the most expensive creatures in the world. And we know that the government takes this into account by letting us take an exemption on our income tax return of $1,000 for every dependent child. Big deal!

But unfortunately many parents don't know that it's relatively simple to turn some parental investment income into kids' income, which will then likely be taxed at a lower rate if it's taxed at all. Every parent saving for a child's education should take advantage of the low or nonexistent taxes on children's income.

All states have a Uniform Gifts to Minors Act or similar legislation which lets you designate as gifts securities purchased or bank accounts established for your children or anyone of whom you become custodian. All you have to do is call a mutual fund or walk into a bank or brokerage office to set up one of these accounts.

These accounts are especially good vehicles for such investments as high-yielding bonds, whose benefits would be largely taxed away if bought in your own name outside of a retirement account. Be assertive in your handling of at least part of your kids' money—you can afford to take some risks with money that might easily have just gone up in taxes.

There is one key point to remember when giving money and securities as gifts to your children: The money you're putting aside really is a gift for your kids. You can't take it back. When the kids reach the age of majority in your state (eighteen or twenty-one or somewhere in between) the money will immediately be theirs to spend as they see fit.

There are ways to limit how the money is spent. The simplest is to spend most of it yourself on items you think are in the child's best interest before the child reaches the age of majority. But you have to be careful in doing this. If you spend the money on simple support of the child—the necessities of life such as food, clothing, and shelter—part of the money you've taken from the trust account will count as income to you and you'll have to pay taxes at ordinary income rates! If you spend the money on expenses other than simple support, however, you need pay no taxes on it.

You could also have a lawyer draw up a more complex trust, which can put any conditions you want on your gift. You can order your child to spend the money only on pilgrimages to Lourdes, if you want. But to do so you'll have to spend a good deal on legal fees.

Know When Cash Flow Isn't Income—When It's Money That's Yours, but You Haven't Seen It for a While

One way to avoid paying taxes is to understand when the "income" you are getting back is only your own money. There are two very popular investments which can easily lead you to pay taxes on income you never received.

1. T-Bills from the Fed—Your Change Is Gonna Come. A lot of people like to buy U.S. Treasury bills directly from the Federal Reserve Bank. "They pay me my interest up front and I like that," they tell me. Folks, that is your *change—not* your interest.

Let's take a simple example. Suppose you go down to the Fed and give them $10,000 (a certified check, of course) to buy a one-year Treasury bill. You don't know what interest they are going to pay—no one will know the interest on this week's T-bills till the weekly T-bill auction in which the big securities houses bid for millions of dollars' worth of T-bills.

When the auction is held, a discount rate is announced and we'll say that the discount rate was exactly 10 percent. You get back a check for $1,000. When the bill matures a year from now, you will get back a full $10,000. The $1,000 difference between the $9,000 you put up (the original $10,000 less your $1,000 change) and the full $10,000 you get back is your interest. So *don't* pay federal income taxes on that first $1,000 until you get the full $10,000 back—next year.

There is more good news. Since you earned $1,000 on a $9,000 investment, your real return was not 10 percent. You really earned 11.11 percent.

Not bad at all, and even better considering that Treasury bill interest is exempt from state and local taxes. But it's not a good deal *if* you forget and pay federal taxes on *both* $1,000 payments.

2. Ginnie Mae Is a Real Looker—But Some of Her Charms Are Just Your Imagination. Another tricky opportunity is a so-called "Ginnie Mae" (Government National Mortgage Association—GNMA) investment. Stockbrokers seem to love to sell these federal government-guaranteed investments but neglect to advise clients about all their complexities.

Ginnie Maes are packages of other people's mortgages which banks and thrift institutions have sold to GNMA. When you buy GNMA mortgage participations you have to face the fact that many people pay off mortgages early. On the average, people move every five years or so. They pay off their old mortgages and then get new ones at their new home bank.

That means that you get, included in your checks from GNMA or the GNMA fund, both interest payments and payments for return of capital on repaid mortgages. If you are not careful to read the fine print on your checks, you could make the mistake of paying taxes on both the interest and the return of principal.

That's one problem with Ginnie Maes. The others are that you never know the real return on these investments until you actually see how long each mortgage lasts before it is repaid and, as with other long-term debt instruments, you can lose money if you want to sell and interest rates have risen since you bought these investments. Often Ginnie Maes do offer a good return. But don't let a broker oversell them to you.

Choose the Right Kind of Income and You'll Come Out Way Ahead

Now you know about the various kinds of income and cash flow you and your family can receive. Seek the right kind of income, and you'll make yourself and your family richer. Only the tax man will cry. (Don't worry, he can stand it.)

Tricks of the Tax Shelter Trade

Before we complete this tax primer, I want to cover three other important approaches to tax sheltering—one very dangerous and the other two extremely safe.

1. How to Lose Your Shirt and Trigger a Tax Audit. You read constantly about millionaires who don't pay a cent in taxes. Perhaps a stockbroker has even offered to let you in on a tax shelter scheme that sounds too good to be true. Can you duplicate the successes of the millionaires?

Maybe—but you'll have to use hard business sense, take substantial risks, accept the significantly increased likelihood of an unfriendly tax audit, and probably pay a large share of your initial investment to the tax shelter promoter. The shelter promoter and the guy who sells the shelter to you are likely to make out fine regardless of whether you win or lose.

But you could be stuck with a big debt that you never counted on. Such apparently well-informed investors as economist and presidential adviser Arthur Laffer, businessman and former Secretary of State Alexander Haig, and hot dog magnate Harold Mayer (former president of Oscar Mayer & Co.) lost tens of thousands of dollars—after taxes—in one recent tax shelter scheme that didn't quite work out as planned. For them, a fancy tax shelter deal just wasn't worthwhile. Similar deals may not be worthwhile for you either. Guacamole's law: Don't count your avocados before they mature.

Basically, a typical tax shelter deal takes advantage of the fact that some kinds of businesses run losses in the first few years of operation, then make big profits later on. A tax shelter promoter can, for example, set up an avocado farm. For the first few years, the business will consist of planting avocado trees, caring for them, and waiting for them to mature. There will be precious little revenue, and certainly no profit. But because the ultimate yield—a crop of avocados—is reasonably predictable, a bank will lend him much of the money he needs to get started.

Say it costs $1 million to get into the avocado business. He borrows 80 percent of the money and sells "limited partnerships" to you and nineteen other investors for $10,000 each to provide the rest of the capital. Legally, partners in a business are in quite a different situation from stockholders in a corporation. When a business suffers a loss, partners in it can deduct that loss from their income taxes in proportion to their ownership of the business. But if the IRS decides that the whole "business" was just a gimmick to generate tax write-offs, it will disallow the shelter and you could wind up owing thousands of dollars in back taxes and penalties.

Suppose the avacado farm runs a loss of $300,000 a year for the first two years. If your $10,000 investment has given you a 1/20 share of the business, you can report a $15,000 loss each year, even though you only put up $10,000 in the first place.

Great. But suppose the Mediterranean fruit fly eats your avocados? Suppose the promoter flies to Brazil with most of the business's money? Suppose the avocado crop comes in as scheduled, but there is a glut of avocados on the market and the business continues to lose money? You'll never get any of your original investment back and you may, depending on how the tax shelter has been constructed, be liable for some or all of the money the promoter has borrowed to get the scheme off the ground.

On the other hand, if the avocado business proceeds nicely and yet never returns you the money you put in, the IRS may decide that your promoter never really intended to make money planting avocados in the first place. Then all your deductions will suddenly become illegal.

The IRS absolutely requires that any investor in a tax shelter be genuinely "at risk" for the full amount of the losses he is writing off, and that write-offs be taken exclusively on investments in genuine, profit-seeking businesses.

These rules cause two horrible possibilities: First, as thousands of tax shelter investors have discovered, when things go wrong you can find yourself deeply in debt. Second, you can find yourself facing an unsympathetic tax auditor. Because many investors try to cheat on the "at risk" provisions and write off losses which don't entail any risks for themselves at all, the IRS has an aggressive program which makes it much more likely you'll face an audit if you write off tax shelter losses.

So if a tax shelter seems too good to be true, don't put your money in it. It can leave you sadder, wiser, and much poorer than when you started.

2. How to Lose Money the Smart Way—Cut Your Losses Short and Let Your Winnings Run Long. But don't give up hope. There is another kind of tax shelter which can turn losses experienced by virtually all investors into profits.

Did the stock you bought fall faster than a brick balloon? Did your municipal bond go bust before you could blink? Did your broker bounce you a bomb off the Big Board and back? Well, cheer up, Bunky! There's nothing like a good quick capital loss to cut your tax bill. In fact, if some of your investments make big gains and others make equally big losses, you can still come out way ahead financially just by knowing when to sell and when not to.

You see, capital losses are deductible on your income tax return under rules roughly similar to those that govern the reporting of capital gain income: Capital losses are fully deductible from income if you sell a stock after holding it for less than six months. But you can deduct only 50 percent of your losses if you hold onto an investment for more than six months.

You can quickly see what a neat deal this provides if you time your buying and selling right: Suppose that last January 1 you bought 100 shares of Complex Computer Corp. and 100 shares of Irrational Information, Inc. Now suppose Complex Computer goes up 20 points and Irrational Information goes down 20 points.

If you sell Irrational Information this year, you can deduct $2,000 from your income tax return right away. And if you then hold Complex Computer and sell it next year, you will pay tax equivalent to the ordinary income tax on only $800. (Remember that long-term capital gains are taxed at only 40 percent of the regular capital gains tax rate. $2,000 × 40 percent is $800.)

Although you made no profit at all in the stock market, you will make a big profit ($1,200 × whatever your tax bracket may be) on the tax consequences of your trades.

There are a few rules to remember regarding capital gains and losses:

1. *When you take a short-term loss, you may not reinvest your money in a "substantially identical" investment within thirty days.* If you do, you will have executed what the IRS calls a "wash sale," and the tax man may assess severe penalties against you when you try to claim a short-term loss.

But the IRS's definition of a "substantially identical" investment is fairly liberal. If you sold your stock in Irrational Information, Inc. and used the proceeds to buy stock in another computer company, you'd have no trouble. And if you simply take some shares in a growth stock mutual fund that failed to grow and telephone the parent company of the mutual fund asking to shift your investment to the same fund family's money market fund, your transfer out of the growth stock fund will certainly qualify as a capital loss.

2. *You report your short-term and long-term gains and losses on a "net" basis.* That is, if your sales of stocks and mutual fund shares during a given year result in $4,000 in long-term gains and $5,000 in long-term losses, you will receive a deduction on your return as if you had suffered a simple $1,000 long-term loss.

3. *The maximum deduction for net short-term or long-term capital losses in any one year is $3,000.* If you lost $12,000 on Amalgamated Moosemobile stock last year and made $5,000 on North American Hatrack, your total net capital loss for the year would be $7,000. But only $3,000 could be deducted this year. The remaining $4,000 would have to be "carried forward"—you could deduct $3,000 of it next year and $1,000 the year after that.

3. Keeping Well Sheltered: Do You Need Income or Just Cash Flow?
Some people, especially senior citizens, think that to get regular cash flow they need to invest in income funds or money funds. They are trapping themselves into paying all their taxes at ordinary income rates, the most expensive kind. These folks are confusing income with cash flow.

Remember that income is any genuine addition to your wealth, such as salary, wages, dividends, and interest. Cash flow is any flow of spendable cash. You pay your bills with cash flow, not income. Most forms of cash flow are genuine income, but others can earn gentler treatment from the IRS. Long-term capital gains, for example, are taxed at only 40 percent of the normal tax rates. And, of course, your own principal has already had the taxes taken out of it.

You can get regular cash flow from your investments without losing the opportunity to enjoy tax-advantaged capital gains taxation.

The service you want to ask for is called a check-a-month plan, and is offered by most mutual fund families. These are well-organized and popular plans. In many cases, the plans actually deposit cash directly into your bank account each month electronically. (No risk of lost or stolen checks.)

Now, just using the check-a-month plan will not guarantee that you will earn some capital gains—you have to manage your money to earn them, but you can get regular cash flow and the opportunity for some tax-advantaged returns if you are willing to invest in growth funds as we explain in Chapter 10 using the Super-SLYC investing system.

Income funds will seldom earn anything other than ordinary income, while growth and aggressive growth funds at least stand a fair chance of earning tax-advantaged returns.

You see, if you manage your investments to take advantage of the stock market mutual funds when interest rates are falling, you are bound to earn some of your return in the form of long-term capital gains. Either some of the fund's distributions to you will be long-term capital gains or you will sell some of the stock fund shares for a profit after holding them for at least six months. Both ways qualify for special long-term capital gains tax treatment.

I've already shown (and I'll show in greater detail in Chapter 10) that an investment program combining both income investments and aggressive growth investments will outperform a simple income-oriented investment program most of the time *in addition* to producing important tax advantages. A check-a-month program lets you pursue this more assertive, intelligent invest- ment strategy while at the same time receiving a stable cash flow.

When the investments grow faster than the withdrawals, the principal grows. When the withdrawals are greater than the income the investment pool has generated, the principal diminishes and you cash in some of your gains. Over the long term, both are likely to happen, depending on how fast you are withdrawing your money. The fund's service representatives can be very help- ful in advising you how much you could reasonably withdraw each month. Either way, the cash flow is constant.

Check-a-month plans may demand that you spend some extra time at the end of the year figuring out just what you paid for the securities the mutual fund has sold to generate cash for you, and therefore how much tax you owe at the reduced capital gains rates. And keeping your funds in capital gains- oriented investments rather than in investments that produce ordinary income does involve some risk. But the effort and the risk are generally worthwhile.

You're Sleeping in a Pile of Cash

Another way some retirees gain a regular cash flow is to sell their houses (without paying capital gains taxes, because they are over fifty-five) to a buyer who agrees to pay them so much a month until they die, after which he will pay off the difference to their estate. This particular type of arrangement is particularly popular when your children want to keep the family home with you in it. You'll get the tax-free income from the sale of the house, and your children will get the house when you pass on.

Those who only need a bit more to live on may choose to use one of the real estate line of credit programs offered by stockbrokers, insurance brokers, and banks where they can borrow on the equity in their home. In effect, this is a second mortgage on which you draw only what you need as you need it.

While the set-up costs on some equity access programs are high, by the time you read this the price war should be on and the set-up fees and interest rates much more competitive. Keep in mind, however, that equity access programs are collateralized loans, with your house as collateral. If you can't pay the loan off in time, you could lose the home you wanted to keep.

When the Tax Man Cometh . . . He's Gonna Leave Still Hungry

Most of this tax shelter stuff isn't very difficult, is it? Now you know some of the rules and tricks of the investment tax game. Be sure to earn the right *kind* of income whenever possible. Claim your capital losses intelligently and don't get stuck with an investment taxed at ordinary income rates when you could have relied on cash flow from your accumulated capital gains.

If you follow this advice you'll beat the tax man to the punch and keep your share of the winnings. It is hard enough to earn money on investments; you ought to keep as much as possible. If you learn how to pay less taxes on your investment earnings, *you will have more money to invest*—automatically. Now that you know how to pay less taxes on money you have *already* earned, you are ready to learn how to save money on your *future* earnings and reduce your current tax bill in the process.

8

Tax Shelters for Very Important Investors

The rich are different than you and me.
—F. Scott Fitzgerald

Yes, they have more money.
—Ernest Hemingway

Until recently, only the very rich had tax shelters. The tradition started back in the Middle Ages, when the tax system was structured backward: the poorest peasants paid the highest taxes, while nobles were exempt from taxes, on the assumption that they needed the money for more important things, like building castles, throwing feasts, and buying expensive jewels.

This tradition of giving tax shelters only to very important investors has continued right down into the twentieth century. While the rich are taxed at a higher rate than others, the government has allowed tax shelters for the very rich on the assumption that it would support "big business."

Old-Style Tax Shelters Were Designed to Keep Lawyers Employed

Of course, the main reason that rich people are the only people with elaborate tax shelters available to them is that only the rich can afford to hire the legal and financial advice necessary to understand them. Most of the tax-shelter schemes involving cattle farms, rutabaga ranches, and oil-drilling operations are so complicated they are beyond the comprehension—much less the budgets—of nearly everybody.

But, fortunately, Congress has realized that ordinary people need to be sheltered from taxes, too. The Internal Revenue Service calls these tax shelters qualified tax-deferred retirement accounts, and, as their name implies, they were intended as retirement vehicles. As their name also implies, they are not tax-free: you'll have to pay taxes on your investment money when you withdraw it, although presumably you'll be in a lower tax bracket when you retire.

You're on Your Own, So Listen Close

In all likelihood, Congress created these retirement plans because of the very real possibility that the Social Security system will collapse within the next twenty years. So even if you're not thrilled at the thought of a tax shelter, you could wind up facing a very bleak retirement indeed if you don't take advantage of these plans.

The Deal of the Century for VIIs

Whatever the purpose of their creation, however, qualified tax-deferred retirement accounts are the deal of the century for the average investor. They're so important to your financial planning, in fact, that I call them tax shelters for Very Important Investors (VIIs)—such as you and your family, You probably know them as Individual Retirement Accounts (IRAs), Keogh plans, and SARAs—the section 401(k) Salary Reduction Plans I've described.

I call them everyone's tax shelters because there's no reason why you can't use them for other long-range purposes than retirement, if you like. If you have a good pension plan, for example, you can use it to save for a house, a boat, or your children's education. In fact, even with the IRS tax penalties for early withdrawal from these plans, your money will accumulate and grow so much faster when it's tax-deferred that it can be worth your while to withdraw your IRA money after as little as seven years.

In this chapter, then, I'm going to show you how to use these tax shelters for Very Important Investors like yourself: how to use them for retirement, how to use them for other long-range goals, and how to make them work as hard as you do.

Tax-Deferred Magic

What makes qualified retirement plans so great? Quite simply, they give you more money to invest on an after-tax basis and allow your earnings to grow much faster than they would with all but the most speculative investments.

First the Bad News . . . For example, suppose you wanted to invest $2,000 and you were in the 30 percent federal tax bracket. If your principal weren't tax-deferred, you'd have to earn $2,857 pretax dollars to invest $2,000.

If that weren't bad enough, watch what happens to your earnings when the tax man takes his yearly toll. Supposing you'd managed to scrape up enough after-tax dollars to put $2,000 into an investment. We'll say for the sake of argument that you put your money into a one-year bank certificate of deposit that pays 10 percent simple interest.

At the end of the year, you'd have earned $200 in interest, which isn't bad. Enter the tax man, who promptly takes 30 percent, or $60, leaving you an after-tax return of $140. Suddenly, your 10 percent return has shrunk to 7 percent! And your state and local tax authorities are probably waiting to take their shares as well.

Now, if that weren't depressing enough, let's see what your real rate of return was. You earned $2,857 and made $140: That's a 4.90 percent rate of return—not counting, of course, state and local taxes. With inflation running at about 6 percent (to be more or less charitable), you lost about 1.1 percent on your 10 percent bank CD. Depressing, isn't it?

. . . Then the Good News. But the picture changes when your principal is deductible currently and your interest is tax-deferred. Since you can deduct your contribution from your taxes, it's easier to find money to invest that way. In fact, if you make one smart investment move, you can actually get the IRS to contribute to your tax-deferred investment.

Here's how to do it. Suppose you make $20,000 per year and you decide that you want to contribute $2,000 to an IRA, one of the most popular tax-deferred investments. You should be paying taxes on $18,000, not $20,000, right?

Now, if you were a single individual who earned $20,000 in 1984, you paid $3,205 in taxes that year. But if you deducted $2,000 for an IRA contribution, you paid only $2,691 in taxes for that year, a savings of $514. If you adjusted your income tax withholding to reflect your true tax rate as I described in Chapter 6, you could start getting part of that $514 back in your next paycheck. In effect, the IRS would be contributing to your IRA.

Tax-Deferred Compounding: Even More Magic

But the tax exemption for tax-deferred retirement plans is only a small part of the investment magic of tax shelters for Very Important Investors. In taxable investments, you'll watch an appalling percent of your investment return eaten away by taxes. But with tax-deferred investments, your money is compounded without taxes—and that makes an amazing difference.

How amazing? If you had invested $2,000 in a fully taxable investment for thirty years at 14 percent and you were in the 25 percent tax bracket, you'd end up with $29,988 after taxes. But if you were in an IRA—which is not the best tax shelter available to you by any means—you'd have $76,425 after taxes. Amazing? Yes. Unbeatable? Not by a long shot. (See Figure 8 for a comparison of the methods of compounding.)

You see, not all of the tax shelters you have available to you are created equal. For example, an IRA is a fine shelter. But you can put more money into a Keogh. And the best shelter of all, SARA, is a real looker.

Meet SARA, the Tax Shelter of the '80s

If you're willing to take a small reduction in your salary (which is essentially the same as contributing some of what you have already earned), you can start a self-directed, tax-deferred retirement account that's even better than an IRA or a Keogh.

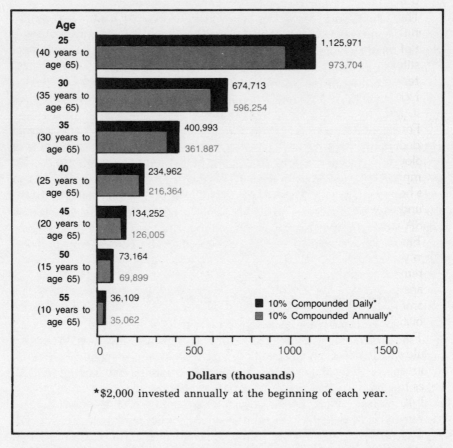

Figure 8. Shopping around: a compounding difference. *(Source: Donoghue's MONEY-LETTER)*

SARA (for *S*alary *R*eduction *A*ccount), known as 401(k) to the Internal Revenue Service, is one of the best deals available today. If your employer offers a SARA, you should take full advantage of it before you even look at any other tax-deferred savings plan, even an IRA, which you can do as well.

Five Ways SARA Is a 10. There are five reasons why a SARA can be better than an IRA.

First, you can contribute more money to a SARA than to an IRA. That means that you'll have more money working for your long-range goals and that your money will grow faster.

Second, under the terms of some SARA plans, your employer will match your contributions. In some cases, your employer will match your contributions dollar for dollar, which will give you a 100 percent return the first year —no matter how well your SARA investments perform.

Third, your money in a SARA is somewhat more accessible than money in an IRA or a Keogh. Most SARAs allow withdrawals from your account in case of an "emergency." While the IRS hasn't issued a ruling yet as to what constitutes an emergency, it's likely that if you need cash for a pressing matter—such as medical expenses, purchase of a primary residence, or even your child's tuition bills—you can get at your money when you need it the most.

Fourth, you can even borrow money from your SARA and pay yourself tax-deductible interest. This is, however, only available in some plans. Ask your employer if you can borrow from your SARA—you may be able to. For example, if you want to withdraw part of your funds to make a down payment on a home or to fund your children's education, you may have a cheap source of funds in your SARA. In some cases, like buying a home, the loans from your SARA may have a longer payback period.

Finally, you can use ten-year forward averaging when you take withdrawals from your SARA. If you choose to take your distributions as a lump sum at retirement, you'll qualify for ten-year forward averaging at tax time. This means your lump-sum distributions will be taxed as if they were your only income and as if the money were paid out in equal annual amounts over the following ten-year period.

For example, using forward averaging, a $100,000 lump-sum distribution would be taxed at only 16 percent if you're in the 40 percent tax bracket. In contrast, IRA distributions are taxed as regular income. That's 60 percent less taxes than you would normally pay on an equal amount of ordinary income and 40 percent more after-tax dollars to live on, and no other self-directed retirement plan available to you offers such a great tax break.

Here's how a SARA works. Your employer designs a prototype plan with a bank, mutual fund, and/or insurance agency. Once your employer's plan is approved by the IRS, you can contribute 2 percent to 10 percent of your pretax income or bonuses to the plan. Your contributions are taken out of your income before you receive your paycheck.

When you file your income taxes, the wages you contribute to your SARA are not considered as income and are not included on your W-2 form. Whatever amounts you contribute to your SARA are tax-deferred until you draw on them. For example, if you earn $30,000 per year and contribute 10 percent of your income ($3,000) to your SARA, you'll pay income tax on only $27,000.

Best of all, you can direct where and when your contributions are invested. Suppose, for example, your plan is set up with a mutual fund family, which is a group of different mutual funds within the same management company. You could split your investment any way you want. You could use the fund family's money fund or stock market growth fund. And you could manage your money as you wish within the limits of the program. In the next few chapters we'll show you how to do it. The important thing is that the choice is up to you, not the pension fund manager.

All SARAs Are the Same Except Where They Are Different. While no two salary reduction plans are the same, there are three basic types of SARAs. An employer can tailor each plan to his company's and employees' needs.

1. Pretax thrift plan. This is the most popular with employees because employers match their workers' contributions. The generally accepted maximum salary reduction for this plan is 6 percent.
2. Salary reduction savings plan. There is no matching of contributions by the employer with this type of plan. In most cases, a salary reduction savings plan can reduce your salary by up to 10 percent.
3. Cash-deferred profit-sharing plan. Like the pretax thrift plan, employers match employees' contributions. However, employees can choose to take the employer's contributions in cash, which means that you can either invest your boss's contributions or spend them. Of course, with the advantages of tax-deferred savings, your best bet is to invest your employer's contributions.

You may begin taking distributions from your SARA six months after you turn fifty-nine. You may also begin taking distributions without penalty when you retire, leave your job for any reason regardless of your age, or suffer financial hardship.

Unlike IRA and Keogh plans, some sponsoring companies allow employees to borrow from their 401(k) plan. The IRS permits loans of up to 50 percent of the account balance or $50,000, whichever is higher. The term of the loan must be no longer than five years, and you must pay interest on the loan as you would with any other loan. Of course, your interest on the loan is tax-deductible. If you don't pay interest on the loan, however, the IRS will consider the loan a distribution, and you'll be taxed accordingly.

Roll Over or Wait? If you leave your job, you can roll over your SARA funds into an IRA or another 401(k). If you take another job and your employer has a retirement plan, you can put your SARA funds in your new employer's retirement plan. This is the best deal. Rolling your SARA into an IRA means giving up the tax benefits of the ten-year forward averaging.

If you are nearing retirement, keep in mind that the pension payments you get from your company are usually based on your salary for the last three to five years you worked. Since a SARA reduces your salary, you probably shouldn't join a company which calculates your pension payments on a reduced salary level. It could lower your pension payments during retirement.

You Can't Do This One Alone. The major catch to a SARA is that your employer must offer one in order for you to open one. But SARAs have become increasingly popular with employers in the last few years, mainly because their contributions to your account are tax-deductible. So if your employer doesn't have one, you should suggest it to him or her. The advantages for your company are substantial—and you'll get the best tax-deferred savings account available.

IRA, SARA's Older Brother

If your company doesn't have a SARA, then you should make the acquaintance of her brother, IRA. For people without SARAs available, the IRA is the best deal to come along in decades. In fact, even if you have a SARA, you can still open an IRA, if you can afford it.

Like SARA contributions, your contributions to an IRA are tax-deductible and your earnings tax-sheltered until you start drawing upon them. Your deduction for your IRA may not exceed $2,000 of earned income or alimony per year. If you and your spouse each earn at least $2,000 per year, you may deduct $4,000 if you file a joint return and have each deposited $2,000 in separate IRAs. If one spouse isn't employed, you may deduct $2,250 each year if you've deposited that amount in at least two IRAs. As long as you don't exceed the maximum of $2,000 for any one of these IRAs, you may divide the money between the accounts however you wish. As I write this, there are several bills before Congress which will allow you to contribute even more to your IRA, making a good deal even better.

Keep in mind that these are the maximum yearly contributions to an IRA, not the minimum. Many IRAs have no minimum initial investment requirements, so you can start small. In terms of investments, $2,000 per year isn't much, and that's the best part about the IRA. Anyone can afford to start an IRA, and most people can afford to contribute the maximum amount.

Unlike a SARA, however, there is a 10 percent IRS penalty on any amount you withdraw from your IRA before you reach retirement age. After the IRS has taken out its penalty, they will also hit you for ordinary income taxes on the amount you have left after the penalty. For this reason, an IRA is a long-term investment—but, as I'll explain later on, not as long-term as you might think.

An IRA Is Not a Bank Account—Unless You Want It to Be. The most popular misconception about an IRA is that it's a bank account. Actually, an IRA is a shelter around an investment, not the investment itself. You can establish your IRA with any number of financial institutions. Banks, S&Ls, insurance companies, credit unions, and brokerage houses all offer IRAs. But you can usually do better at some place other than a bank or thrift.

Bank IRAs Are a Trap. If you have already set up an IRA at your bank, you have probably gotten yourself into a trap. Most bank IRAs have three major problems. First, since most IRAs are placed in eighteen-month certificates of deposit, you could lock into a rate that will look horribly low by the end of six months. Unless you honestly feel that interest rates have peaked, you're better off with a variable-rate IRA, such as one offered by money funds and bank money market deposit accounts. Also, if you started your IRA between January and April, as most people do, your IRA certificate matures just when you are least likely to think about moving your IRA.

Second, there are substantial early withdrawal penalties as with most bank CDs. If you try to move your IRA from a bank before the CD matures, you will have to pay three to six months' interest to move into another IRA account elsewhere.

Worst of all, if you decide to withdraw your IRA before retirement and your IRA is in a bank CD, you'll have to pay the CD's early withdrawal penalty, the 10 percent IRS penalty—and then you'll have to pay ordinary income taxes on the amount you've withdrawn. If you do have a bank IRA, the best you can do is to mark your calendar and make sure you withdraw your money when the account matures—your bank should notify you—and move your account then.

So What Should I Do? The best place to move your IRA is to a no-load mutual fund family. If you name the fund family as the trustee of the account, you can switch your IRA investments as often as the fund's management permits to take advantage of changing market conditions. Best of all, you'll be able to take advantage of my Super-SLY and Super-SLYC system, which I describe in Chapters 9 and 10.

Of course, if you haven't contributed the full $2,000 to your bank IRA, you can simply start an IRA with a no-load mutual fund whenever you like. You can have two IRAs—or sixteen, if you want—provided that your total contribution to all of them isn't more than $2,000 for the year.

Double Your Treasure. Don't forget that you can set up an IRA for this year until April 15 of next year. You have 15½ months in which to set up your IRA, and the sooner you get your money in the sooner your earnings will be tax-sheltered. A lot of people setting up their first IRA in the spring will make a double contribution if they can afford it—one for the tax year just ended and one for the next tax year.

Looking into a Keogh

If you're self-employed or have a business on the side, you should investigate a Keogh account. Opening a Keogh account is one of the best moves a self-employed person can make now because you can contribute more money to a Keogh than an IRA, although you can open an IRA in addition to your Keogh.

The best way to explain a Keogh account is to compare it with an IRA. Like an IRA, a Keogh is a tax shelter around an investment—not necessarily a bank account. You can open a Keogh account in a wide variety of investment vehicles, including mutual funds and brokerage accounts.

As with an IRA, the money you contribute to your Keogh plan is tax-deductible and any money that the investment earns is tax-exempt until you begin to draw on it. You must be at least fifty-nine and a half before you begin to draw on the funds in your IRA or Keogh account without incurring a 10 percent tax penalty on any funds you withdraw (only what you take, not the full balance in the account, however).

However, *you* must be self-employed to open a Keogh account. If you are only self-employed part-time, you can also start a Keogh. For example, if you work at Allied Moosemobiles during the day and make money on the side making tiny sweaters for the flea market, you can put the money you make in your second job into a Keogh. Remember, you can have an IRA and a Keogh at the same time, if you can afford it.

One of the advantages of a Keogh over an IRA is that you can generally contribute more to a Keogh than to an IRA. The amount you can contribute to your Keogh depends on how you decide to structure your Keogh program.

Define the Contribution or the Benefits. The most widely offered type of Keogh is a defined contribution plan. Under a defined contribution plan, the amount you may put into your Keogh account is a certain percentage of the net taxable income you make from your self-employment. For the tax year ending December 31, 1983, you could contribute either $15,000 per year or 15 percent of your net self-employment income, whichever is the smaller sum. For any subsequent tax year, you can contribute the lesser of $30,000 or 25 percent of your self-employment income.

You may also open a defined benefit plan, which means that your contributions are determined by the amount you wish to receive per year during your retirement. Because the rules governing a defined benefit plan are extraordinarily complex, suffice it to say that you can generally contribute more to this type of plan and that you should always consult a professional tax adviser before you open a defined benefit Keogh account.

Although it's not true of IRAs, you must open your Keogh account before the end of the year, although you may contribute to your Keogh up until the deadline for filing your taxes. For example, for 1985 you must open your Keogh account by December 31, 1985. You may continue to contribute to your Keogh up until April 15, 1986, however.

Everybody Gets in on the Act. Keep in mind that if you have employees, you must provide coverage for them under certain circumstances. Generally speaking, if you opened a Keogh before January 1, 1984, and you have employees who have worked for you for three years or more, they must qualify for your Keogh benefits. To the IRS, a year of employment means that your employee has worked 1,000 hours over a twelve-month period. If you started after 1983, however, you must provide coverage for anyone who is over twenty-five and has worked for one year or more.

While contributions to your employees' accounts are deductible business expenses, you should consult a professional adviser to make sure you know your obligations. In some cases, other types of retirement and benefit plans might be more appropriate for you and your employees.

When you reach age fifty-nine and a half, you may begin drawing on your Keogh account. You may also, in some cases, roll over your Keogh account into another qualified retirement plan such as an IRA. In any case, you are not required to begin drawing on your Keogh account at fifty-nine and a half. In fact, the longer you can manage without doing so, the longer your money will have to grow.

Once you start to draw on your Keogh—and you must begin doing so by age seventy and a half under most conditions—it will be taxed as ordinary income. Since most people have a lower tax bracket when they have retired than when they are working, this can be a significant tax advantage.

If you're eligible for a Keogh, you should look into opening one now, no matter what your age. The tax advantages are significant, but the real advantage is having a nest egg for your retirement. Otherwise, you may have only Social Security to count on—and if you're wise, you won't.

A Warning—You Must Withdraw from Your Tax Shelter or Pay the Consequences

If you do not begin drawing upon your tax shelters by age seventy and a half, you will find that the IRS will assess a harsh penalty of 50 percent of what they say you should have withdrawn. By the time you reach this age, you must either take a lump-sum distribution or regular distributions based upon the IRS's actuarial tables.

An Alternative: Variable Annuities

If you're looking for another tax-deferred investment for your child's education or for other major long-term goals, you might consider investing in a variable annuity. But it pays to do your homework before you invest in one of these products, and you should always look at other tax-deferred investments, such as IRAs, Keoghs, and SARAs before you even think about a variable annuity.

An annuity is a contract between you (the annuitant) and an insurance company. You can invest in a variable annuity by paying either a lump sum or monthly installments. If you pay by monthly installments, your payment can be as low as $25.

Your insurance company will invest your money in either stocks, bonds, or mutual funds, and the earnings on the annuity will be tax-deferred until you begin to draw on it. Best of all, you can direct where you want the money invested within the company's stable of mutual funds, so you can take advantage of changing market conditions.

You can withdraw all funds from your annuity without penalty after ten years or when you reach age fifty-nine and a half. Most insurance companies require that you begin to take distributions by the time you reach age eighty-five. When you withdraw your funds, you can either take a lump-sum payment and use regular income averaging to pay taxes or you can take monthly payments.

Variable annuities are complex, and they involve more fees than an Individual Retirement Account (IRA) or Keogh. But variable annuities have several payout and investment advantages.

First, you can use a variable annuity to salt away additional retirement money. If you already have an IRA or Keogh, you can tax-defer additional funds for your retirement nest egg.

Second, because an annuity is an insurance product, there is a mortality guarantee written into the contract. This means that if your payout schedule is based on your life expectancy and you outlive the designated payout schedule, payments will continue.

Finally, you can choose several different options for receiving distributions when you retire. If you choose a life annuity, you will receive payments until your death. If you buy a life annuity with a "period certain" and die before the period stipulated in the contract, your beneficiary collects the balance of the account over a five-, ten-, or twenty-year period. In a joint-survivor annuity, the income from the annuity is guaranteed for your life as well as your surviving spouse's life as long as she or he lives.

Most annuities have deferred sales charges, so 100 percent of your money is fully invested until you begin receiving distributions. Because you contribute after-tax money to an annuity, only the investment earnings are taxed as ordinary income upon distribution. When you retire, you can roll over your IRA or Keogh into a variable annuity that will immediately begin paying you monthly income while the earnings in the account grow tax-free until distribution. Finally, with a variable annuity your benificiaries will avoid the costs of probate court when your estate is settled. They may still have to pay estate taxes on the distributions, however.

Compare the costs when you shop for a variable annuity. The charges can total up to 5 percent a year, depending on the annuity contract you choose. If, for example, you have the mortality guarantee of lifetime payments, the insurance company will deduct from 0.8 to 1.5 percent annually.

There are also early withdrawal fees (surrender charges) if you take out more than 10 percent per year from your account before ten years have passed or if you're not yet fifty-nine and a half. The fees range from 6 to 1 percent, depending on how long you have held the annuity. In addition, the IRS levies a 5 percent tax if you make early withdrawals.

There are switching fees if you change from one fund to another in your variable annuity, and state taxes on premium payments can amount to as much as 2 percent when you start to take distributions. Some companies also charge investment advisory fees for mutual fund account management.

Variable annuities can be an excellent deal, but they're not for everyone. You need to consider you financial needs at retirement, your taxes, and your estate. You also need to watch fees very carefully, and decide whether the relatively high fees justify the return. Before you invest, talk to your accountant, financial planner, or insurance agent to see whether this source of tax-deferred earnings is for you. Shop around carefully, read the fine print carefully, and don't be swayed by sales pitches.

How to Make the Most of Your Tax-Deferred Investments

By now, you should have decided which of the many tax-deferred investments are right for you. Your first choice should be a SARA, if your company offers one. If not, open an IRA. If you're self-employed, open a Keogh before anything else, then look to opening an IRA. You should use variable annuities only if you don't have employment income and you have an insurance expert who can explain carefully your choices (these are very complicated and confusing investments).

Keep in mind that you can mix and match all of these plans to suit your needs. For example, if you have employment and self-employment income, you could open an IRA and a Keogh. If your company offers a SARA, you could have an IRA as well. The more money you can put into these plans, the faster your money will grow and the more you'll have for your long-range goals.

The Rate's the Key

The real benefit of investing in an IRA or any tax-deferred investment is the ability to take the money you would have paid in taxes each year and reinvest that money for your own benefit. You don't have much control over how long your investment money will be in your tax shelter because you must start withdrawing between the ages of fifty-nine and a half and seventy and a half. You cannot control how much you can invest because that amount is generally set. Therefore, the rate of return is the most important factor you can control.

Guaranteed Rates Guarantee Less

For example, suppose your long-range goal was to have $1 million after taxes when you retire. That's a big goal, and not one that anyone can guarantee. But you have no chance whatsoever of reaching that goal if you settle for low fixed rates. (See Table 9.)

For example, it would take you seventy-seven years to accumulate 2 million pretax dollars in your IRA if you chose a passbook savings account for your IRA trustee. At that rate, you'd have to start your IRA thirteen years before you were born if you were planning on retiring at sixty-five—an obvious impossibility.

If you averaged 10 percent in your tax-sheltered investment, you'd have to start your IRA at seventeen in order to get $2 million before taxes, because it would take forty-eight years to get that much.

You can do better if you put your IRA in a no-load mutual fund that offers

Table 9   What a $2,000 Investment from Your *Gross* Income Will Be Worth After Taxes Under Different Tax Sheltering (and Unsheltered) Options*

Your Tax Rate	Your Annual Pretax Rate of Return	Your Years Before Withdrawal	IRA with Withdrawal After Age 59½	IRA with 10% Penalty for Withdrawal Before Age 59½	Thrift Plan with 25% Employer Match	Thrift Plan with 50% Employer Match	Thrift Plan with 100% Employer Match	401(k) Plan with 50% Employer Match	Non-IRA, Capital Gains-Producing Investment	Non-IRA, Non-capital Gains-Producing Investment
10%	6%	5	$ 2,409	$ 2,141	$ 2,890	$ 3,432	$ 4,516	$ 3,613	$ 2,384	$ 2,341
10%	6%	15	4,314	3,834	5,033	6,004	7,945	6,471	4,213	3,962
10%	6%	30	10,338	9,190	11,811	14,137	18,789	15,507	9,997	8,719
10%	10%	5	2,899	2,577	3,441	4,094	5,398	4,349	2,855	2,770
10%	10%	15	7,519	6,684	8,639	10,331	13,714	11,279	7,290	6,556
10%	10%	30	31,409	27,919	35,515	42,582	56,716	47,114	30,225	23,882
10%	14%	5	3,466	3,081	4,079	4,859	6,418	5,199	3,339	3,258
10%	14%	15	12,848	11,421	14,634	17,525	23,307	19,272	12,406	10,675
10%	14%	30	91,710	81,520	103,354	123,989	165,259	137,565	88,114	63,303
25%	6%	5	2,007	1,740	2,257	2,633	3,386	3,011	1,957	1,869
25%	6%	15	3,595	3,116	3,745	4,419	5,767	5,392	3,385	2,903
25%	6%	30	8,615	7,467	8,452	10,067	13,298	12,923	7,904	5,618
25%	10%	5	2,416	2,094	2,640	3,093	3,999	3,624	2,324	2,153
25%	10%	15	6,266	5,430	6,249	7,424	9,774	9,399	5,789	4,438
25%	10%	30	26,174	22,684	24,913	29,821	39,636	39,261	23,707	13,132
25%	14%	5	2,888	2,503	3,083	3,624	4,707	4,332	2,749	2,471
25%	14%	15	10,707	9,279	10,413	12,420	16,435	16,060	9,786	6,707
25%	14%	30	76,425	66,235	72,024	86,353	115,013	114,637	68,933	29,989
30%	6%	5	1,874	1,606	2,059	2,387	3,043	2,811	2,336	1,720
30%	6%	15	3,355	2,876	3,356	3,943	5,117	5,033	3,121	2,595
30%	6%	30	8,041	6,892	7,446	8,863	11,677	12,062	7,224	4,810

30%	10%	5	2,255	1,933	2,393	2,787	3,577	3,383	2,152	2,154
30%	10%	15	5,848	5,013	5,537	6,561	8,607	8,772	5,314	5,099
30%	10%	30	24,429	20,939	21,796	26,071	34,621	36,644	21,666	18,575
30%	14%	5	2,696	2,310	2,779	3,250	4,194	4,044	2,540	2,234
30%	14%	15	9,993	8,566	9,164	10,913	14,410	14,990	8,960	5,691
30%	14%	30	71,330	61,140	62,834	75,317	100,282	106,995	62,939	23,131
38%	6%	5	1,659	1,391	1,757	2,014	2,529	2,489	1,596	1,448
38%	6%	15	2,972	2,492	2,774	3,235	4,156	4,458	2,709	2,145
38%	6%	30	7,122	5,973	5,991	7,095	9,302	10,683	6,228	3,709
38%	10%	5	1,997	1,391	2,019	2,328	2,948	2,996	1,882	1,675
38%	10%	15	5,180	4,344	4,486	5,288	6,894	7,770	4,581	3,057
38%	10%	30	21,637	18,147	17,240	20,594	27,301	32,456	18,537	7,536
38%	14%	5	2,388	2,002	2,322	2,692	3,432	3,581	2,213	1,880
38%	14%	15	8,851	7,423	7,331	8,703	11,446	13,277	7,694	4,321
38%	14%	30	63,178	52,988	49,434	59,227	78,812	94,767	53,764	15,063
50%	6%	5	1,338	1,071	1,336	1,504	1,838	2,007	1,271	1,159
50%	6%	15	2,397	1,971	1,998	2,297	2,897	3,596	2,117	1,558
50%	6%	30	5,743	4,595	4,090	4,808	6,243	8,615	4,795	2,427
50%	10%	5	1,611	1,288	1,507	1,708	2,111	2,417	1,488	1,276
50%	10%	15	4,177	3,341	3,111	3,633	4,677	6,266	3,541	2,079
50%	10%	30	17,449	13,960	11,406	13,587	17,949	26,174	14,160	4,322
50%	14%	5	1,925	1,540	1,703	1,944	2,425	2,888	1,740	1,403
50%	14%	15	7,138	5,710	4,961	5,853	7,638	10,707	5,910	2,705
50%	14%	30	50,950	40,760	32,344	38,713	51,450	76,425	40,960	7,612

*Assumes tax rate at return is same as tax rate during accumulation period.

Source: Reprinted with permission from *The IRA Book*, by Roger Krughoff and the Center for the Study of Services (*Consumers' Checkbook* magazine).

free telephone switching. While no one can guarantee that you'll average more than 10 percent, you at least have the ability to move with the different markets for the highest rates of return. Why trade away the possibility of high returns for a bank account?

If You're Young, Don't Be Afraid to Take Some Risks

I think that taking a little risk with your IRA money can pay off in the long run, particularly if you're young and have plenty of time to make up for any losses you may suffer.

If you use a mutual fund family that offers switching between its stock funds and money funds for your IRA trustee, you can take some limited risks. For example, if you move your IRA money into a stock market growth fund and decide that if it declines as much as 10 percent from its highest price you will switch back into a money fund, you will limit your losses. Would you accept a controllable 10 percent risk to earn 20 percent or 30 percent average returns in the long run? If so, then you're on the way to higher average returns and a better retirement.

If you feel that you need the security of an insured account, make sure you get the best rate available. If you have your IRA in a variable-rate bank account, remember that you'll only get what the bank wants to pay you for your money —which is not the same as what your money is really worth. (See Tables 10 and 11.)

If You Can't Afford an IRA or Keogh, It Can Pay to Borrow

If you want to contribute the full $2,000 to your IRA or Keogh, then don't be afraid to borrow the money from your local bank. It's perfectly legal, provided you have at least $2,000 in employment (or self-employment) income for the year.

As an added bonus, any interest you pay on your IRA or Keogh loan is tax-deductible. So you can deduct the amount of the loan and the interest. That's one of the smartest moves you can make.

Know When to Hold 'Em and When to Fold 'Em

Some people feel that IRAs are too long-term for them to even consider. "Why should I lock up my money for thirty years in an IRA?" they ask. And for most people, locking up money for a long time causes a very squeamish feeling indeed.

But the truth is that the penalties for early withdrawal from an IRA are not as harsh as they sound. In fact, you can withdraw your money from an IRA

Table 10   IRA Versus Thrift Plan

Case 1

Annual return on investment: 13%
Time period: 30 years
Tax bracket: 45%
Employer's matching rate: 25% of employee's contribution

	IRA	Thrift Plan	
			($900 has been
Employee's deposit	$ 2,000	$ 1,100	taxed away)
Employer's deposit	+0	+275	
Total deposit	$ 2,000	$ 1,375	
Value of deposit after 30 years	$78,232	$53,784	
Less: employee's contribution of aftertax dollars	−0	−1,100	
Taxable portion of account	$78,232	$52,684	
Less: ordinary income tax on account	−35,204	−23,708	
Value of deposit after tax if withdrawn after age 59½	$43,025	$30,076	
Less: 10 percent penalty tax for early withdrawal	−7,823	−0	
Value of deposit after tax if withdrawn before age 59½	$35,205	$30,076	

Case 2

Annual return on investment: 7%
Time period: 10 years
Tax bracket: 25%
Employer's matching rate: 50% of employee's contribution

	IRA	Thrift Plan	
			($500 has been
Employee's deposit	$ 2,000	$ 1,500	taxed away)
Employer's deposit	+0	+750	
Total deposit	$ 2,000	$ 2,250	
Value of deposit after 10 years	$ 3,934	$ 4,426	
Less: employee's contribution of aftertax dollars	−0	−1,500	
Taxable portion of account	$ 3,934	$ 2,926	
Less: ordinary income tax on account	−984	−732	
Value of deposit after tax if withdrawn after age 59½	$ 2,950	$ 3,694	
Less: 10 percent penalty tax for early withdrawal	−393	−0	
Value of deposit after tax if withdrawn before age 59½	$ 2,557	$ 3,694	

Source: Reprinted with permission from *The IRA Book*, by Roger Krughoff and the Center for the Study of Services (*Consumers' Checkbook* magazine).

Table 11   IRA Versus Capital Gains-Producing Investment

Case 1

Annual return on investment: 13%
Time period: 30 years
Tax bracket: 45%

	IRA	Capital Gains-Producing Investment Outside an IRA	
Your investment	$ 2,000	$ 1,100	($900 has been taxed away)
Value of investment after 30 years	$78,232	$43,027	
Taxable portion of account (total balance minus your contribution of aftertax dollars)	$78,232	$41,927	
Less: tax on account when withdrawn (used) if withdrawn after age 59½	−35,204	−7,547	
Aftertax value of account if withdrawn (used) after age 59½	$43,078	$35,480	
Less: 10 percent penalty tax for early withdrawal	−7,823	−0	
Aftertax value of account if withdrawn (used) before age 59½	$35,255	$35,480	

Case 2

Annual return on investment: 7%
Time period: 10 years
Tax bracket: 25%

	IRA	Capital Gains-Producing Investment Outside an IRA	
Your investment	$ 2,000	$ 1,500	($500 has been taxed away)
Value of investment after 10 years	$ 3,934	$ 2,951	
Taxable portion of account (total balance minus your contribution of aftertax dollars)	$ 3,934	$ 1,451	
Less: tax on account when withdrawn (used) if withdrawn after age 59½	−984	−145	
Aftertax value of account if withdrawn (used) after age 59½	$ 2,950	$ 2,805	
Less: 10 percent penalty tax for early withdrawal	−393	−0	
Aftertax value of account if withdrawn (used) before age 59½	$ 2,557	$ 2,805	

Source: Reprinted with permission from *The IRA Book,* by Roger Krughoff and the Center for the Study of Services (*Consumers' Checkbook* magazine).

in as little as seven years and make as much money as you could in a taxable investment.

The actual formula for determining when it's worth taking the IRS penalties is quite complex, and I've relegated it to the back of the book for my more technical-minded readers (see Appendix 5). But if you look at the table in Appendix 5, you'll get a fair idea of when it's worthwhile for you to take the penalties and withdraw your IRA money.

Now, unless you know you have a wad of cash on which to retire, you shouldn't go spending your IRA money frivolously. But if you have an emergency, it's comforting to know when you can dip into your retirement nest egg.

Tax Shelters for Very Important Investors: Keystones to Savings Plans

SARAs, IRAs, and Keoghs are keystones of your lifetime savings plan. No other type of investment offers the combination of tax advantages and earnings that these plans offer.

Quite simply, the more you contribute to these plans, the greater tax breaks you get. The greater the tax break, the easier it is to invest more.

Best of all, the money you invest in these plans can find you more money to invest than any comparable taxable investment. The faster your money grows, the more money you'll find to invest.

9

Super-SLY Money Market Investing

Some of the easiest money you will ever find in your quest for money to invest is the money your money can find for you in the money market.

For many first-time investors, the first cautious step is discovering the wonders of the "retail money market." "Retail" means that this portion of the money market is for everybody (including those with only a few dollars to invest) and "money market" means that this is where you can earn an honest free market return on your savings.

We've Come a Long Way, Baby

I sometimes forget how far we have all come in such a short time. It was not until 1972 that most people were allowed to earn money market returns through the first money funds. Bank customers had to wait for six-month money market certificates until June 1, 1978—and even then, you needed $10,000 to get money market rates. As recently as 1975, it was actually illegal for a bank to open a passbook savings account for even a small corporation like mine. That certainly has changed!

Now there is nearly $2 trillion ($2 million million) in the retail money market, and people like you and me can earn those high money market yields that all the banks and money funds advertise. And we accept it as if it had always been available. (See Table 12. The dates chosen represent three phases of the retail money market: before the 1978 introduction of the six-month money market certificate; before the 1982 introduction of money market deposit accounts and Super NOW accounts; and today [retail money market].)

Table 12   The Retail Money Market (All Figures in Billions of $)

	January 1978	November 1982	March 1984
Checking accounts	$242.8	$240.6	$239.6
NOW accounts	4.2	101.5	134.1
Super NOW accounts	N/A	N/A	37.8
Retail repos	N/A	10.3	1.2
Passbook savings	489.1	363.4	307.1
MMDA	N/A	N/A	392.8
MMC	N/A	$440.4	*
Small saver certificates	N/A	247.8	*
All-saver certificates	N/A	19.5	N/A
Other consumer CDs	$401.8†	156.9	$820.8
Total consumer CDs	401.8	864.6	820.8
Money funds (general purpose)	4.2	194.4	145.4
Money funds (institutional)	N/A	47.9	41.2
$100,000 jumbo CDs	148.8	340.4	346.1
Total retail money market	$1,290.9	$2,163.1	$2,466.1

N/A—Not available.
*—All CDs deregulated. Comparable statistics not available.
†—Pre-deregulation CDs, mostly under 6% yields.
Source: Donoghue's Money Fund Report.

What Does Super-SLY Stand For?

The SLY part is easy. I have alluded to that earlier in the book. SLY stands for safety, liquidity, and yield.

We designed the SLY investment strategy for my *Complete Money Market Guide* in 1981. Now we have added new tax-free investments and new deregulated bank money market accounts and certificates of deposit. *Voila*—Super-SLY.

Tax-free money market investments are important because most money market investments generate ordinary income, which means that the tax man can run off with much of your earnings before you have a chance to enjoy them. By using tax-free investments in the SLY strategy, you get to keep more money for yourself and less for that all-time spendthrift, Congress.

The Deregulation Derby

Banks have been deregulated since my *Complete Money Market Guide* came out. In essence, the federal regulators have done for the banking industry what they did for the airline industry. Remember what fun that was? You could get great deals on tickets to exciting places—and you could also get stuck in some godforsaken airport halfway across the world because the airline went out of business before you could use your ticket to get home.

The federal regulators have started to remove the regulations on banks so there is no longer a "highest interest rate allowed by law" or a formula which determines the highest interest rate banks can pay. Basically, this means that banks are allowed to offer the best deal they can—if they wish. But finding the best deal in town requires a lot of research and effort, and most banks use these new powers to avoid ever being "the best deal in town." Given the chance to compete, many banks decline the offer.

You see, banks don't have to give you any particular rate. They can give you any rate they want to. And when a bank offers an astoundingly great rate, it means that they have an astoundingly great need for deposits. In fact, for many depositors, "the best deal in town" from banks is usually available only from the weakest banks and savings institutions or from your stockbroker, who can do the shopping nationally for you. You can take advantage of these banks if you don't exceed the $100,000 limit on federal deposit insurance. If you have more, you should be much more cautious about getting a high rate from a bank.

Safety Is a Prime Concern . . .

All of which brings us back to the SLY system. Let me spell out the general guidelines for you.

Safety means that you should never invest in anything that is not either insured or offered by a well-regulated financial institution.

Federal deposit insurance from the Federal Deposit Insurance Corporation (FDIC), the Federal Savings and Loan Insurance Corporation (FSLIC), or the Federal Credit Union Share Insurance Corporation (FCUSIC) is essential. I would not put my money in any bank without such insurance because of the record number of bank failures in the past few years (forty-eight in 1983 alone and sixty more by October of 1984).

. . . But Know the Rules of the Road

You think you couldn't get burned in a bank failure? Think again. There are two ways you could get caught: by investing in uninsured bank retail repurchase agreements, or repos, or by investing more than $100,000 in a bank account.

People who were lured by the high yields of retail repos illustrate the problem. Repos are normally safe investments, if the repo is set up properly.

To put it simply, a repo is a cross between a security and a collateralized loan. Many money funds use very short-term repos for their overnight cash. The repos money funds use are always set up properly, as required by law, and are safe investments.

Several years ago banks used to offer repos to investors to get around the federal regulation that prevented them from paying more than 5.5 percent on a liquid savings account. Some banks still offer them. But investors at a bank in Mt. Pleasant, Iowa, were unpleasantly surprised to find that the repo wasn't set up properly—the bank had no collateral behind the repos, and deposit insurance didn't cover the investments. Those poor souls ended up high and dry when the bank failed. They had to stand in line with the rest of the bank's creditors to get back what was left of their savings. They simply trusted their bank too much and didn't know what they were getting into.

The other way to lose money in a bank is to keep more money in your bank than insurance covers. Federal regulators are casting a cold eye on the plight of large depositors—in fact, large depositors at two failed banks recently got paid between thirty-five and fifty-five cents on the dollar on the uninsured portion of their deposits, the portion above $100,000.

Most bank money market deposits are safe, but you've got to keep your eyes open all the time—even when you're dealing with your friendly neighborhood bank. You can, however, arrange things so you get more insurance bang for your buck.

Insurance You're a Fool Not to Buy

Federal deposit insurance of various types insures each account up to $100,000 per account per customer. That means that if you and your spouse each have accounts at a bank totaling $100,000, you are both insured in full. It also means that, if you open a third account, jointly, in both of your names, you could deposit another $100,000 and be fully insured. In addition, if each of you had $100,000 in an Individual Retirement Account (IRA) or Keogh account (for those who are self-employed) that account would be fully insured as well. Of course, if you were to spread identical accounts around other banks, that too would increase your insurance.

If you have larger accounts in your bank and you want to get additional information about the bank, I'd suggest getting their financial reports and reviewing them with your accountant, attorney, or stockbroker. Or, you could consult with a reputable bank credit analyst such as Cates Consulting Associates, Inc., Keefe Bruyette and Woods, Inc., or IBCA Bank Analysts, Ltd., all of which are based in New York City.

Safety Without Insurance

Safety can also be found in uninsured accounts as long as they are properly regulated. I am particularly impressed with the Securities and Exchange Commission's regulation of mutual funds in general and money funds in particular. As far as I have seen, the SEC has been clearly on the side of the investor. In every enforcement action involving a money fund with which I am familiar, investors have received more than they deserved rather than less. In fact, I know of one case where some investors felt the SEC was so unfair that investors tried to give money back to the money fund's investment manager.

You can also get safety through diversification. Money funds are fully diversified. That means that if one of a fund's investments bites the dust, there are often enough other quality investments to make up the difference—without losing money for their investors. This same quality of regulation and safety extends to the regulation of unit investment trusts, a nonmanaged type of mutual fund.

Is diversification better than insurance? It's hard to say. Of course, if you just can't live without insurance, there are two money funds, offered by Vanguard and Travelers, that are insured privately for more than $2 million per account. Because of the insurance premiums, however, these funds don't yield as much as uninsured funds, and I feel the lost yield and the insurance are unnecessary. No money fund investor has ever lost a penny. Banks can't claim that good a track record.

A final factor that adds to safety is government guarantees. Surely, the guarantee of the full faith and credit of the U.S. government behind the repayment of T-bills is the greatest type of safety you can get. If they don't have the money to pay you back, they'll print it. What that printed money will be worth is hard to say, but having a lot of devalued money is better than no money at all.

If you can't afford to buy Treasury securities directly (the minimum denomination Treasury bill is $10,000), you might consider investing in a government-only money fund, which invests only in ultrasafe government securities. These funds don't yield as much as other funds, but if peace of mind is foremost on your investing agenda, you might consider one. Capital Preservation Fund is one of the most popular government-only funds because of its conservative investment portfolio. Their toll-free phone number is 1-800-227-8380 (in California, 1-800-982-6150).

That, in essence, is safety. You can get safety in three ways: insurance, diversification, and government guarantee. Safety is an important factor in investing because sometimes, and for some people, a good night's sleep is the best investment return available. The investments we will be discussing under the Super-SLY system all qualify as safe investments.

Liquidity: When You Need It in a Hurry

Liquidity is the ability to get at your money when YOU need it, not when they want to give it back to you. SLY investments allow you, in most cases, to get your money back without penalty within twenty-four hours.

Obviously, money market mutual funds which will transfer your money back to your bank account within twenty-four hours (assuming you authorized them to do so on your request in the first place) fit the bill as SLY investments. So do bank money market deposit accounts, which allow you a limited amount of checks each month.

Bank CDs, which are required to have an early withdrawal penalty, do not qualify as truly SLY investments for that reason. Of course, if you hold them to maturity and are comfortable with tying up your money for the term of the CD, you will want to consider them as part of your investment strategy. Treasury bills do not have early withdrawal penalties, but they do have fees and commissions attached to them, if you choose to sell before maturity. Still, some investors are willing to trade off a bit of liquidity in exchange for the safety and state tax benefits T-bills offer.

Yield: The Right Way

Finally, *yield* is the name of the game. Since we are talking only about investments that are highly safe and liquid, we can concentrate on getting the best yield on our money. And, as I noted earlier, the best place to go for yield is probably not your bank.

The $19.5 Billion Rip-Off—Still in Progress

As I write this chapter, bank money market deposit accounts are costing savers an average (on an annualized basis) of $4.91 billion a year in lost interest. That's $4,910,000,000, if you need to see it spelled out. That's how much more savers would earn if they all invested in only an average money market mutual fund. It works out to 125 basis points more (1.25 percent) on the average. That's a lot of money. (Figure it out for yourself. That's $125 a year on a $10,000 investment. Not a fortune, but a good dinner for two.)

In fact, and I feel I must point this out again to drive home the point, those people who are keeping money in passbook savings accounts are giving up $14.61 billion a year in additional interest they could be earning if they, too, would move their money into money market mutual funds.

That's a total of $19.5 billion in easy-to-earn interest savers have missed in passbook savings accounts and money market deposit accounts alone, not to mention CDs and Super NOWs.

It's not that I have anything against banks. Many offer competitive yields on some very attractive products. But most seem to follow a marketing strategy of "creative mediocrity." I can see them saying to themselves, "There are so many of our customers who will settle for a mediocre product because they trust us—why should we offer a better product on which we will make less money?" They're right, except for the fact that some depositors are very discriminating and learn how to tell the difference between mediocrity and excellence.

Down-to-Earth Advice from the "Guru"

Allow me to give you some basic suggestions as to where to go to get the highest yield.

1. The riskiest money fund is only slightly riskier than the safest money fund, so you might as well invest in the funds with consistently high yields. Of course, if you're extremely conservative, you might consider a government-only money fund, such as Capital Preservation, which invests only in Treasury securities, such as T-bills.
2. If you can find an insured money market deposit account that pays more than a money fund, take it. But don't take your eyes off it.
3. Never invest in anything you don't understand. If you're not certain about an investment, don't jump into it.

Examine Figure 9, and keep the following in mind:

1. *Buy the line—not the points.* When you invest in a money fund, you essentially buy the line describing its yield. As rates rise, your returns rise; as they fall, your returns fall. When you buy a U.S. Treasury bill, you must buy a point on the line, since you are buying a fixed-rate investment. As interest rates rise, not only will your return not rise but the market value of your investment will decline.
2. *Being able to compete and choosing to compete are different concepts.* The banks and thrifts have been crying in their beer for a long time about how they were restricted and could not compete on a "level playing field." Now they can compete, and, as you can see, MMDAs are now paying well below money funds and even further below U.S. Treasury bills (to which the once popular six-month money market certificate yields were once tied).

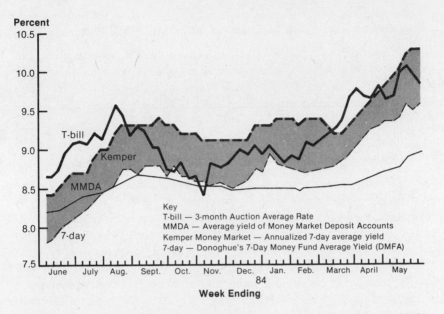

Figure 9. Money market yields, June 1983–June 1984. *(Source:* The Federal Reserve Board; *Bank Rate Monitor,* Miami Beach, FL 33140)

You've Made a Good First Move

"OK, Bill," you say, "I took your advice and all of my money is in Kemper Money Market Fund, the highest-yielding money fund over the past five years. What else should I be doing? Isn't that enough?"

Well, for a passive investor, you aren't doing badly. You have learned that money funds are on the average a better investment than the bank MMDAs.

You're finding out that the money funds don't charge all of those nuisance service charges for checks, for deposits, for asking how much you have in your account, or for transferring money to a CD. Most money funds are free of service charges.

You have dealt well with the deposit insurance issue. You know that you need insurance on your bank deposits because banks fail, because banks take risks with your money, and because uninsured bank depositors have lost money. No one has lost money in a money fund.

But, you still ask, "Is that all there is?" Of course not. Keep reading. You still have a lot to learn. You can still save money on taxes and add some timing and finesse to your money market investing. After all, more is better than less, isn't it?

Paying Too Much in Taxes Is Not SLY, It's Dumb

Do you really find paying taxes a pleasant experience? OK, stop laughing. I'm serious. There are ways to earn higher after-tax returns on money market investments than you are earning. Tax-free money funds pay dividends which are exempt from federal income taxes. In some states there are funds whose dividends allow you to avoid state and local taxes as well.

People Who Have Money Like to Keep It

Tax-free money funds are another good deal in the money market that more and more people are discovering. In the spring of 1984, as people began to shift back into the money market from the declining stock market, 35–40 percent of that money was invested in tax-free money market funds. Those people were exercising their patriotic duty to avoid unnecessary taxes.

Tax-free money funds invest in short-term obligations of tax-exempt entities—such as cities, states, and municipal authorities. Unlike the popular tax-free bond funds, these funds invest their money, on average, for less than three to six months at a time. By doing so, most can maintain a stable or constant price per share, allow investors to redeem their shares at any time, and still pay daily dividends which are exempt from federal income taxes. Some even offer check-writing privileges.

Less Can Be More—Sometimes

Tax-free money funds pay lower yields than taxable money funds but, if you are in a 44 percent or higher tax bracket, tax-free money funds are for you.

Of course, you must be in a high enough tax bracket so that the lower actual yields on tax-free money funds can generate higher after-tax returns for you. As a rule of thumb, you must be paying a marginal rate of 44 percent or higher to make tax-free money funds right for you. That currently translates into a taxable income of over $55,300 if you are single, over $85,600 if you are married, filing jointly, over $42,800 for married, filing separately, or $60,600 for a single head of household.

Incidentally, the tax barriers I mentioned above change when interest rates change. Since this book will be published some time after I write this, and since interest rates (and tax rates) are subject to constant change without notice, here's how to figure out whether tax-free funds are worthwhile to you at the time you read this.

First, you should look at what you would get in a taxable fund. Use the average for all taxable funds as a convenient figure, or use the yield of a taxable fund you're looking at.

Now look at the average yield for all tax-free funds, or the average yield for a tax-free fund you want to invest in. To determine the taxable equivalent yield (in other words, what you'd have to get in a taxable investment to equal the performance of a tax-free fund), use the following equation:

$$\text{Taxable equivalent yield} = \frac{\text{tax-free yield}}{1 - \text{your highest tax bracket}}$$

For example, suppose you were in the 50 percent tax bracket and you were interested in a taxable fund that paid 9 percent and a tax-free fund that paid 5 percent. You'd be better off in the tax-free fund because the taxable equivalent yield of the tax-free fund would be 10 percent (.05 divided by .50 = .10).

Somebody Does It Better—But Only in Three Great States

If you think tax-free funds are a good deal, double tax-free and triple tax-free money funds are available in three states—Massachusetts, California, and New York. So if you find yourself saying "Pass the schrod," "Fer sure," or "I love New York" a lot, you have something to look forward to. If you don't know what those things mean, you probably shouldn't mess with these funds anyway.

Double and triple tax-free money funds work for even more taxpayers because they are exempt from state and local taxes as well. If you live in one of these states and want to make sure that a double tax-free investment is right for you, use the following formula to determine your taxable equivalent yield:

$$\text{Taxable equivalent yield} = \frac{\text{tax-free yield}}{1 - (\text{maximum federal tax bracket} + \text{maximum state tax bracket})}$$

What About Other States?

Be a bit thankful if your state doesn't offer double tax-free money funds. After all, the reason these funds appeared in California, Massachusetts, and New York is that those were the only states which had the combination of a lot of short-term borrowing by in-state tax-exempt authorities and immorally high state and local income taxes which make these special investments very attractive.

Just be thankful if your state taxes are low or nonexistent.

When You Invest Can Be as Important as Where

"What about timing?" you say. I thought you would never ask. Yes, the timing of your investments is very important. Here are a few rules for market timing in the money market.

Rule 1 is easy to remember: "When interest rates are rising, invest in a liquid investment whose rates will rise with the general level of interest rates (money funds and insured money market deposit accounts seem to fit the bill best) and when interest rates are falling, invest in the highest negotiable fixed rate money market investment with the longest maturity you can find."

Rule 2 is important to remember: "Do all you can to cut the taxes on whatever you invest in."

Rule 3 is important if you want to stay liquid: "Don't lock up your money too long. It usually doesn't pay." Combined with rule 1, this can be a little confusing, but usually a good maturity to pick is in the six-to-eighteen-months range depending on how good a deal you can get and how long you are willing to lock up your money, if you choose a nonnegotiable bank CD as your investment.

Rule 4: "Don't take any risk for which you are not amply compensated."
Those are the basic rules for money market timing.

What to Do When Interest Rates Rise

Let's start by assuming that interest rates are generally rising. There are only four types of investments you should consider:

1. Traditional (taxable) money funds
2. Tax-free money funds
3. Double and triple tax-free money funds
4. Insured money market deposit accounts
(Sorry, but the banks cannot offer tax-free investments.)

The guidelines to use in selecting the right type of investment for you are as follows:

1. *Check out the double tax-frees first.*
2. *Then check out the tax-free money funds.*
3. *If you still haven't found a home, then find a high-yielding money fund.*

If you are not in a sufficiently high tax bracket to qualify for tax-free money funds, you should identify the highest-yielding taxable money fund and compare its performance over the past few months with the highest-yielding money market deposit account you can find and choose the higher-yielding of the two. If that turns out to be the insured money market deposit account, watch it closely since the bank is not obliged to stay competitive.

(One small caution: If you intend to use the checking privilege extensively, you will want the money fund, since the banks currently permit only three checks a month on MMDAs. In any case, watch for the imposition of service charges by your bank, especially for services you are likely to use.)

4. *Stick with a winner as rates rise.*

Stay in the investment of your choice, especially if you think interest rates are going to continue rising.

Questions and Answers for the Curious

Q. How can I find the highest yielding accounts?

A. You could look at the table in your newspapers, which may or may not answer your questions. The Donoghue Organization, Inc. provides tables to over sixty-five newspapers around the country on the largest taxable and tax-free money funds. If you can't find a table where the names of the money funds are spelled out in English (our competitors don't) look in *Barron's,* the national investment weekly. Tables on local insured money market accounts are carried by many newspapers, but yields reported are not well-standardized.

There are two newsletters available which are especially designed to guide you in this area: *Donoghue's MONEYLETTER* (Box 540, Holliston, Mass. 01746; $87 for 24 issues, samples free on request). *100 Highest Yields* (published by Advertising News Service of Miami Beach, available from the Donoghue Organization, Box 540, Holliston, Mass. 01746; $84 a year for 52 weekly issues) covers the insured money market accounts nationally including coverage of the $100,000+ account special rates. (Subscription prices are, of course, subject to change without notice.)

Q. What about bank CDs?

A. Sometimes it makes sense to lock in today's yield for the next two or three months if you think you can afford to have your money locked up and if you think you will average a higher return by doing so. A word of caution: Yields on bank products, CDs included, can be very misleading and the only way to compare them is to ask how much you will get back at maturity. The other alternative is to subscribe to *100 Highest Yields,* which reports standardized yields for various maturities.

Q. How can I find names and addresses of the most competitive banks and money funds?

A. This information is in the National Consumer Money Market Directory, which is available for $12 from NCMMD, Box 540, Holliston, Mass. 01746. It contains not only the details and toll-free numbers for both taxable and tax-free money funds but also details on how to buy CDs from the nation's top-yielding banks and thrifts.

Q. What about Treasury bills? Aren't they exempt from local and state taxes?

A. You are quite right. U.S. Treasury bills do pay interest which is exempt from state and local taxes, and it has been proven that a strategy of simply rolling over three-month Treasury bills will produce very nice returns.

However, your money is not as liquid as in money funds. You cannot redeem $100 from a $10,000 T-bill. If you want your money early you will probably have to pay a broker for selling the bill for you and that will cut into your yield. However, if you can afford to have the money tied up for a few months, it is a strategy that seems to work well for some investors, especially in states where taxes are high.

Q. Aren't money funds which pay higher returns taking greater risks?

A. Technically, that is true. But practically, no one has ever lost money in a modern money fund—so no one has had to worry about the risk.

My feeling is that the worst probable risk of a money fund investment losing money is less than one chance in 100,000. In such a case you might lose 1 percent, but there is a better than fifty/fifty chance that you would get it back in a day or so or before you even knew about it.

Why do I say this? With the money fund industry's track record of safety, a large loss is highly unlikely. Even with the problems of Continental Illinois National Bank, which made too many bad loans and had to be rescued by the federal banking regulators, no money fund had invested in that bank for almost two years before the problems came to a head.

Some risk could occur if interest rates rose abruptly and the value of a money fund's assets declined. Since money funds put their money in short-term investments, that risk is slight. The worst case situation I can imagine would show up first as a decline in the $1 per-share price to $.99.

In fact, Merrill Lynch Ready Assets Trust, the nation's second-largest money fund, has declared a small but negative dividend on about ten days in its history, and few even noticed.

Actually, if you hear about a money fund's price falling from $1 to $.99 in a rising rate market, grab as much money as you can and invest it in that fund. In the next day or so, it is likely that the fund will recalculate it's yield back to $1 per share and that is equivalent to earning 365 percent for a day. That's a no-risk bonanza, but you have to act fast. It's a one-day phenomenon.

Q. What about bonds and bond funds? Don't they promise higher yields?

A. Repeat after me: "When interest rates *rise,* bond prices *fall."* Now quickly, read that again. Never invest in a bond or bond fund when interest rates are rising. It is possible to have your "higher yields" completely obliterated by larger losses in principal.

While you may fully and realistically expect and plan to hold your investments to maturity, why would you want to worry about your investments declining in value and worry that you may have to sell them at a loss? Why would you want to earn high taxable returns (on which you would have to pay federal, state, and local income taxes as well) at a time when you are experiencing offsetting principal losses which you can deduct only if you sell and take a monetary loss?

If all of that sounds unattractive, I guess you get my point. Do not buy bonds when interest rates are rising.

Q. What if interest rates fall? And how do I know when interest rates are falling?

A. Now we can get to the next section of the SLY strategy.

How to Get a Handle on Money Market Trends

Sometimes the money market seems to make little or no sense. One day, interest rates are up. Next day, rates are down. The stock market seems to respond to the movements of the money market, but some days the money market seems to have a mind of its own. How do you know which way the money markets are moving so you can know what to do?

Sometimes the most obvious answer is the hardest to believe. Who knows the most about which way interest rates are moving? The Federal Reserve? If they did, they would never tell any of us. Economists? Are you kidding? If all of the economists in the world were lined up end to end, they couldn't reach a conclusion. Who, then?

If I wanted to know what the smartest minds in the money market actually believed about interest rate trends, I would look at how they manage their money. If they are buying shorter- and shorter-term investments in hopes of reinvesting their money sooner at higher rates tomorrow, I would believe that they thought that interest rates were rising.

If I thought they were buying longer- and longer-maturity securities in anticipation that interest rates were about to fall, I would assume the reason for locking in today's rates was that today's would be higher than tomorrow's rates, or at least that was what they believed.

Where could I get this valuable information? How can a humble citizen like me get the pros to tell me what they really believe? The answer is that this information is public information readily available to all.

Each week, in Donoghue's Money Fund Table in sixty-five or more major newspapers, you will find the average maturity for each of the major money funds. The average maturity is the average amount of time before each of the money fund's investments mature, weighted by the amount of dollars invested in each investment. (See Figure 10.)

The average maturiy number, in and of itself, is not particularly significant. The shifts in the average maturity from week to week, however, are important, especially if they continue to move in one direction. If you were to follow the average maturity of the whole money fund industry, the last figure in the table, you would have an idea of the interest rate expectations of money fund managers.

The average maturity of the money fund industry is published in our money fund table once a week and is released on Wednesday afternoons. So don't get confused as some of my readers have who see the table in both Friday's and Sunday's *New York Times* and say "The average maturity didn't change". It's simply the same table for the same period—they just publish it on two different days.

If, for example, money fund average maturities averaged thirty-four days at the end of one week, and then over the next few weeks shifted to thirty-three days, thirty days, twenty-eight days, etc., that would be a good indication that the money funds thought that interest rates would be rising in the near future. What does that mean to you? Keep your money in money funds and ride those increasingly high yields as interest rates rise.

What if the money fund average maturity moved in coming weeks from thirty-four days to thirty-six days to forty days to forty-two days? That would mean that interest rates will be falling and that money market investors like you should be locking in today's high yields.

If you felt strongly that interest rates were about to fall dramatically, you might want to buy a T-bill or a six-month CD to lock in some high returns. You are unlikely to pick the absolute high point in interest rates, so instead of investing, say, your full $20,000, you could buy a $5,000 CD each week for four weeks. You are sure to pick up some of the higher returns and will probably average a higher rate this way than by committing your money all at once. If rates were falling fast, you might want to invest more sooner.

Donoghue's Money Fund Average Maturity does not necessarily forecast rates, but it can serve to confirm the direction of interest rates. After all, moving with confidence, you will make the money-making decisions. If you waver, you will miss all the opportunities. It's much more attractive to tell the folks at tonight's cocktail party that you committed your money because of a well-known and accepted market indicator than simply a guess. A missed opportunity is better forgotten.

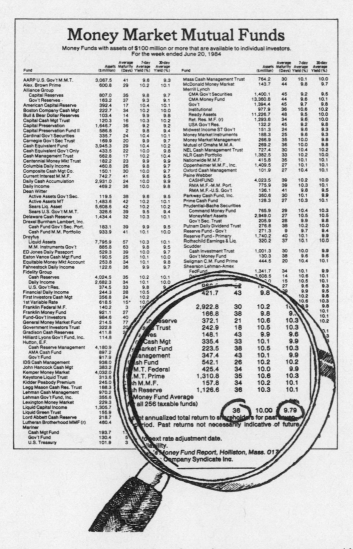

Figure 10. Money market mutual funds, with emphasis on average maturity (days) and 30-day average yield (percent). Donoghue's 30-day Money Fund Average is used as a SLYC indicator for predicting stock market trends, and Donoghue's Money Fund Average Maturity is used as a SLY indicator for predicting interest rate trends. *(Source: Donoghue's Money Fund Report)*

Turning the SLY Indicator into a Super-SLY Indicator

Do you want to go the Donoghue's Money Fund Average Maturity indicator one better? Why not select a leading money fund that seems to beat the averages and whose investment management style seems to be based heavily on timing their investments to swings in the money market rates?

We decided to track the average maturities of several of the leading money funds over the past year to see if their investment strategies' success was explained, at least in part, by managing their average maturity to stay in tune with interest rate movements. (See Figure 11.)

Of the five top-performing money funds of the past five years (Kemper Money Market Fund, Dreyfus Liquid Assets, American Capital Reserve Fund, T. Rowe Price Prime Reserve, and Prudential Bache's MoneyMart Assets), only Dreyfus Liquid Assets seemed to serve as an effective Super-SLY indicator of money market trends. Its average maturity was longer when interest rates went up (locking in higher yields) and shorter when interest rates went down. The others seemed to be less in tune with money market interest rate trends and gave more attention to investment in more assertive money market investments.

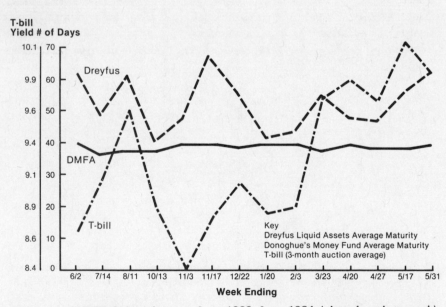

Figure 11. SUPER-SLY indicators, June 1983–June 1984 (plotted peak to peak). (*Source:* The Federal Reserve Board)

While all the top funds follow creative investment policies, only Dreyfus Liquid Assets' average maturity seems to be more helpful in forecasting interest rates than Donoghue's Money Fund Average.

Therefore we are recommending that in addition to Donoghue's Money Fund Average, which seems to be a solid interest rate trend indicator in more volatile times, you might well want to watch the average maturity of Dreyfus Liquid Assets, which seemed to give clearer trend calls in the "sidewise" or less dramatically volatile market of 1983–84. Which will serve you best in the future? I would watch both closely.

Investing "After the Fall"—or What to Do When Interest Rates Decline

When you see the average maturity of the money fund industry starting to grow, that is your signal to lock in today's high yields.

There are several attractive alternatives available to you when interest rates fall: bank CDs, Treasury bills, and Unit Investment Trusts in the taxable income field and federal project notes and Municipal Unit Investment Trusts for those of you who prefer to deal in the tax-free investment arena.

Avoid the temptation to invest in individual issues (other than government-guaranteed project notes and Treasury bills). When you invest in individual issues, you lose out on diversification—and diversity spells safety to most investors. If you don't believe me, think of all the poor souls who invested in Washington Public Power Supply bonds. They don't call 'em WHOOPS for nothing.

Another warning: Don't invest in anything with maturities of three years or longer. Longer-term investments will lock you into high yields, which is great if you buy near the peak and interest rates decline. But that advantage can be negated when you can't get at your money without a penalty.

Riding the Yield Curve

You can make higher returns when interest rates fall than when interest rates are rising. That is because when interest rates fall two wonderful things happen; the yield on negotiable fixed-rate investments, such as bonds, stays high and the value of those same investments rises.

For example, if I bought a Treasury bill earning 12 percent for the next six months and interest rates fell to 10 percent, not only would that Treasury bill continue to earn 12 percent, but I could sell it for more than I paid for it and, if the cost of selling it wasn't too high, I could make a profit.

The Two Best Choices

The key to making this strategy work is to buy something that has a low transaction or selling cost and that can be sold. For all intents and purposes there are only two practical investments that work that way and meet Super-SLY criteria. The first is a U.S. Treasury bill, and the second is a Unit Investment Trust such as Corporate Income Fund—Short-Term Series, which is created by Merrill Lynch and sold through most stockbrokers.

Treasury bills may be bought at your local Federal Reserve Bank without a fee but with some inconvenience and loss of interest between the time when you arrange for the certified check and when you actually start earning interest on your T-bill. Banks and stockbrokers can help you avoid this problem, typically for about a $35 fee. The critical point in dealing in T-bills is being able to sell them when you want to take an extra profit. That is best done with a bank or stockbroker, since the time required to sell a T-bill registered at the Fed can eliminate most of your benefits.

While the Treasury bill has transaction costs at both ends of the transaction (buying and selling through a stockbroker), the UIT has a fee only at the purchase end of the transaction. Typically the fee is 3 percent and the yield you are quoted on the unit investment trust takes that fee into consideration.

Unit investment trusts are unmanaged mutual funds sold in $1,000 "units" to investors. These funds invest in all sorts of securities, from top-grade U.S. commercial bank CDs and EuroDollar CDs to tax-free municipal bonds, all of which mature on a given date. The ones that invest in munibonds are called "MUITS." The securities are purchased by the sponsor, most often a group of major brokerage houses, and units are sold each week or so through many brokers, including many not affiliated with the sponsor.

These UITs and MUITs are issued irregularly in response to market demand so they may not always be available exactly when you want them. However, the fact that Merrill Lynch is willing to buy them back from you at any time at the current market value allows you to avoid the early withdrawal penalties of bank CDs. While there is a load or fee paid to the broker who sold them to you, all yields are quoted after that fee is taken into account and these UITs can often offer highly competitive yields on a very liquid investment.

Another choice is an intermediate-term bond fund. Some no-load mutual fund families offer mutual funds which invest in bonds of various maturities in a number of separate portfolios within one fund. You can invest, for example, in a short-term portfolio which buys bonds with less than one year to maturity, an intermediate-term portfolio which invests in one- to three-year notes or bonds, or a portfolio which invests in longer-term bonds.

Since all of these funds' investments are fixed-income investments whose value increases with falling interest rates and decreases with rising interest rates, they are good investments in different markets. The longer the maturity of the portfolio, the greater the return in the right market.

In a rising rate market, the money market portfolio will provide increasing returns and stable per-share values. In a falling interest rate environment, the intermediate- and longer-term portfolios will increase in value while providing fairly stable returns.

For Super-SLY money market investors, the intermediate-term portfolios allow the investor the opportunity to earn higher total returns (dividends plus increase in principal value) than the short-term portfolios. Of course, you must sell the shares of the fund when interest rates start to rise again to capture the appreciation in value of your investment.

These intermediate-term bond funds do come in three distinct flavors: taxable government bond funds, taxable corporate bond funds, and tax-free municipal bond funds. Remember, capital gains on all three are fully taxable, albeit at much more favorable rates.

Government bond funds invest in U.S. Treasury obligations: Treasury bills, notes, and bonds. The interest paid on these bonds is tax-exempt at the state level, and the fund may be able to pass this benefit on to you. Capital Preservation Fund usually can give you the latest news on how their U.S. government securities fund dividends are being taxed in your state.

Corporate bond funds invest in long-term obligations of corporate businesses. They usually pay higher rates than government and tax-free authority bonds, although their dividends are fully taxable.

Municipal bond funds invest in obligations of tax-exempt authorities, municipalities, states, and the like. Their dividends are usually lower than those of corporate or government bond funds but, of course, their federal income tax exemption makes their after-tax returns very attractive. Some of these funds offer returns that are exempt at the state tax level as well if they invest heavily in obligations within your state.

As with all mutual fund investments, avoid bond funds which are sold by brokers, since the stock and insurance brokers will charge you a load or commission. No-load mutual funds are just as well-managed and are free. While a small commission—say, 5 percent—might not seem much, when you want to get out two months down the line to get back into a money fund, that 5 percent commission will look more like 30 percent on an annualized basis. Watch out for back-end loads or redemption fees as well. Read the fine print and deal with a no-load mutual fund. (See Table 13.)

Now You CDs, Now You Don't

If you must buy a federally insured CD to sleep at night, shop around for a good one. Your shopping list should include Citibank–New York, Citibank–

Table 13   Selected Short-Term and Intermediate-Term Bond Funds

Tax-Free Funds	Taxable Funds

Fidelity Limited Term Muni Fund
  Fidelity Investment Corp.
  82 Devonshire Street
  Boston, MA 02109
  (800) 225-6190
	Capital Preservation TNT (Treasury Note Trust)
	  Benham Management Corp.
	  755 Page Mill Road
	  Palo Alto, CA 94304
	  (800) 227-8380

USAA Tax-Exempt Intermediate Fund
USAA Tax-Exempt Short Term Fund
  USAA Investment Management Co.
  9800 Fredricksburg Road
  San Antonio, TX 78288
  (800) 531-8181
	Fidelity Government Securities
	  Fidelity Investment Corp.
	  82 Devonshire Street
	  Boston, MA 02109
	  (800) 225-6190

Vanguard Muni Intermediate Fund
Vanguard Muni Short-Term Fund
  Vanguard Group
  Drummers Lane
  Valley Forge, PA 19482
  (800) 523-7025
	Midwest Income Short-Term Government Fund
	  Midwest Advisory Services
	  522 Dixie Terminal Bldg.
	  Cincinnati, OH 45202
	  (800) 543-0407

	T. Rowe Price Short-Term Bond Fund
	  T. Rowe Price Associates, Inc.
	  100 E. Pratt Street
	  Baltimore, MD 21202
	  (800) 638-5660

	Twentieth Century U.S. Government Fund
	  Investors Research Corp.
	  650 17th Street, Suite 6000
	  Kansas City, MO 64112
	  (816) 531-5575

South Dakota, Dean Witter, Merrill Lynch, and a major big city newspaper.

Why? Because the range between the lowest one-year CD and the highest one-year CD available to you can be quite wide. By buying a CD through your stockbroker, you can have the advantage of a professional shopping for the highest rates and standing ready to repurchase the CD if you have to get at your money. There is no need to get hit with an early withdrawal penalty from your bank if you do not want to. Avoid your bank and avoid the problems.

When you are shopping for rates, remember that *100 Highest Yields* always has the latest information on CDs in a concise, consistent form. (See Figure 12.)

A Liquid Alternative

Another technique that can be exciting, albeit for a brief time, is to invest in Merrill Lynch Ready Assets Trust when interest rates are falling fastest.

Which banks and thrifts are paying the highest current yields, according to 100 HIGHEST YIELDS?

Where are they located?

Only banks and thrifts with federal insurance are listed.

Who has the highest-yielding money market account in America? How does that compare with the average MMA yield?

What is the ANNUALIZED REAL YIELD on six-month CDs (The annual rate of return over the next six months?)

What is the AVERAGE ANNUAL YIELD for the top one-year CDs? Banks and thrifts don't calculate it that way, but 100 HIGHEST YIELDS is the ONLY source of yield calculations which allows the investor to fully and accurately compare return on investment for periods longer than one year.

Highest JUMBO CD rates for investors with $100,000 or more.

How do top money fund performers compare with average-performance money funds?

Which are the highest yields among money funds which invest only in government securities?

Which are the top-performing, broadly-based money bunds (those that do not restrict their investments to only government securities)?

How do federal tax-free money fund yields compare with taxable yields?

Which tax-free money funds (those that invest solely in short-term federal income tax-exempt issues) are earning the most?)

Only money funds available to ALL types of investors are included. Funds which cater only to institutional investors are excluded, and smaller funds not normally listed in Donoghue's Money Table are included.

Money funds whose sponsors are temporarily subsidizing the fund's yields are noted.

HIGHEST MONEY MARKET YIELDS

BANK/THRIFT YIELDS*

(Highest yields reported by federally-insured banks and thrifts as of July 18, based on stated rates and method of compounding for lowest minimum deposit available. Figures in parentheses are average annual effective yields offered by 50 large banks and thrifts in the top 5 markets. Individual yields for 2½-year and 5-year CDs are average annual interest earned over entire life of account, not "annual effective yield" which would only show interest earned the first year.)

MMDA Annual Effective Yield (Nat'l Avg. 9.22%)
Gill Savings, Hondo, Texas	12.13%
Resource Savings, Denison, Texas	12.13
Maximum Savings, Cabin John, Md.	12.00
Butterfield Svgs., Santa Ana, Cal.	11.80
Westlands Bank, Santa Ana, Cal.	11.63

6-Month CD Real Yield   (Nat'l Avg. 10.74%)
(Real yields are for 6 months only, and do not assume reinvestment for additional 6 months to earn advertised "annual effective yield.")
Amer. Divsifd. Svgs., Costa Mesa, Cal.	13.61
Chase Manhattan, N.Y.	13.31
Western Fin. Savings, Orange, Cal.	13.03
Eureka Fed'l S&L, San Francisco	12.90
Western Savings, Houston	12.90

1-Year Annual Effective Yield (Nat'l Avg. 11.10%)
Western Savings, Houston	13.74%
Unity Savings, Beverly Hills, Cal.	13.37
Grand S&L Assn., Dallas	13.37
Butterfield Savings, Santa Ana, Cal.	13.34
Western Financial, Orange, Cal.	13.31

2½-Year Avg. Annual Yield (Nat'l Avg. 12.99%)
(Average annual interest earned over entire life of account).
State S&L Assn., Lubbock, Texas	15.61%
County Svgs. Bk., Santa Barbara, Cal.	15.15
Investors Savings, Minneapolis	15.08
Unity Savings, Beverly Hills, Cal.	15.08
Citicorp Savings, San Francisco	15.04

5-Year Avg. Annual Yield   (Nat'l Avg. 15.61%)
(Average annual interest earned over entire life of account)
Grand S&L Assn., Dallas	19.33%
Citicorp Savings, San Francisco	18.66
County Svgs. Bk., Santa Barbara, Cal.	18.64
Virginia Beach Fed'l S&L, Virginia	18.64
Pyramid S&L Assn., Santa Francisco	18.51

$100,000 CDs (Real yields to maturity)
1-month
American S&L, Beverly Hills, Cal.	13.51%
Butterfield Savings, Santa Ana, Cal.	13.00
Santa Barbara S&L Assn., California	12.88

3-month
American S&L, Beverly Hills, Cal.	13.64%
Butterfield Savings, Santa Ana, Cal.	13.14

6-month
American S&L, Beverly Hills, Cal	13.71%
San Francisco Fed'l S&L	13.60
Cont. Svgs. of Amer., San Francisco	13.30

MONEY FUND YIELDS**

(10 highest 30-day yields for period ended July 11)

Government-only Money Funds (Avg. 9.67%)
American Treasury Shares k	10.89%
Cardinal Gov't Securities	10.39
Hutton Gov't Fund	10.38
Lehman Gov't Fund, Inc.	10.26
Pacific Horizon Funds/Gov't k	10.23
Government Investors Trust	10.17
Mariner Gov't Fund	10.16
First Variable Rate	10.10
Seligman Cash Mgt. Gov't	10.09
Vanguard M.M.T. Gov't	10.09

General Purpose Money Funds (Avg. 10.07%)
CIMCO Money Market Trust k	11.10%
Money Mart Assets	10.75
Prime Cash Fund	10.70
USAA Money Market Fund	10.70
Hutton Cash Reserve Mgt.	10.69
Capital T Money Fund k	10.68
Vanguard M.M.T. Prime	10.65
Transamerica Cash Reserve	10.64
Trinity Liquid Assets Trust	10.64
Financial Daily Income	10.60

Fed'l Tax-Free Money Funds   (Avg. 5.46%)
Reserve N.Y. Tx-Ex/N.Y. k	6.35%
Reserve Tx-Ex/Res. Interstate k	6.30
Value Line Tx-Ex Fund k	6.24
Reserve Tx-Ex/Interstate k	6.05
Lexington Tx-Fr/M.F.	5.95
Daily Tx-Fr Income Fund	5.94
Hutton Muni Cash Res. Mgt.	5.81
Reserve N.Y. Tx-Fr/Res. N.Y. k	5.81
Vanguard Muni Bond Fund M.M.	5.76
First Investors Tx-Fr M.F. k	5.71

Addresses, phone numbers and names of national consumer money market contact officer of federally-insured high-yielding bank/thrift MMDAs and CDs, and money funds, are available at $12 from National Consumer Money Market Directory, Box 402608, Miami Beach, Fla. 33140.

Money fund yields represent annualized total return to shareholders for past 7- and 30-day period. Past returns are not necessarily indicative of future yields. Investment quality and maturity may vary among funds. k-manager absorbing a portion of fund's expense.

* Source: 100 HIGHEST YIELDS
Miami Beach, Fla. 33140. 800/327-7717

** Source:
DONOGHUE'S MONEYLETTER,
Holliston, Mass. 01746. 800/343-5413

© CONSUMER FINANCIAL NEWS SERVICE INC.

Figure 12. Banks versus money funds: Who offers the highest yields in the country?

You see, MLRAT, or "the RAT fund" as it is called by its detractors, has two unique characteristics. First, it has by far the most conservative and traditional accounting method of any money fund existing today. Rather than try to stablize the yield of the fund by any of the SEC-approved methods, MLRAT reflects the full appreciation in value associated with a rapid decline in interest rates in its yield.

When interest rates fell precipitously in April 1980, MLRAT registered a monthly average annualized yield of 22.2 percent and was paying dividends at over 20 percent annualized rates for five weeks. Everyone in the press ignored it and said it would end soon and was strictly a freak accounting phenomenon—but it was a *real* yield.

So, if rates begin to decline dramatically, transfer your money directly into MLRAT and enjoy the short but exciting special ride. Don't forget that this means that, when interest rates rise, MLRAT yields will be lower than average.

Are You Ready for Super-SLY Now?

Now you have a good handle on how to track interest rate trends, how to take advantage of them to lock in high rates, how to avoid taxes if you are in a relatively high tax bracket, and how to avoid locking up your money unnecessarily.

You have taken an objective look at most bank CDs and have rejected most of them out of hand. You have seen how to find bank and thrift CDs which do warrant your attention and how to get your broker to look for you. You have looked the question of safety in the face and found that there were many ways to be safe and that taking a little risk can get you a lot more yield. You have also seen that what "everybody is doing" is not necessarily the best for you.

Start building your lifetime savings program on your hidden cash resources, invest what you have wisely, and keep in touch. By the time this book is published and finds its way into your hands it is likely that some of the fine points will have to be updated. We invite you to write to us at the Donoghue Organization, Inc., Box 540, Holliston, Mass. 01746, for a *free Super-SLYC Update.*

You are learning to be Super-SLY. At this point, you should have become a confident Super-SLY investor. But there is more to come.

10

Super-SLYC Investing
for Patriotic Investors

Want to join the parade and become a Patriotic Investor? You're welcome to become one of us. Listen up and we will tell you why the Super-SLYC investors are so jubilant.

What Does SLYC Stand For?

SLYC (pronounced "slick"), as you may know, is an acronym for safety, liquidity, yield, and catastrophe-proofing. The SLYC system is a long-term, relatively conservative system for managing your investments. It allows you to incorporate both stock market and money market mutual fund investments into your wealth-building plan.

As with any investment system that involves the stock market, the SLYC system does involve some risks. If you don't want to manage your money actively, or if you don't want to take any risk whatsoever, then you'd probably be better off following my SLY system outlined in the previous chapter. If you're not sure how much risk you can take, skip back to Chapter 2 and take my little quiz to determine what kind of investor you are.

But if you're attracted by the higher yields that the SLYC system can offer, and you are willing to put in the little extra effort to learn about stock market investing, then read on.

The SLYC Funds: All in the Family

Mutual fund "families" are the best deal to hit the financial markets in decades. A fund family is a group of different funds—such as money funds, stock funds, bond funds, and precious metals funds—all offered by the same management company. Many of these fund families offer telephone switching, which allows you to call up your fund's service representative and exchange all or part of your shares of one fund for shares of another to stay in tune with the investment markets.

Of the many fund families around, only a few meet the SLYC criteria. Here are the guidelines for a SLYC fund family:

1. The family must have both an aggressive growth fund and a money fund. These two types of funds are the heart of the SLYC strategy.
2. Both funds must be no-load funds—that is, they may not have sales charges associated with them. Why start any investment program with 3–8 percent loss by paying someone to do what you can do yourself?
3. The no-load growth fund must have at least $50 million in assets. When a growth fund has at least this much as its investment pool, it has enough money to move in and out of the market easily—and handle the redemptions when its investors want to move out quickly. At that level the mutual fund distributors are making enough money from the fund to assure that shareholder services are top-notch.
4. The fund family must allow telephone switching (or a convenient alternative like a Western Union wire) between the growth fund and the money fund, so you can move in (and out) of the stock market quickly. With telephone switching, your investment money never needs to be more than twenty-four hours away from your bank account.
5. The fund should provide free exchange privileges or charge no more than $5 to exchange as many shares as you wish.

At present, there are thirty-six funds in eighteen fund families that meet the SLYC criteria. I've listed them in Appendix 6 for your reference. Now let's see how to take advantage of the opportunities they offer.

Safety and Liquidity First

As with the SLY system, SLYC investors are concerned with the safety of their investments. The SLYC system offers safety in two different ways: the safety of money market investments when interest rates are rising (see Chapter 9 for a detailed explanation of money market investments) and the safety of diversified, well-regulated stock market mutual funds that allow you to switch out instantly when the market starts to turn sour.

You see, for many investors, especially those investing in stock market mutual funds, *liquidity is safety*. Liquidity gives you the ability to take your losses in a declining stock market and turn your investments back on the positive track by simply making a phone call to your mutual fund family. Since there is no need to tie up your money to earn high returns, liquidity is a factor that you can build into all your investment strategies.

Yields Are Getting More Than Your Money Back

High yields consistent with safety are the ultimate goal of investors, and SLYC investors are no exception. The SLYC investment strategy focuses on a commonsense, get-me-in-the-right-market-at-the-right-time approach to investment while keeping an eye open to avoid unnecessary risks. The high yields in the SLYC system come with market timing, avoiding predictable losses and taking advantage of the top performing funds in the hottest markets, which I'll explain shortly.

Catastrophe-Proofing: Creative Paranoia

Catastrophe-proofing is the final element of the SLYC system. The economy ultimately may have to face one of two potential economic disasters: hyperinflation or hyperdeflation. Both are threats to your investments and both present investment opportunities.

Hyperinflation, or having interest rates go through the roof, is a very real threat. Continued high federal budget deficits could drive business borrowers into a competitive, high interest rate environment. If the government decides to print money to pay off investors, the value of money will decline catastrophically. The result will be a stunted recovery or inflationary pressures on the economy.

This is a scenario that has taken place before. A classic example was during the Weimar Republic in Germany before World War II. Back then, you needed an entire wheelbarrow full of money to buy a loaf of bread.

In fact, there's a story about a fellow who went to the store with a wheelbarrow full of money. He left his cache outside the store to get some bread. When he came back, he found he'd been robbed—someone had stolen the wheelbarrow and dumped the bills. The wheelbarrow was worth more than the money.

If inflation were to go through the roof, there is only one effective risk-reduction strategy: an "insurance" position in gold bullion coins. You see, when paper money becomes worthless, the value of hard assets, such as gold, rises dramatically. If inflation rises into the 20 or 30 percent range, the value of gold as a storehouse of value could expand twentyfold and a 5 percent position in gold coins could insure your entire portfolio against loss.

I recommend bullion coins because, unlike gold bars, you won't need to get them assayed, or tested for weight and purity, as you will with most gold bars. In addition, bullion coins don't have a collector's value, so you won't take any large losses because of trends and fancies in the rare coin market.

Most gold bullion coins come in sizes based on one ounce, which is both more affordable than most bars and more convenient to use, if you have to: It's easier to buy bread with a coin, or part of a coin, than it is to shave off part of a gold bar.

Keep in mind that this is a long-term insurance position, so don't put more than 5 percent of your assets into gold. If gold is below $400 an ounce, that's historically cheap—so take your insurance position and forget about it.

People ask me frequently, "Are you recommending gold mutual funds?" The answer is that they are often good investments, but they invest in gold stocks, not real bullion gold. In a time when people distrust paper money, they certainly won't trust stock certificates. If there is a collapse of our economy, as some people love to predict, only gold will do the job for you.

Where to Store Your Gold Reserves

When you buy your gold, store it in your bank safe deposit box. Even if your bank fails, you'll still be able to get to your holdings because the trust departments of banks are insulated significantly from losses of the banks with which they are affiliated.

Of course, some people prefer to use what are called "midnight gardeners" or "nightcrawlers," which are long polyurethane tubes designed to be filled with gold coins and buried in your backyard.

What you do is get a post-hole digger and dig a hole in the woods or your back yard and bury the gold. Then you bury some scrap metal elsewhere so the folks with the metal detectors don't beat you to it. And then send me the map for safe keeping (only kidding)!

Seriously, however, you should keep your gold in a safe deposit box and avoid those deals where gold salespeople pay you interest on your money if you will take delayed delivery of your gold. "Earn interest on your gold investments," read the ads. They are using your money to speculate in gold. If they lose, as some have, there can be no gold to deliver. Deal with a reputable broker/dealer or a bank and take physical delivery of your gold or at least store it in your broker's vault.

Beating the Hyperdeflation Hype

The other half of the catastrophe-proofing process is the protection against hyperdeflation, or a sudden and precipitous drop in interest rates to 1 or 2 percent. A lot of people forget that, back in the late thirties, investors actually paid a premium for U.S. Treasury bills. They would pay more for the Treasury bills than they got back.

With all of the bank failures going on at the time and even with the new FDIC insurance plan, they were obviously looking to Will Roger's observation, "I'm not so much concerned about the return *on* my money as the return *of* my money."

Long-term government bonds are an excellent hedge against hyperdeflation. As I write this, five-to-thirty-year government bonds are paying 13–14 percent. If interest rates fell to 1–2 percent generally, the value of a bond on which the federal government had agreed to pay 13–14 percent could sky-rocket, insuring your entire portfolio. Once again, 5 percent of your investment portfolio should be the maximum commitment you should make.

While hyperinflation is a much more likely economic disaster than hyper-deflation, you now know how to protect yourself from both disasters.

Back to SLYC

SLYC is a strategy based on the assumption that, in the long term, the stock market and money market are closely related. Just reading the daily newspaper can confirm that assumption, but it takes a lot of detailed study to turn that assumption into a workable investment system.

A few years ago, I put together a team of experts with nearly seventy-five years total experience studying mutual fund performance and, after we had combined our experience and built it into an econometric model, we came to this simple conclusion: *When interest rates rise, the stock market falls.* When interest rates fall, the stock market takes off. We were all a bit surprised at how simple the model was, and we have come to believe in it confidently.

You see, the market value of a stock is its net present value (which is a statistical term for what you would pay today to buy an investment that would pay a given return in the future) discounted at some rate you could earn without taking any risk.

The future value on which a stock's net present value is based is an expected stream of future dividends and/or some expected growth in the value of your investment. Put simply, the market price of a stock is based on the amount of return that traders and investors feel they will earn on that stock in the future.

An important factor in determining what a stock is worth is what alternative investments are paying. The higher the yields on the alternative investments, particularly riskless ones, such as Treasury bills or insured bank certificates of deposit, the lower the value of the stock market investments. After all, why should you buy a stock with a possible 10 percent rate of return when you can get a guaranteed 10 percent rate of return elsewhere?

For example, if, as was true in August 1981, thirty-month bank CDs were paying investors 19 percent or more, stocks which paid an average of, say, 5 percent weren't worth much. You would have had to buy them at a deep discount to earn a 19 percent return.

When Rates Fall, Opportunities Rise

As interest rates decline, the attractiveness of the stocks increases and those that look best (partly because they looked worst as interest rates rose) are the aggressive growth stocks. These stocks are often investments in out-of-favor industries which have a potential to rebound dramatically, small high-tech firms which could be gobbled up by a larger firm at inflated prices, or firms which are just basically on a fast track because of aggressive management.

Few aggressive growth stocks are known to the general public before they take off. "I've made millions on these stocks—in hindsight," an investor friend once told me. You know the feeling. I'd say to myself, "If I had just thought to buy that stock a year ago, I'd be rich today." Well, unfortunately, you can't invest with hindsight, and the hardest tasks for investing in aggressive growth stocks is picking them before they take off. I, for one, prefer to leave that task to the professionals who manage aggressive growth stock mutual funds.

So the SLYC strategy is to invest in money funds which will hold their principal value ($1 per share, usually) while continuing to pay higher and higher daily yields as interest rates rise. When rates begin to decline, then I recommend switching into aggressive growth mutual funds for the fast ride.

How Do I Know When to Switch Investments?

That is the strength of the SLYC system. It tells you when to get the "itch to switch." As you might expect, it is based on the trends of interest rates. The following table explains the basic strategy using Donoghue's (30-day) Money Fund Average as the basic indicator of interest levels.

The first step is to determine where interest rates are and allocate your investment dollars between aggressive growth funds and money funds, as indicated.

As you look over Table 14, notice that the moves between the stock market and the money market are gradual. There are two major reasons for this. First of all, the SLYC system is, by definition, a relatively conservative system. It's not designed to move you in every time there's an uptick in the stock market or out every time there's a small downturn. All we want here is to catch the major upturns and avoid the major collapses. If you want fast, in-and-out trading, the SLYC system just isn't for you.

The reason for this is simple. First of all, the stock market can be so volatile that no amount of market timing can allow you to miss all the downturns and

Table 14

Donoghue's (30-day) Money Fund Average	Stock Market	Money Market
Rising Rates		
Below 10%	100%	0%
10%–11%	75%	25%
11%–12%	50%	50%
12%–13%	25%	75%
Above 13%	0%	100%
Falling Rates		
13%–12%	25%	75%
12%–11%	50%	50%
11%–10%	75%	25%
Below 10%	100%	0%

catch all the upturns. Second, there's nothing wrong with being a cautious investor in the stock market. If there's a 100 percent bull market in one year, I'm perfectly happy to settle for 60 percent in the middle of it.

The gradual movement in and out of the stock market helps you to smooth out some of the bumps along your investment avenue. As you move into the stock market, you still get money market returns to increase your returns and make up for any minor losses that an unsettled early bull market might have. As you move out of the market, your increasing money market investment will help protect you from any downturns—and, of course, your fund serves as a handy "escape route" if the market turns sour before the SLYC indicators tell you to move out. Nothing's perfect, and common sense should always prevail. But more on that later: For now, look at Table 14 and familiarize yourself with the SLYC barriers.

One important caveat here: *Never* invest new money in the stock market if interest rates are rising. For example, suppose you decide to follow the SLYC system and interest rates are at 12 percent and rising. You should invest all of your money in the money market until rates peak and start heading back down past 13 percent. If interest rates are falling from 12 to 11 percent, on the other hand, you can confidently put 50 percent of your money into a stock fund.

Where Does the "Super" in Super-SLYC Come In?

When I first described the SLYC system in my *No-Load Mutual Fund Guide,* I pointed out that no mechanical system could anticipate all market movements and that therefore you had to add some common sense to your investments. I pointed out, perhaps too enthusiastically, that the five-year track record of the SLYC system was exciting—in fact, over the five years ended December 31, 1983, it was a whopping 28 percent rate of return. (That assumed you switched your investments between the average money fund and the average yielding SLYC fund based soley on the level of Donoghue's Money Fund Average.)

Now, the money market interest rate swings have been pretty wide and clear for most of the past six years. Mid-1983 through mid-1984 was an exception. Interest rates moved within about a 3 percent range (stable for most recent times) and even Donoghue's Money Fund Average Maturity stayed most of the time in the thirty-four- to forty-day range and did not make the same clear calls on interest rates. Consequently, these two indicators were of little help during that period.

To make the SLYC system a bit more "super," we found that we have to be a bit more concrete about adding some common sense to the system. To accomplish that goal we formulated our "stop-loss rule":

> When you are 100 percent invested in stock market mutual funds, you should calculate the market value of your portfolio each month. If you lose 10 percent from the highest recent valuation, assume the bull market is over and sell all your stock investments and return to the money market.
>
> Stay 100 percent in the money market until interest rates rise and peak over 13 percent, then return to the SLYC system.

How Much Better Is Super-SLYC?

Recalculating the five-year track records to May 31, 1984, lowers some of the returns but reasserts the power of SLYC and Super-SLYC. If you simply bought equal shares of each of the SLYC funds and held for the five-year period you would have averaged 15.85 percent annual returns. Using the basic SLYC strategy would have raised your average annual rate of return by 6.9 percentage points to 21.94 percent. Adding the commonsense stop-loss rule would have increased your returns to 25.31 percent—that's nearly 60 percent higher returns than a buy and hold strategy and over 15 percent more earnings than the SLYC strategy alone. (See Figure 13.)

When the Market Dives, Head for the Shore

The reason for this commonsense caution is that the market is really telling you that it is too riddled with confusion and uncertainty to decide on a clear direction. Under those conditions, it is likely that interest rates will begin to climb. Once you have moved into a 100 percent money market position, never move back into the stock market in a rising interest rate environment. Wait

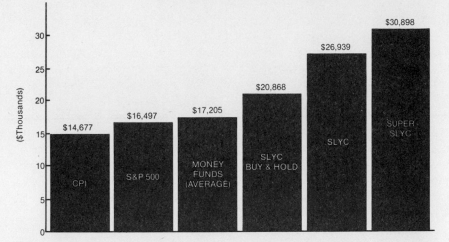

Figure 13. What $10,000 would grow to over five years. CPI: based on the percent change of the Consumer Price Index for urban wage earners. S&P 500: based on Standard & Poor's index of 500 leading stocks with reinvestment of dividends and capital gains. (*Sources:* Standard & Poor's Corporation; Federal Reserve Board; *Donoghue's MONEYLETTER.*)

until interest rates peak *over* 13 percent and start to fall again and then move into the market as the table indicates. (See Table 15.)

Customizing SLYC

Now, once you've gotten the idea that the SLYC system is predicated on the assumption that interest rates dominate the stock market, you can add some of your own ideas and preferences. The SLYC system isn't written in stone, and you should feel free to tailor it to your own particular needs as an investor. No system works perfectly for everyone.

For example, suppose you buy the basic premise of SLYC but just don't feel comfortable investing in an aggressive growth fund. I recommend aggressive growth funds because that's where you can get the best rate of return in a rising stock market.

But aggressive growth funds tend to move as fast downward as they do upward. So if the downside risk of an aggressive growth fund scares you, you might consider a growth-income fund, which will give you lower losses in a down market. Of course, you'll also have to accept less growth and, unfortunately, a higher amount of fully taxable dividends.

Another alternative in a falling rate market is a bond fund. As I explained in the previous chapter, the principal value of bonds increases when interest rates are falling. While the returns on a bond fund won't be quite as spectacular

Table 15   A Walk Down Super-SLYC Street (Beginning July 1980)

Month	DMFA	Portfolio		Stock Price	MF Yield	Total Investment	Div. & CG Per Share
		%MM	%SM				
1	8.5%	0	100	11.62	8.58	$14,007	
2	8.2	0	100	12.43	8.54	14,983	
3	9.2	0	100	13.04	9.37	15,719	
4	10.5	0	100	13.51	11.04	16,285	
5	12.3	25	75	14.96	12.63	4,114/13,525	
6	15.6	75	25	14.65	16.37	13,410/4,318	
7	17.1	100	0	12.57	17.92	17,993	
8	16.3	100	0	12.45	16.62	18,242	
9	15.1	100	0	13.68	15.68	18,480	
10	14.1	100	0	13.83	14.16	18,698	
11	15.6	100	0	14.33	15.39	18,938	
12	16.9	100	0	13.63	16.85	19,204	
13	17.1	100	0	13.09	17.33	19,482	
14	17.2	100	0	11.72	16.47	19,749	
15	16.6	100	0	11.19	17.05	20,030	
16	15.4	100	0	12.37	15.38	20,286	
17	14.0	100	0	12.49	13.66	20,517	
18	12.1	100	0	11.91	11.96	20,722	
19	12.0	75	25	9.93	12.10	15,698/5,014	1,552
20	13.1	75	25	9.69	13.09	15,869/4,892	
21	13.5	100	0	9.47	13.60	20,997	
22	13.7	100	0	10.09	13.83	21,239	
23	13.5	100	0	9.73	13.74	21,482	
24	13.1	100	0	9.27	13.46	21,723	
25	12.9	100	0	9.19	13.41	21,966	
26	11.0	75	25	10.14	11.76	16,636/6,059	
27	9.7	50	50	10.42	10.49	11,447/11,661	
28	9.2	0	100	12.36	9.70	27,410	

Source: Donoghue's Money Fund Report.

as those of an aggressive growth fund during a raging stock market, they won't be quite as depressing when interest rates fall, either. If you're in a high tax bracket, however, a tax-exempt bond fund can produce some feisty after-tax capital gains distributions when interest rates are falling as well as very tempting long-term capital gains if you hold your shares for one year or longer.

When You Make the Plunge—Look Before You Leap

Buy Low and Sell High. Embodied in that simple statement is our whole investment strategy in a nutshell. The only shortcoming is that you need to know *when* to buy and *when* to sell.

There is no hard and fast guide as to when to sell—you will know when you have earned enough, won't you? But how would you like a surefire strategy on how to buy investments cheaper? It comes in two parts; first, avoid the middleman and, second, invest regularly and patiently.

Avoid the Middleman. It seems so obvious when the statistics show that no-load funds often average higher returns to investors than load funds and that investment information is so readily available that everyone should invest in no-load mutual funds. Right? Wrong.

Most people who invest in mutual funds (other than the money funds which are nearly all no-load) invest in *loaded* mutual funds. What's a load? A load is a broker's commission which can be as much as 8.5 percent. That means that if you invest $10,000 you pay the broker $850 simply for filling out the forms for you.

For a whole lot less money you could have bought a copy of my last book, *William E. Donoghue's No-Load Mutual Fund Guide* ($3.50 in paperback) and made your own decision. You could have used *Donoghue's Mutual Fund Almanac* (only $23.00) to review the performance of over 900 mutual funds and picked the fund you felt was best for you. You could have subscribed to *Donoghue's MONEYLETTER* (only $87 a year) and followed the SLYC funds' performances as you went along. They are all a lot cheaper than $850, and you will learn something in the process.

The bottom line is you could have accomplished your goals for a whole lot less money and been more confident in your actions as well. So avoid load funds like the plague. For you the load is a waste of money; for your friends who need to be led through life on a golden leash, give them your broker's phone number.

Low-Loads, Lemons, or Lemonade? In recent years, a new breed of mutual fund has emerged—the low-load fund. It charges a lower entry fee (around 2–3 percent) which buys no personal investment advice but does buy a lot of, in some cases, well-earned hype.

This new breed of mutual fund started with the highly touted Fidelity Magellan Fund which, at the time, had the top five-year track record in the field—up 518 percent over the five years through 1983.

"Magellan has charisma," said Fidelity's management, "let's charge for it." Investors flocked to the fund and the gamble paid off for Fidelity. The low-loads paid for the aggressive advertising campaign and then some. But they were not satisfied.

"Maybe it's not Magellan that has the magic, maybe it's Fidelity," they pondered. So they launched Fidelity Mercury Fund which had *no* track record. You guessed it. It sold like hotcakes. An ounce of charisma is worth a pound of performance.

Are low-load funds a good deal? Fortunately, many are. It takes some top performance-oriented managers to make a low-load fund sell or the premium they charged investors to get in the door will blow up in their faces. As I write this, Magellan is *down* over 15 percent since the first of 1984. Will investors notice? That's the gamble Fidelity has taken. Should you join them in that gamble? Perhaps.

For every low-load Magellan at Fidelity there is a no-load Discoverer Fund at Fidelity with similar performance. So those who knew about Discoverer saved the cost of the load and kept a lot more flexibility to switch out of this high performer when it falters.

Even olympic marathoners slow down eventually. Who wants to pay another fee just to get back into a fund after its price has fallen? No, folks, no-loads are the answer. It's only common sense.

Patience Is Prudence and Consistency Can Be a Blessing

Every investment adviser I know will tell you that his investment strategy will work for you—most of the time. I would certainly not promise, nor would you believe, anything more.

On the other hand, there is an investment strategy which works all of the time. It guarantees you that if you invest money on a regular basis in equal amounts, you will have bought shares of a mutual fund cheaper than the average price per share over the period during which you invested. The strategy is called dollar cost averaging, and believe me, it works. For example, if you had $2,000 to invest and you invested $200 each Friday for the next ten weeks, you would find that you would have bought your shares at a lower price than the average price during that period.

This strategy works best in a short-term declining market and in a long-term uptrend. It takes guts to continue investing into a declining market and continue seeing those short-term losses, but be patient and you will find that when the market rises you will have locked in some very low prices and big profits.

Dollar cost averaging is no guarantee that you will make money in the stock market. It is a guarantee that you will have lower-priced shares in your portfolio, which does mean that you have bigger profits or smaller losses, either of which is an improvement over most people's experience.

Of course, one reason that dollar cost averaging works so well with no-load mutual funds is the absence of an investment charge. If you tried the same thing with an individual stock you would find it cost you much more to buy frequently in smaller amounts. Why not just avoid the cost altogether?

Sell High—On an After-Tax Basis

With the recent change in the tax laws, it makes a lot of sense to take your losses before they run over six months to get full credit for them. Capital gains, on the other hand, should be allowed to continue to run for over six months to qualify for the long-term capital gains treatment and be taxed at 40 percent of your maximum ordinary tax rate. The after-tax profits are where you find new money to invest.

Spreading Your Risk

Another commonsense investing strategy is to diversify your investments so that you are spreading the risks among several investments. When I am investing in the stock market while interest rates are falling or low, I normally spread my money among several mutual fund families since it is hard to decide which growth fund will grow fastest. I then try to stay in funds near the head of the list of top-performing SLYC funds we publish regularly in *MONEYLETTER*. Why invest in losers?

Now It's Time to Start Waving the Patriotic Flag

As we discussed earlier, tax avoidance is a key element of patriotic investment. There are several ways to avoid taxes creatively, many of which I have outlined in Chapters 8 and 9. Let's see if we can work some of these tax-reduction and avoidance strategies into our SLYC system to make it Super-SLYC. (Remember: while tax avoidance is patriotic, tax evasion is illegal. Patriots don't cheat, but they don't waste money on unnecessary taxes either.)

Investing for Growth and Avoiding Taxes

As I pointed out in Chapter 8, the highest taxes you will ever pay are on ordinary income and short-term capital gains which you realize on investments you sell within six months of when you bought them.

The best kind of money you can make is long-term capital gains, on which the tax is calculated at 40 percent of your maximum tax. If that maximum tax is 50 percent, the tax on long-term capital gains is only 20 percent—that's at least 80 percent tax-free money. If you pay lower tax rates, you would pay even less taxes on long-term capital gains.

If you embark on an investment program which includes investments in stock market mutual funds, at least some of the profits you will earn are likely to be in the form of long-term capital gains.

If you invest only in the money market, you will never earn long-term capital gains. So incorporating growth mutual funds in your investment strategy is not only smart, it's patriotic. If you follow the SLYC investment strategy, you will probably find yourself earning some profits which qualify for special treatment.

Some More Super-SLYC Common Sense

When interest rates begin to rise and the Super-SLYC system begins to call for a sale of your aggressive growth stock funds in favor of money market mutual funds, the true Super-SLYC investor hears a bell ring in his patriotic little head which says, "Can I pay less taxes if I wait out the market a bit?" and he starts checking out the tax-free money funds.

Patience Pays

Patience can be a virtue. It's often hard to sit back and watch the value of your investments decline unless you see that the government will share part of the loss with you. There are times patience can be a virtue.

Suppose you have been invested in stock market funds for five months and you have seen, as was possible in the bull market of 1982–83, a 100 percent increase in the value of your shares from, say, $10 a share to $20 a share. If you sell now you will pay taxes (let's assume the worst, 50 percent) of $5 a share, leaving you with only $15 a share to invest in your money fund.

On the other hand, if you waited one more month, you could sell the shares and pay only 20 percent taxes. So waiting can make you a bit of money. In fact, if the price per share falls to as low as $16.30 a share, you will still end up with $15 a share after taxes, since 80 percent of the $6.30 profit is still $5. The bottom line in this case is that you can stand a decline of 37 percent of your profits before selling. Read that again. We are talking about 37 percent of your paper profits, not the share price.

Now, this is only one case where it's better to hold your investment before selling. Many other times, it's better to run for cover and live to invest another day. Of course, you can learn a lot about investing by losing a bit of your money. I'd rather learn by reading about it than experiencing it. But you should realize that if you are near the magic qualifying point for capital gains treatment, you should figure out the tax consequences before you switch.

Don't Take the SLY Out of SLYC

When it comes time for you to bail out of your stock market investments, don't forget to take advantage of the opportunities of the SLY system. You'll want to look closely at both tax-free and double tax-free money funds before you look at a taxable money fund or a money market deposit account.

If you're not sure what to do when interest rates rise, then skip back to Chapter 9 and review the advantages of the SLY system. But before you invest any money, read on to the next chapter, where I will regale you with the foremost rules of investing: those that make the most common sense.

11

Your Guide to Commonsense Investing

Common sense is an all too uncommon commodity in today's world. I am constantly amazed at the reckless abandon Americans show in investing their hard-earned money. A little common sense could go a long way toward building a better life for all of us.

The Wrong Place at the Wrong Time

Look at the highly popular bank money market deposit accounts (MMDAs). When they were first offered, they looked attractive with $2,500 minimums, convenient access to your money, and money market returns. On the other hand, 48 percent of the people who invested in them told researchers that "growth or growth and income" was their primary goal.

MMDAs surely provide money market sized income returns, although they are seldom competitive with "real" money funds' returns. But rest assured they will provide no growth in the value of your principal. Only stock or bond market investments can do that. Those folks who invested in MMDAs for growth are simply in the wrong place.

Take the bull market of 1982–83, for example. MMDA owners earned less than 10 percent fully taxable returns on their money while growth stock mutual fund investors earned ten times that amount or more—a large portion of which qualified for long-term capital gains treatment. I'll leave you to decide which is better—a 10 percent return netting you between 5 and 8.5 percent or a 100 percent return netting you at least 80 percent?

Which was better? If you were willing to take a little risk and pick your time to buy and sell, you got a lot more return. But if growth was your goal, MMDAs were the wrong place. Of course, getting real growth entails a bit of risk and a few sleepless nights—and, of course, the opportunity to participate in a bull market happens only once or twice a decade.

Commonsense Investing Is the Way to Go— You "Auto" Get That Right

Well, you are certainly not going to make the mistakes those folks made. So let's try to tie together some of what we have learned in this book into a plan.

Commonsense investing is like learning to drive a car for the first time. It takes some practice and maybe a few dented fenders, but we all seem to get the hang of it. Ready to go out for a spin?

Acquiring the Right Vehicle. First you need a vehicle. That's why we went through the whole process of finding money to invest: reassessing the role of each of our assets and thinking about what we want to do with them, developing a CASHPLAN to allow us to squeeze as much investible cash out of our cash flows as possible, taking a good look at ourselves to decide just how powerful an investment vehicle we want to drive, getting to know the rules of the road, and deciding what our desired destination will be. The money we found and will continue to find is our vehicle to drive to prosperity.

Greasing Up the Gears. The SLY and SLYC systems are the gear system choices we can select. If we want to pretty much drive on automatic, the money market will give us a smooth ride. On the other hand, if we decide we are the "we're-gonna-be-in-control, give-me-five-on-the-floor" types, we will obviously pick the SLYC system. If we use the SLYC system, the ride will be a bit bumpier but professional management will smooth out the ride a bit.

Fueling Up for the Ride. The financial markets, however, must provide the fuel for our ride. Sometimes we will get some supersonic aviation fuel and the Wall Street ride will be wild and wooly, suited only for a James Bond movie. Other times we will find the market provides us only enough fuel to just crawl along in the money markets.

Getting the VIP Treatment All the Way. The next step in commonsense investing is to improve our chances of getting those pesky state and federal government cops (read taxing authorities) to escort us on our charge down the financial highway instead of constantly pulling us over just when we get up some speed.

To supercharge our ride to prosperity we are going to assure ourselves of the VIP treatment previously available only to the rich and famous. We're going to knock down the toll booths and clear the highways by using every tax shelter we can find that won't tie up our money too much.

A Little Creative Paranoia Won't Hurt. Even when we venture out onto the real life highways, we wouldn't think of foregoing the precaution of insurance. That's what the catastrophe-proofing of our Super-SLYC system is for. That's also why we have had several discussions of the safety of various investments, so we know where the real potholes and blind curves lie.

A Little Fine-Tuning Pays Off Big. Just like driving a car, after you have learned the basics, there is more to learn: how to fine-tune the car, how to maintain your shiny new vehicle, how to drive defensively, when *not* to drive at all, and how to keep other people from distracting you and spoiling your ride.

That's what the rest of this chapter will be talking about, fine-tuning. This is your course in commonsense investing, where we review the fine points of investing and some neat little tricks you can use to soup up your investment vehicles.

The VIP Treatment: Learning to Tax-Shelter What You Earn

No matter what kind of returns you can earn, you owe it to yourself to tax-shelter at least part of them. Although tax shelters usually entail making some commitment to tie some strings around your money, you don't need to tie down your money too tightly.

Let's consider the three most popular tax shelters—tax-free investments, Individual Retirement Accounts, and 401(k) Salary Reduction Programs—and see when to use each.

Tax-Free Investments. These normally make sense only to the rich and/or patient (although overtaxed folks like New Yorkers love 'em too).

Short-term, highly liquid tax-free money funds pay only about half the return of taxable money funds, although their returns are higher on an after-tax basis for some investors in high tax brackets.

Long-term tax-exempt bond funds (called municipal unit investment trusts, or MUITs) offer higher returns, but you must pay a broker a commission and must hold them for the long term and take the risk of their value shrinking in a rising rate market or your broker's commission eating up a large portion of your return. On the other hand, if you didn't need the principal, you could stand a 10 percent-plus tax-free income for quite a while. These tax-free investments do not permit you to defer taxes on your principal, however.

Commonsense investing says tax-free money funds are for money you must keep liquid—and then only if you are in a sufficiently high tax bracket. MUITs are for long-term investing and can be attractive to just about any tax bracket, especially when they are paying about the same as money funds.

Commonsense investing also says that tax-free money funds are more vulnerable to rapidly rising interest rates because their average maturities are longer than taxable money funds. While investors in a 50 percent tax bracket will nearly always choose tax-free money funds, those with tax brackets in the lower 40 percent range should watch the relationships between the taxable and tax-free funds to see which is better for them.

Individual Retirement Accounts (IRAs). These are clearly for long-term savings goals, although the higher the returns you earn in these accounts, the sooner you could feel free to withdraw your money in an emergency without having the 10 percent early withdrawal penalty become a detriment to your investment strategies. That is why we recommend adopting a Super-SLYC Investment strategy for your IRA and why we suggest you avoid low-yielding bank IRAs.

Commonsense investing says that IRAs are for money you can afford to lock up for a relatively long term, and which you do not expect to draw upon in less than ten or fifteen years.

Commonsense investing says that for that reason, if you have your money in a bank IRA, you should immediately transfer it (as soon as you can avoid a bank-imposed early withdrawal penalty, if you chose a CD) into a no-load mutual fund family. You are free to change your IRA trustee as frequently as you wish without penalty.

401(k) Salary Reduction Plans. SARAs are my true love as long-term investment vehicles. Not only are they tax-sheltered but, like an IRA, they allow you to defer the taxes on the money you contribute.

Although you cannot establish your own 401(k) Plan (your employer has to do it), this would be my first choice for a tax shelter.

If you are fortunate enough to have an employer who offers such a plan, you should check it out carefully to see what the terms are and what choices of investments are offered. You might be wise to encourage your employer to include a few of the top no-load mutual fund families in your choices. (If you have a choice, Fidelity, Stein Roe, Founders, Dreyfus, Vanguard, T. Rowe Price, Scudder, and Financial Programs would be good choices.)

Commonsense investing says if you have some good choices of investments and a rather liberal 401(k) plan you should put your first long-term savings money in your 401(k) plan, and only after you have fully used up your limits to save should you start putting money into your IRA.

There are five reasons for this advice (depending of course on the terms of your specific plan):

1. You can often contribute and tax shelter more than $2,000 a year, so this is a good chance to take some of your already-invested long-term savings money and get it under a tax shelter.

2. Your employer can match all or part of your contributions. If your employer chooses to add to the pot on, say, a profit-sharing or a fixed percentage of your contribution basis (although we know you earned whatever you get) it's all gravy. After all, if you didn't contribute, you wouldn't get it at all.

Think about it. If your employer contributes only 50 percent of your contribution, you just got a 50 percent return this year even before you start earning money on your investments and you have 50 percent more assets to earn you tax-deferred returns in future years. That's nothing to sneeze at.

You would be wise to investigate the vesting rules to see how long you are expected to stay before your employer's portion is yours, but still it's a good deal even if you can contribute only your own money.

3. You can often borrow part of the money from the plan and *pay yourself tax-deductible interest.* This means that you can make the mistake of overenthusiastically funding your account and still avoid the early withdrawal penalties while you catch up with your enthusiasm.

4. You can often withdraw money for emergencies without paying early withdrawal penalties. Emergencies still have not been defined by the IRS, but buying a home or sending the kids to college appear to be within the expected definitions of emergencies—they sure fit my definition of a real emergency.

5. When you retire you will qualify for a ten-year forward averaging tax treatment, which means simply that *you will have more after-tax money* with which to enjoy your golden years.

That's the one I like—*gold* for the golden years.

Commonsense investing says your IRA is still a pretty good deal if you don't have access to a Keogh or 401(k) program, but if you do, even the best IRA can wait in line.

You've Probably Got More Tax Shelters Than You Can Use. Think about it. You've got a lot of tax shelters available to you. All you have to do is have $2,000 a year employment earnings to qualify for a $2,000 IRA account. You can hike that to $2,250 if you are married and you set up a "spousal" account, to $4,000 if you are both working and earning $2,000 or more.

If your employer sets up a 401(k) program, you can contribute roughly 6–10 percent of your income into that program in addition to your IRA contributions. If you make $25,000 that means that you can tax shelter up to $4,500 all by yourself, $2,500 in your employer's program and $2,000 in the IRA of your choice. When was the last time you invested $4,500 a year?

Add in the tax-free investments, long-term capital gains, and U.S. Treasury bills and you have a lot of at least partially tax-sheltered money.

When to Borrow to Invest—Supercharging the Superchargers

You can convert your investment vehicle into an airplane if you are willing to borrow to invest, which is known as leveraging. But as we all know, driving a car takes your full time and attention.

Now you know why I am usually against leveraged investments. Seldom are situations so attractive and opportunities so clear that I would recommend that you borrow to invest. Even if I could forecast the future accurately, I would never recommend that you put all of your investment dollars at risk. I'm just not a betting man.

But think about this. If I could find a situation where *both* the interest and principal on the money you borrowed were deductible on your next tax return *and* where the investment you could buy was fully tax-sheltered, would you be willing to give it a try? I would.

That is exactly the situation with your 401(k) Salary Reduction Program. Even if your employer makes no matching contribution at all (an unusual situation), you can't lose if you borrow money to maximize your allowable investment in your 401(k) program.

The principal amount you contribute is fully deductible on your next income tax return (you can even reduce your withholding by claiming one exemption per $1,000 that you can contribute if you want).

The interest you pay on the amount you borrow is fully deductible as well. In fact, what you save in income taxes by this strategy could pay for much of the interest if you plan properly.

The earnings on the money in your 401(k) program are fully tax-deferred. You pay taxes on them only when you have to withdraw the money. In fact, if the loan gets too heavy for you to handle, you can borrow part of the money back from your 401(k) account (if your plan permits you to do so) and pay yourself tax-deductible interest!

Of course, if you overdo this, you will have to repay the 401(k) program over the time permitted by the plan and probably forgo some of the contributions you can make in the future, so don't get too ambitious. But it is a no-lose situation.

Some of you are probably thinking that there is something wrong with this good deal. Somewhere in the back of your mind you remember that you cannot deduct interest on money you borrow to invest in a tax-exempt invest-ment. You are right—but we are talking about a tax-deferred investment. You are not avoiding taxes. You are simply deferring them.

Where to Borrow to Invest

Before you even think about borrowing to invest, you should go back to your CASHPLAN and your inventory of assets and reread the first few chapters of this book, which should show you that you already have the money to invest.

You Bet Your Life. The obvious place to look for money to borrow to invest are policy loans on any whole life insurance policies that you might still hold. Pre-1978 policies offer loans at 6 percent or less. If you haven't already taken advantage of this cheap money, funding your 401(k) should inspire you to do so.

Introduce IRA to SARA. Another place for those of you still employed and over fifty-nine and a half years of age is to withdraw the money from your IRAs, since after that age you can withdraw without tax penalty and usually without bank penalties if you are still in a bank or thrift IRA. You will have to declare as income any withdrawals, but you can then deduct them as you contribute them to your 401(k). The reason you would do such a switch is that you will get more favorable tax treatment when you finally withdraw the money from your 401(k) and you can borrow the money back if you need it without paying income taxes currently.

Give Your Credit Union Credit Where Credit Is Due. Don't forget your credit union as a source of convenient and cheap loans. Shop around a bit. Remember, you probably qualify for the credit union at work and one in your community as well.

Passbook Savers, Out of the Closet. One final time: Clear out your passbook savings accounts. I hate to repeat myself, but so many people still have them and never seem to get around to making such an obvious decision.

When to Repay Loans

If you are able to find more money to invest than you know where to invest (a highly unlikely situation), the question comes up, "Which loans do I repay and which do I keep on the books?"

The rule of thumb for loans is *keep the cheap and pay the rest.* When choosing between paying off a loan and investing, the rule of thumb is *if the interest is high, repay the dough; if the interest is low, go with the flow.*

Pay off any loans where the interest you save is more than what you can reasonably expect to earn on your investments. If it is a toss-up, repay the loan and improve your credit rating. Of course, you should *never* repay a sub-10 percent mortgage any faster than you have to.

Knowing Why You Are Investing Can Make a Big Difference in How You Invest

There are four basic types of Super-SLYC investors, each of which has different goals and strategies: tax-qualified investors (most of us fall in this as one of our categories), high-tax-bracket investors, growth and income investors, and strictly money market investors.

Tax-Qualified Investors. Nearly all investors should have at least one tax-qualified investment program (IRA, 401(k), or Keogh). These investment strategies are very straightforward and simple—"more is better than less": No matter which investments are growing money fastest, those are the ones in which you should invest.

There may be two subsets of this group of investors: passive investors and active investors.

Passive investors will want to follow funds designed to be actively managed between stock and money market positions by the managers—that is, internal switch funds. These types of funds are usually restricted to qualified investors or have stated policies that they will not consider tax implications of their actions.

These investors don't want to have the bother of managing their investments.

Active investors will want to follow a more aggressive switching strategy using no-load switch funds to take maximum advantage of top-performing market segments such as gold, high-tech, and energy. Once again this is a pure "more is better than less" market strategy.

An investor who has rolled over his or her pension plan into an IRA is a good example of an investor who must actively manage his or her money and who has sufficient dollars to bother.

High-Tax-Bracket Investors. These investors are mostly in the 40–50 percent tax brackets and are very concerned about after-tax returns. They will want to follow tax-free money funds, tax-exempt bond funds, and maximum capital gains funds.

Once again there are two markets: the conservative, retired, more passive income-oriented investor and the aggressive young professional who is long-term growth oriented and will monitor his or her investment closely.

Conservative, mature investors are concerned with the following:

1. Where can I get the highest after-tax return in tax-free money funds or taxable money funds?

2. When should I stay short and when should I go long with part of my money?

3. Which is better for me, to earn 5 percent after-tax on a tax-free money fund or 10 percent after-tax on a MUIT?

These investors should watch cautiously the credit ratings and diversification of their tax-free investments and avoid getting too greedy. They often need to be reminded that rates will not rise forever. These are often people who have made their bundle and who simply want to live comfortably off their savings without having to take excessive risks. They may also want to avoid the vagaries of the stock market.

4. Where are the fairly certain stock market opportunities for large capital gains? A good opportunity is a good opportunity.

Aggressive investors will eschew the 100 percent tax-free 5–10 percent returns in order to make 80 percent tax-free capital gains in the 50–100 percent range when the opportunities present themselves. They are stock market rather than bond market oriented. For these people, aggressive stock market funds will be very attractive.

Income-Oriented Investors in Lower Tax Brackets. These people are best served with the long-term basic SLYC strategy, which will earn them some capital gains. Most of the time, however, they are simply seeking to earn money market rates without taking principal risk. When a bull market comes along, these folks will need to be educated to take some known risks in exchange for capital growth and a chance at long-term capital gains.

Money Market Investors. These folks are the most risk-avoiding class of investors. They will not invest in the stock market. Most are not in sufficiently high enough tax brackets (except maybe in New York City) to take advantage of tax-free money funds.

Their interest is in locating the top money funds, the top bank CDs, and knowing when Treasury bills are a good deal. They need maturity advice. They need to know when to lock in part of their money in twelve-, thirty-, or sixty-month CDs or Treasury securities. (See Figure 14 to find your place on the risk pyramid.)

Each of these types of investors gets a lot of special attention in the pages of *MONEYLETTER.*

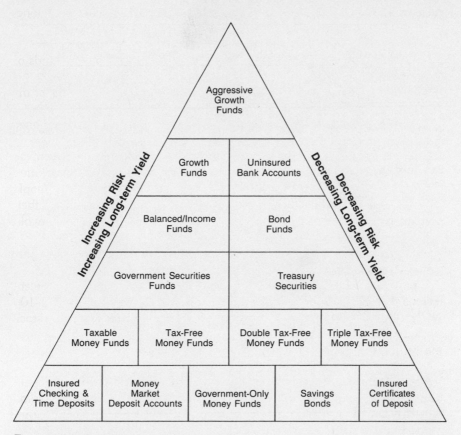

Figure 14. Risk pyramid.

A summary of the investment alternatives which should be considered for each of these different types of investors is given in Table 16.

Check-a-Month Plans Work Both Ways

I hope I have impressed upon you a very important concept—that you must learn to regularly "pay yourself first." A lifetime savings plan requires discipline, and you should never break that pattern. Even when you must raid the cookie jar for a rainy day, you should continue to save regularly.

Check-a-month programs are very helpful in adding the discipline we all need. If we set up a program with our no-load mutual fund family to draw a regular amount out of our checking program each month, we can always

Table 16

Investment Alternatives	Type of Investor			
	Tax Qualified	High Taxes	Growth & Income	Money Market
Money market				
Tax-free money funds	no	yes	(1)	(1)
Double tax-free money funds	no	yes	(1)	(1)
Taxable money funds	yes	no	yes	yes
Project notes	no	yes	no	(1)
Treasury bills	yes	yes	yes	yes
Brokered CDs	yes	no	yes	yes
MUITs	no	yes	(2)	no
Bank CDs (1, 6, 12, 30, and 60 months)	(2)	no	(2)	yes
Bank MMDAs	(2)	no	(2)	(2)
Stock market				
Series funds (investment by market sector)	no	yes	yes	no
Aggressive growth & maximum capital gains funds	yes	yes	yes	no
Gold funds	yes	yes	yes	no
Internal switch funds for tax-qualified money	yes	no	no	no
Insurance investments				
Gold bullion	(3)	yes	yes	yes
Long-term government bonds	no	yes	yes	yes

(1)=Depends on your tax bracket; (2)=permitted but seldom a good deal for yield of liquidity reasons; (3) =not permitted.

vary the amount to fit our capacity to save but the pattern should never be broken during our saving years.

The check-a-month program works in the other direction too. During our retirement years we need cash flow with which to pay our bills, and a check-a-month program is ideal to provide a regular flow of money each month.

It works both ways. Best of all our cash flow needs don't interfere with our commonsense investing principles of safety, liquidity, high after-tax yields and catastrophe-proofing.

What About Those Catastrophe-Proofing Investments?

We haven't forgotten the gold bullion and long-term U.S. government bonds we recommended. They are both subject to special tax treatments.

Bullion gold, which we hope will rise in value to offset hyperinflation, qualifies for long-term capital gains treatment if you hold it for six months or longer.

Our long-term U.S. government bonds, which we hope will appreciate if we experience hyperdeflation, pay interest which is exempt from state and local taxation. Of course, any long-term capital gains will be taxed at 40 percent of your maximum income tax. So you win two ways.

Not bad for investments that are only insurance against catastrophes!

The Wisened Old Philosopher Muses for the Masses

Once you get around to placing your investments, you should reread Chapters 9 and 10. While they will give you more than a little guidance on the mechanics, I have found that some philosophical guidance is useful to novice investors. Ah yes, the wisdom of the ages is so well condensed into clichés that a few words to the wise will help you keep more of that money you have worked so hard to find to invest.

The Five Best Risk-Reduction Strategies

Let's look at the top five commonsense strategies for reducing investment risks.

Stay as Liquid as Possible. In today's highly volatile and confusing markets, liquidity (the ability to get at your money quickly and without unnecessary transaction costs) *is* safety. If you were standing in front of a truck careening down your street, you would want the ability to move quickly.

It only makes sense not to tie up your money. That's a big reason why I strongly recommend using no-load mutual funds with telephone exchange privileges. If you have no "load" (broker's commission) to forfeit by getting out of your investments, and if getting out of the way of a declining stock market is only a tollfree telephone call away, you are highly liquid.

Buying a load fund of any kind is buying psychological handcuffs. The idea that you will lose any "value" you got for the stockbroker's fee will keep you from selling when you should. A fund which requires you to write them to sell your shares requires too much advance planning to be convenient.

Don't Invest in Anything You Do Not Understand. Simple, common sense, but advice many ignore. If you do not understand what you have bought, you simply won't know what to do with it. Too often we let high-pressure salespeople run our lives. Take charge of your life. If you make

204 Guide to Finding Money to Invest

mistakes, at least you will learn from them. You won't learn much from your broker's mistakes except not to deal with brokers.

Ask a lot of questions—it's *your* money. If it's so good, would the broker buy it? How hard is it to sell if I want out? What similar investments can I get without paying a stockbroker? (The broker will never tell you, but *Donoghue's MONEYLETTER* can.)

Use All Kinds of Insurance. Insurance is an interesting concept. It does not necessarily mean that all of the risks are covered, only that the most obvious risks are minimized at less cost than if the risk came home to roost.

For example, FDIC insurance would not have been sufficient to cover all the losses in bank accounts during the Depression. I feel sure that $99,000 in a bank is safer than $99,000 in a money market mutual fund—but I would not pay much for the insurance to make them equal.

On the other hand, I feel that if the amount we were talking about was $101,000, I would feel safer in a money fund than in a bank. The risk of loss in a money fund is, in my opinion, probably 1 in 100,000 that I might lose 1 percent of principal while retaining most of my dividends earned. The FDIC guarantees to pay only the first $100,000 of my deposits.

How about the Standard & Poor's–rated money funds? Does a high rating make them safer? Not much. The S&P rating system is highly controversial, and knowledgeable people in the field question S&P's methods and assumptions. It's better than nothing, but common sense tells you it's a lot of work to evaluate what even they will tell you is a small risk.

To get an assertive investment return, you have to learn to take common-sense risks. Insurance simply is not a big factor in commonsense investing.

Don't Buy a Car If You Don't Intend to Learn to Drive. It's only common sense that you familiarize yourself with the rules of the road when you start to invest.

Before you invest in a mutual fund of any type, read the prospectus. It is your "driver's manual."

When investors first put money in a money fund, I frequently get letters telling me, "I tried to switch my money out of the stock fund (or I tried to get my money out of the money fund) as you said, but they told me I can't. What happened to your so-called good advice?"

The answer is that you stopped listening and learning too soon. Some money funds, such as the Stein Roe group in Chicago, will not allow you to switch more often than once a month, so you have to wait a month before using the privilege.

Other funds (like Kemper Money Market Fund), if you invest by check, will not permit withdrawals for thirty days, although your money is invested promptly. If you wire the money from your bank to the fund, you will have no such problem. It's all in the prospectus. Read it or call and ask the fund's service representatives.

Let Your Winnings Run and Cut Your Losses. This old stock market adage is usually the exact opposite of what most investors actually do. When your investments are increasing in value, don't sell off and take the profits; let the profits run up even higher.

On the other hand, if your investments are decreasing in value, take the losses and run for cover. Since we are talking about no-load mutual funds for the most part, you are very liquid and adjusting your portfolio means incurring some very small costs, usually no more than $5 per transfer, although it could create a taxable event.

The worst enemy to face for most investors is the "break even" mentality —"I'm going to hold onto my investment until I at least break even." Folks who take this attitude seldom break even and if they do they wait a long time and miss the opportunity to recoup their capital faster in another investment.

My father lost 20 percent of his life's savings waiting to break even, which he never lived to see. He would have been better advised to forget the load he had paid and put his money back in his savings account. Of course, that was before money funds and telephone switch funds.

Getting the Family in on Your CASHPLAN

I hope you are getting the point that maybe you should buy a copy of this book for each member of the family. That way you can expect each family member to understand what it takes to squeeze every dollar out of your cash resources. It will also give them some better understanding of how to organize their own cash flows.

Of course, if you can agree to act as a team and operate the family as a company with each member holding shares based on some common agreement, you can cut a lot of expenses. For example, you can spread some of the investment capital and taxable income to younger members who are in lower tax brackets. Using the very liberal gift tax exemptions to move money around the family, you can save a lot of taxes.

The key to sharing family income is to work out some written agreement on how to issue shares to each family member, how each member can cash in his or her shares when they set up a separate family, and who gets what share of the family's investment income. Of course, the trouble comes when you cannot agree who will keep the books.

One Final Warning

Before you charge out and start implementing your new investment strategies, allow me to give you one final word of caution. *Anyone who can guarantee you a specific yield is making more on the deal than you are. There are no guarantees attached to the investment strategies I have described in this book, but the odds are with you that in the long run you will do better than if you did not take my advice.*

In the investment markets nothing is constant; everything is in a state of flux. I have given you some insights into the behavior of financial markets so you can see the forest *and* the trees.

I have also shown you that when we tested our strategies against the real world of the past five years they stood tall. Amazingly, money funds beat the stock market averages, both of which beat inflation. Adding the SLYC switching system improved on money funds alone, Super-SLYC with some commonsense stop-loss controls got an even better return, and switching among the funds at the top of our list got still better returns. Each step improved our five-year performance. (See Table 17.)

We feel that you now have a good idea of what range of returns you should expect as realistic. You also know that the Super-SLYC strategy should outperform the alternatives by a reasonable margin most of the time, regardless of what actual returns the markets offer us.

With commonsense investing guidelines to follow and a strong strategy for *finding money to invest,* you should make the most of your opportunities.

You've Got the Route and the Loot to Boot

By now you must have a long list of lemons to be liberated. You've assessed your assets, listed your liabilities, noted your net worth, created your CASH-PLAN, whittled your withholding, dealt with your deductions, blasted your tax bill, resurrected your investment returns, sheltered your savings, jostled your cookie jar, and discovered you are a minor money mogul with moolah.

You have found that this book contains "everything that is known or can be known" about finding money to invest. Hermetically sealed in a mason jar on Funk & Wagnall's porch, these secrets have been handed down through the centuries with the sole purpose of helping you gather up the gold that is coming to you for putting up with the garbage it took to earn it.

Seriously, folks, by now you have a solid background in the fine art of squeezing investable money from your hidden cash resources, which turned out, to your surprise, to be juicier than you first suspected. You've sold off or redeployed most of your lazy assets and have started to systematically manage

Table 17 Top Performing Switch Funds Based on Donoghue's SLYC System

Fund	1983 Assets ($ Millions)	What $10,000 Grew to 1979–83	Fund Family	Money Funds
Stein Roe Special Fund	145.1	51,235	Stein Roe & Farnum	SteinRoe Government Reserves SteinRoe Cash Reserves
Stein Roe Capital Opportunities	292.5	46,026	Stein Roe & Farnum	SteinRoe Tax-Exempt Money Fund
Founders Special Fund	94.5	43,726	Founders Mutual Depositors Corp.	Founders Money Market Fund
(Vanguard) Explorer Fund	260.0	42,723	Vanguard Group	Vanguard M.M.T. Federal Vanguard M.M.T. Insured Vanguard M.M.T. Prime Vanguard Muni Bond Fund, M.M.
Columbia Growth Fund	145.5	40,104	Columbia Management Corp.	Columbia Daily Income Fund
Dreyfus Growth Opportunities	415.0	39,894	Dreyfus Service Corp.	Dreyfus M.M. Instruments Government Dreyfus Liquid Assets Dreyfus Tax-Exempt Money Fund
T. Rowe Price New Era Fund	485.1	39,598	T. Rowe Price Associates	T. Rowe Price U.S. Treasury Money Fund T. Rowe Price Prime Reserve
T. Rowe Price New Horizons Fund	1,355.4	39,360	T. Rowe Price Associates	T. Rowe Price Tax-Exempt Money Fund
Value Line Special Situations Fund	337.9	39,337	Value Line Securities, Inc.	Value Line Cash Fund
Bull & Bear Capital Growth Fund	76.1	39,038	Bull & Bear Group	Bull & Bear Dollar Reserves

Source: Donoghue's Mutual Funds Almanac (15th ed.).

your finances. The tax man is now as close to a friend as he is ever going to be. You're on your way.

Now it's up to you. You've got to go back and patiently reread this book to make sure you've got your "to do" list as complete as possible and make sure you understand each money management move you want to make. You've got to discipline yourself to take charge of your life.

But now you have the greatest tool to do the job—knowledge.

Glossary

accrued interest   The interest due on a bond or other fixed-income security that must be paid by the buyer of the security to the seller.

amortization   The gradual reduction of any amount over a period of time.

annuity   A contract where the buyer (annuitant) pays a sum of money to receive regular payments for life or a fixed period of time.

asked price   The asked price of a fund share refers to the net asset value per share plus sales charge, if any. The asked price of a stock refers to the price at which the seller is willing to sell.

asset   Any item of value. Several types, including: *tangible asset*—an item that can readily be assigned a dollar value (hard assets fall into this category, but it is usually reserved for gold and silver); *current asset*—an item that can be turned into cash in a year or less; *fixed asset*—an item used for business, such as machinery; *intangible asset*—an item that cannot be readily assigned a dollar value, like the goodwill of a business.

automatic reinvestment   Allows shareholders to receive dividend distributions in the form of new shares instead of cash.

automatic withdrawal   See check-a-month plan.

balance sheet   A financial statement showing the dollar amounts of a company's or person's assets, liabilities, and owner's equity.

balanced fund   A mutual fund which has an investment policy of "balancing" its portfolio, generally by including bonds, preferred stocks, and common stocks.

balloon payments   Dollar amounts of earlier payments are smaller than dollar amounts of later payments.

bankers' acceptances   Short-term noninterest-bearing notes sold at a discount and redeemed at maturity for full face value. Primarily used to finance foreign trade. BAs represent a future claim on a U.S. bank that provides lines of credit to U.S. importers. BAs are collateralized by the goods to be sold and are guaranteed by the importer's U.S. bank.

basis point   One hundred basis points equals 1 percent. Term used to describe amount of change in fixed-income rates. An increase from 8 percent to 10 percent would be a change of 200 basis points.

bear market   The opposite of a bull market. It is a sustained period of falling stock prices accompanied by a period of poor economic performance known as a recession.

beta   Used to analyze the price volatility of securities. Standard & Poor's Index is set at a beta of 1; anything assigned a beta above 1 is considered to be more volatile than the index, anything below 1 has less volatility than the S&P Index.

bid   The price at which someone will buy a security.

big board   The New York Stock Exchange.

blue chip   The common stock of a large, well-known corporation with a relatively stable record of earnings and dividend payments.

bond   A security representing debt, a loan from the bondholder to the corporation. The bondholder usually receives annual interest payments with principal being refunded at maturity.

bond fund   A mutual fund whose portfolio consists primarily of bonds. The emphasis is normally on income rather than growth.

breakeven   1. The point where the value of A becomes equivalent to the value of B. 2. The point where income equals expenditures.

broker   A person in the business of effecting securities transactions for others. He receives a commission for his services. Closed-end investment company shares are usually bought and sold through brokers.

bull market   A stock market that is characterized by rising prices over a long period of time. The time span is not precise, but it represents a period of investor optimism, lower interest rates, and economic growth.

call   An option contract that gives the holder the right to purchase a particular security from another party at a prespecified price during a fixed period of time.

capital gain   A long-term capital gain is a profit from the sale of a capital asset, such as a security, that has been held for over six months and is taxed at a lower rate (40% of the seller's tax bracket). A short-term capital gain is the profit from selling an asset in less than six months and is subject to the ordinary federal income tax rate.

capital growth   An increase in the market value of securities.

capital loss   A loss from the sale of a capital asset. Half of a long-term capital loss is tax deductible. All of a short-term capital loss is tax deductible. The time period determining short- and long-term is the same as with a capital gain.

certificate of deposit (CD)   Generally short-term debt instrument certificates issued by commercial banks or savings and loan associations. (Euro CDs are issued by foreign branches of U.S. banks; Yankee CDs are issued by U.S. branches of foreign banks.)

check-a-month plan   An arrangement many open-end companies have which enables investors to receive fixed payments, usually monthly or quarterly. The actual payout is determined by the investor.

churning   Excessive trading of securities in an account by a broker who does not have the best interest of the client in mind.

Clifford trust A trust set up for ten years or more. Income from the trust is paid to a specified party (often children of the person setting up the trust). At the end of the trust the assets revert back to the person who set up the trust.

closed end management company A company that issues a fixed number of shares that usually must be traded in the secondary market.

collectible A physical object which has value by virtue of its rarity or intrinsic or artistic value.

commercial paper Unsecured promissory notes of corporations, with maturity up to 270 days. Used as a money market instrument.

commission The fee paid to a broker for buying or selling securities as an agent.

common stock Securities that represent ownership interest in a corporation.

consumer price index (CPI) Index that analyzes the change in prices for consumer goods and services over time.

conversion privilege *See* exchange privilege.

correction Used in conjunction with a bull market. It is a sustained period of stock price declines in the midst of long-term rising stock prices. Corrections are usually followed by another period of rising stock prices. A major correction refers to a decline of 10 percent or more in the widely accepted stock market indexes.

custodian The organization—bank or trust company—which holds in custody and safekeeping the securities and other assets of a mutual fund or individual.

DIDC (Depository Institutions Deregulation Committee) The regulatory committee charged by Congress with phasing out interest rate restrictions on bank deposits.

dealer A person or firm who regularly buys and sells securities for others from his or her own account of securities. In contrast, a broker acts as an agent for others. Frequently, broker and dealer functions are synonymous.

debenture A bond secured only by the general credit of the corporation.

debt instrument Any instrument that signifies a loan between a borrower and a lender.

deep discount bond A bond that is selling below 80 percent of its par (face) value. The face value of a bond is usually $1,000.

demand deposit Basically, the money that has been deposited into checking accounts. Since the customer can remove money on demand, it is called a demand deposit. Used in calculating the money supply.

discount The amount by which a preferred stock or bond may sell below its face value.

distributions Dividends paid from net investment income and payments made from realized capital gains.

distributor The principal underwriter—either a person or company—that purchases open-end investment company shares directly from the issuer for resale to others.

diversification The mutual fund policy of spreading investments among a number of different securities to reduce the risk inherent in investing. Diversification may be among types of securities, different companies, different industries, or different geographical locations.

diversified investment company To be so classified, the Investment Company

Act requires that 75 percent of a fund's assets be allocated so that not more than 5 percent of its total assets are invested in one company. In addition, it can hold no more than 10 percent of the outstanding voting securities of another company.

dividend   A payment from income on a share of common or preferred stock.

dollar cost averaging   Method of investing equal amounts of money at regular intervals regardless of whether the stock market is moving upward or downward. The theory is that the investor's average cost will be lower than if he invested larger amounts irregularly over the same amount of time.

employee stock ownership plan   A plan where employees systematically buy out the owners of their company, eventually spreading ownership to all employees in the plan.

equity   Represents stock ownership of a company.

equity fund   A mutual fund that invests in stocks.

Eurodollars   Dollars held by U.S. banks in foreign countries.

exchange privilege   The right to take all or some of the shares of one fund and put them into another fund within the same family of funds. This is considered a sale and new purchase for tax purposes. (Same as a conversion privilege.)

FDIC (Federal Deposit Insurance Corporation)   The federal agency which insures deposits up to $100,000 at member banks. FDIC also makes loans to buy assets from member banks to facilitate mergers or help prevent bank failures.

FSLIC (Federal Savings and Loan Insurance Corporation)   The federal agency established to insure funds on deposit at member S&Ls.

face value   The value that appears on the face of a bond. This is the amount the issuing company will pay at maturity, but it does not necessarily indicate market price.

family of funds   The various mutual funds all managed by the same investment company. One fund may manage several different funds, each with different objectives, such as growth, income, or tax-exempt funds.

Fannie Mae   Nickname for Federal National Mortgage Association (FNMA).

Federal Home Loan Mortgage Corporation   Promotes development of secondary market for conventional residential mortgages. Participation certificates (PCs) and guaranteed mortgage certificates (GMCs) are sold in $100,000 denominations with thirty-year maturities. Many mutual funds hold these in their portfolios.

Federal National Mortgage Association   A publicly owned corporation that buys home mortgages on the secondary market by selling FNMA debentures (a long-term unsecured debt instrument) or notes (similar to a debenture but matures in less than ten years).

fiduciary   An individual or corporation who is entrusted with certain assets for some specified purpose. Also known as trustee, executor, guardian, etc.

float   The time lag in the check-writing process. It is the number of days it takes a check to show up in your checking account as either a debit (when paying a bill) or a credit (when depositing money).

Freddie Mac   Nickname for Federal Home Loan Mortgage Corporation (FHLMC)

front-end load   A sales charge for buying into a mutual fund.

Ginnie Mae   Nickname for Government National Mortgage Association (GNMA).

Government National Mortgage Association A government-owned corporation that buys home mortgages from private lenders at prices that are lower than are available in the market, packages the mortgages into GNMA bonds, and sells them to private investors at the prevailing market price. The difference in the prices is subsidized by the government.

growth fund A mutual fund with growth of capital a primary objective, to be obtained principally through investments in common stocks with growth potential. This type of fund will generate long- and short-term capital gains rather than pay dividends.

growth-income fund A mutual fund with the objective of providing both income and long-term growth.

holding company A company that owns and manages other companies.

IRA *See* Individual Retirement Account.

IRA rollover A term used if you take your money out of one investment and put it into another. A rollover involves the individual receiving the money and reinvesting it again. Rollovers must be completed within sixty days and are only allowed once a year. This is *not* an IRA transfer. A transfer is allowed at any time; however, you do not receive the money. It goes directly from one investment to another.

illiquid An asset that is hard to sell, so the owner may not be readily able to obtain cash quickly.

income fund A mutual fund with current income as its primary objective.

index A measurement used to determine trends in the market.

Individual Retirement Account A retirement plan that can be opened by any employed person. Up to $2,000 may be invested each year and will be tax-deferred until withdrawal at age fifty-nine and a half or later. Can be self-directed or part of a company plan.

interest Periodic payments made to a lender of money by the borrower for use of the money.

investment company Generic term including mutual funds, unit investment trusts, and other types of companies principally engaged in the business of investing the funds of their shareholders.

investment objective The specific goal, such as long-term capital growth, or current income, which the investor or mutual fund pursues.

Keogh plan A retirement program for self-employed individuals and their employees based on tax-saving provisions. A Keogh plan may be funded with mutual fund shares. A self-employed individual may put up to $30,000 a year into a Keogh.

leverage Investing with borrowed money to obtain higher earnings. Using debt will magnify the profits or losses and increases the amount of risk. (*See* margin.)

liability Any debt owed by a company or individual. Usually broken down into current liabilities (due in one year or less) and long-term liabilities (over one year).

line of credit Allows preferred customers to borrow up to a predetermined maximum amount of money.

liquid Easily convertible into cash or exchangeable for other values.

load A portion of the offering price that goes towards selling costs such as sales commissions and distribution. A front-end load is charged when buying into a fund. A back-end load is charged when getting out of a fund.

management company   A company that manages the day-to-day operations of a portfolio. *See* open end and closed end management company. (Also called an investment company.)

management fee   The amount paid to the administrator and/or investment adviser for its services.

margin, buying on   Buying securities on credit from your broker.

market price   The last reported price at which a security has been sold.

market rate   A general term used to describe the current interest rate on a given instrument.

maturity   The time period stipulated on a promissory note for when the note comes due and will be paid off.

money market fund   Mutual funds investing in short-term, relatively riskless money market instruments—bank certificates of deposit, bankers' acceptances, commercial paper, and short-term government securities.

municipal bond fund   Unit investment trust or open end company whose shares represent diversified holdings of tax-exempt securities issued by state, city, and local governments, the income from which is exempt from federal taxes.

mutual fund   An open end or closed end investment company which pools the money of many people whose investment goals are similar and invests this money in a wide variety of securities.

net asset value per share   The market worth of an investment company's shares. Derived from taking their total resources—securities, cash and any accrued earnings—then deducting liabilities and dividing by the number of shares outstanding.

no-load fund   Investors purchase shares directly from the fund, rather than through an investment dealer or broker; therefore the fund does not charge the investors for sales comissions that a load fund would charge.

NOW account   A negotiable order of withdrawal account. An interest-bearing checking and savings account.

odd lot   The usual amount when buying shares of stock is 100 shares (a "round lot"). When you buy less than 100 shares it is called an odd lot. Commissions will vary with the number of shares bought.

offering price   The lowest price at which someone is willing to sell. (Also called asked price.)

open end management company   An investment company that will continuously sell shares and then redeem shares whenever the present owner wishes to sell them.

option   The right to buy (call option) or sell (put option) a fixed quantity of a security, at a fixed price, within a specific amount of time.

options fund   A mutual fund which sells options on shares it owns to increase its income.

ordinary income   Income taxed at the maximum rate schedule, such as employment income or income from a business.

par value   A security that will sell at face value. If the face value of a bond is $1,000, and it is being offered at par, you can buy it for $1,000.

payroll deduction plan   An arrangement whereby an employee may accumulate shares in a mutual fund by authorizing his employer to deduct and transfer to a fund a specified amount from his salary at stated times.

penny stocks   Any stock that is very low-priced and often speculative.

periodic payment plan   An arrangement by which an investor can purchase mutual fund shares periodically in large or small amounts, usually with provisions for the reinvestment of income dividends and the acceptance of capital gains distributions in additional shares.

portfolio   The mix of investments owned by an investment company or an individual.

preferred stock   A type of stock that receives a dividend at a specified rate when the company declares a dividend. This type of stock is known as preferred because the company must pay its declared dividend on preferred stock before paying any on common stock, and in the event of bankruptcy, preferred stockholders are entitled to payment before the common stock stockholders.

premium   The amount by which a bond or preferred stock sells above its face value.

profit   The difference when the selling price is higher than the cost.

prospectus   The official booklet which describes a mutual fund and offers its shares for sale. It contains information as required by the Securities and Exchange Commission on such subjects as the fund's investment objectives and policies, services, investment restrictions, officers and directors, how shares can be bought and redeemed, its charges and its financial statements.

proxy   When a shareholder with voting rights transfers this right to someone who will then vote according to the wishes of the shareholder. Usually done if the shareholder cannot be present at the meeting.

put   An option contract that gives the holder the right to sell a particular security to another party at a prespecified price during the term of the option.

qualified retirement plan   A private retirement plan that meets the rules and regulations of the Internal Revenue Service. Contributions to a qualified retirement plan are in almost all cases tax-deductible and earnings on such contributions are always tax-sheltered until retirement. Most company pension plans are qualified retirement plans.

recession   A sustained decline in business activity represented by a drop in the Federal Reserve Board's index of industrial production.

recovery   An increase in business activity after a recession. A recovery occurs when economic activity in this country and worldwide attains the same level as before a recession.

redeem   To buy back shares from the present owner. *See* redemption price.

redemption price   The amount per share the mutual fund shareholder receives when he cashes in his shares (also known as "liquidating price" or "bid price"). The value of the shares depends on the market value of the company's portfolio securities at the time.

reinvestment privilege   A service provided by most mutual funds for the automatic reinvestment of a shareholder's income dividends and capital gains distributions into additional shares.

return, rate of   Yield.

risk The uncertainty associated with a particular investment.

rollover Reinvestment of funds into a similar investment.

round lot The accepted standard number of shares used to trade stocks is 100. It is also the number of shares to which prevailing broker commission rates apply.

sales charge The amount charged in connection with public distribution of fund shares. It is added to the net asset value per share in computing the offering price and is paid to the dealer and underwriter.

savings and loan association (S&L) A financial institution that accepts time deposits and uses this money primarily for financing home mortgages. Some S&Ls are stock corporations. These are often chartered and regulated on the state level. Many S&Ls are mutually owned by their depositors, who receive dividends from the associations' profits.

Securities and Exchange Commission (SEC) An independent agency of the U.S. government which administers the various federal securities laws for the protection of the shareholder.

short sale The sale of a security which is now owned, in the hope that the price will go down so that it can be repurchased at a profit. The person making a short sale borrows stock in order to make delivery to the buyer and must eventually purchase the stock for return to the lender.

speculative An investment that is considered to have a high degree of risk.

tax-deferred Income on which tax is levied only when it is distributed.

tax-exempt securities Usually refers to municipal bonds that are exempt from federal taxes. Some municipal bonds, known as triple exempt bonds, are also exempt from state and local taxes depending on the state laws where the bond was issued and where the buyer of the bond resides.

tax-free fund A mutual fund whose portfolio consists of securities (usually municipal bonds) exempt from federal income tax.

tax shelter An investment used for deferring taxes.

Treasury bill (T-bill) Short-term debt issued by the U.S. government at a discount from its face value. Maturities are three months, six months, and one year. Minimum order $10,000, then multiples of $5,000.

Treasury bond Issued with maturities of around twenty or thirty years (generally over ten years) with $1,000 as the lowest denomination issued.

Treasury note Debt obligations with maturities of not less than one year and not more than ten years. Lowest denomination issued is $1,000.

trustee The institution which maintains administrative control over another's assets; a commercial bank, savings and loan association, mutual savings bank, trust company, or stockbroker.

Truth-in-Lending Law A federal law stating lenders must specify the terms and conditions of the loan to the borrower.

underwriter The organization which acts as chief distributor of a mutual fund's shares; it is often the same as or affiliated with the advisor.

unit investment trust (UIT) A type of mutual fund that buys a fixed number of debt obligations and sells them to investors in units. Most common types of obligations are GNMAs, municipal bonds, and utility obligations.

variable annuity   An insurance annuity contract under which the dollar payments received are not fixed but fluctuate with the market. Most frequently investors will have a choice of stock, money, or bond funds.

volatile   Used to describe a stock whose price can increase or decrease rapidly.

withdrawal plan   A mutual fund plan that allows a specified amount of money to be withdrawn at specified intervals.

Yankee dollars   U.S. dollars in U.S. branches of foreign banks.

yield   Income received from investments, usually expressed as a percentage of market price; also referred to as return.

zero coupon bond   A bond sold at a discount which matures in more than one year. Used for tax shelter purposes.

Market Indexes

American Stock Exchange Index—Measures the change of the average share price of stocks listed on the American Stock Exchange.

Donoghue's Money Fund Average (DMFA)TM—The average yield on all taxable money funds for both a seven- and thirty-day period. DMFA (thirty-day yield) is used as a mutual fund switch indicator by SLYC investors.

Donoghue's SLYC Index—An index of thirty-six no-load growth and aggressive growth funds with at least $50 million in assets. Index includes only mutual fund families that permit telephone switching between their money funds and equity funds. The index was originally priced at $100 on January 1, 1983 and represents the average percent gain in net asset value of the thirty-six funds with dividends and capital gains reinvested.

Dow Jones Bond Average—Consists of ten industrial corporations and ten public utilities.

Dow Jones Industrial Average (DJIA)—An index representing the average stock price performance of thirty "blue-chip" industrial companies.

Dow Jones Municipal Bond Yield Average—A changing average showing the yields on municipal bonds in fifteen major cities.

Dow Jones Utilities Average—Made up of fifteen geographically diverse public utilities.

Forbes 500—Index based on the stock prices of the 500 largest companies (according to sales).

New York Stock Exchange Index—Measures the change of the average share price of stocks listed on the New York Stock Exchange.

Standard & Poor's 500—An index of stock performance representing 400 industrial, 20 transportation, 40 financial, and 40 public utility stocks.

Value Line Index—An index of stock performance of 1,500 companies.

Wilshire 5000 Equity Index—The total price of all stocks for which daily quotations are available. Quotations taken from the New York Stock Exchange, American Stock Exchange, Over-the-Counter, and the regional stock exchanges.

Suggested Reading

Books

Berlin, Howard, M. *The Dow-Jones Guide to Buying and Selling Treasury Securities.* Homewood, Illinois: Dow-Jones Irwin, 1984.

Donoghue, William E., and Thomas Tilling. *William E. Donoghue's Complete Money Market Guide,* New York: Harper & Row, 1981; New York: Bantam, 1982.

Donoghue, William E., and Thomas Tilling. *William E. Donoghue's No-Load Mutual Fund Guide.* New York: Harper & Row, 1983; New York: Bantam, 1984.

Egan, Jack. *Your Complete Guide to IRAs and Keoghs.* New York: Harper & Row, 1982.

Hardy, C. Colburn. *Dun & Bradstreet's Guide to Your Investments.* New York: Lippincott & Crowell, 1984.

Hyman, Henry A. *The Where to Sell Anything and Everything Book.* New York: A World Almanac Publication, 1981.

Malkiel, Burton. *The Inflation-Beater's Investment Guide.* New York: W.W. Norton & Company, 1980.

Pope, Alan. *Successful Investing in No-Load Mutual Funds.* New York: John Wiley & Sons, Inc., 1983.

Porter, Sylvia. *Sylvia Porter's New Money Book for the 80's.* Garden City, New York: Doubleday & Co., 1979.

Van Caspel, Venita. *The Power of Money Dynamics.* Reston, Virginia: Reston Publishing Company, Inc., 1983.

Booklets

Hunt, James H. *Taking the Bite Out of Insurance.* National Insurance Consumer Organization, 344 Commerce Street, Alexandria, VA 22314.

Krughoff, Robert. *The IRA Book.* Center for the Study of Services (*Consumers' Checkbook* magazine), 806 15th Street, NW, Suite 925, Washington DC 20005.

Government Publications

Consumer's Resource Handbook. Write to Consumer Information Center, Pueblo, CO 81009 or call 1-303-948-3334. This handbook has tips on what to do when you have a complaint, who to get in contact with, and how to follow up.

Individual Retirement Accounts. IRS publication 590, available from your local IRS office.

IRAs & Keoghs: New Opportunities for Retirement Income. Available from the Federal Reserve Bank of Philadelphia, P.O. Box 66, Philadelphia, PA 19105. Make sure to send a self-addressed, stamped envelope.

Your Federal Income Tax for Individuals. IRS publication 17, available from your local IRS office.

Magazines and Journals*

AAII Journal, published monthly except for August and December by the American Association of Individual Investors. Price: $40. Subscription: Subscription Information, American Association of Individual Investors, 612 N. Michigan Ave., Chicago, IL 60611.

Changing Times, published monthly by The Kiplinger Washington Editors, Inc. Price: $15. Subscription: Circulation Director, Changing Times, Editors Park, MD 20782.

Fact, published monthly by *Fact* Magazine. Price: $18. Subscription: Circulation Director, FACT, 711 Third Avenue, New York, NY 10017.

Money, published monthly by Time, Inc. Price: $25.95. Subscription: Money, P.O. Box 2519, Boulder, CO 80322.

U.S. News & World Report, published weekly by U.S. News & World Report. Price: $36. Subscription: U.S. News & World Report, Subscription Department, P.O. Box 2629, Boulder, CO 80322. News You Can Use and Money Matters sections.

Newsletters*

Bank Rate Monitor's 100 Highest Yields. Published weekly by Bank Rate Monitor. Price: $84. Subscription: Box 540, Holliston, MA 01746.

Donoghue's MONEYLETTER. Published twice a month by the Donoghue Organization, Inc. Price: $87. Subscription: Box 411, Holliston, MA 01746.

Donoghue's Money Fund Report, Executive Edition. Published monthly by the Donoghue Organization, Inc. Price $195. Subscription: Box 411, Holliston, MA 01746.

Fundline. Published monthly by David H. Menashe & Company. Price: $60. Subscription: P.O. Box 663, Woodland Hills, CA 91365.

Growth Fund Guide. Published monthly by Growth Fund Research, Inc. Price: $79. Subscription: Growth Fund Research Bldg., Box 6600, Rapid City, SD 57709.

Prime Investment Alert: An Advisory for No-Load Investors. Published monthly by Prime Financial Associates. Price: $60. Subscription: P.O. Box 8308, Portland, ME 04104.

Switch Fund Advisory. Published monthly by Schabacker Investment Management. Price $125. Subscription: 8943 Shady Grove Court, Gaithersburg, MD 20877.

Telephone Switch Newsletter. Published monthly by Dick and Douglas Fabian. Price: $117. Subscription: Box 2538, Huntington Beach, CA 92647.

*All subscription prices listed are for one year.

222 **Suggested Reading**

United Mutual Fund Selector. Published monthly by United Business Services. Price: $98. Subscription: 210 Newbury Street, Boston, MA 02116.

Annual Publications

Donoghue's Mutual Funds Almanac. The Donoghue Organization, Box 540, Holliston, MA 01746. Covers the performance of 850 mutual funds. Price: $23.

Mutual Fund Fact Book. Investment Company Institute, 1775 K Street, NW, Washington, DC 20006. An industry overview.

National Consumer Money Market Directory. Box 540, Holliston, MA 01746. Price: $12.

No-Load Mutual Fund Directory. No-Load Mutual Fund Association, 11 Pennsylvania Plaza, Suite 2204, New York, NY 10001. Covers some no-load mutual funds (does not include performance data). Price: $2.

Newspapers*

Barron's. Published every Monday by Dow Jones & Co. Price: $71. Subscription: Barron's, 200 Burnett Road, Chicopee, MA 01021.

Wall Street Journal. Published daily (except weekends and holidays) by Dow Jones & Co. Price: $101. Subscription: The Wall Street Journal, 200 Burnett Road, Chicopee, MA 01021.

*All subscription prices listed are for one year.

Addresses and Phone Numbers

Before calling the numbers below, check your yellow pages to see if there is an office closer to you.

Automobiles

AutoCAP (National Automobile Dealers Association)
8400 West Park Dr.
McLean, VA 22102
703-821-7144

> Automotive Consumer Action Plan, sponsored by the National Automobile Dealers Association, handles disputes with car dealers that cannot be resolved between the buyer and dealer. Contact AutoCap for the address of a local dealer that sponsors AutoCAP.

Auto Safety Hotline
National Highway Traffic Safety Administration
U.S. Department of Transportation
400 Seventh St., SW
Washington, DC 20590
800-424-9393
202-426-0123

Banking

Comptroller of the Currency
Office of Consumer Affairs
490 L'Enfant Plaza, SW
Washington, DC 20220
202-447-1600

> For problems with federally chartered banks (those that have national or N.A. in or after the bank name).

Federal Deposit Insurance Corp.
Office of Consumer Affairs
550 17th St., NW
Washington, DC 20429
202-393-8400
    Complaints about banks that are "FDIC" insured.

Federal Home Loan Bank Board
Office of the Secretary
1700 G St., NW
Washington, DC 20552
202-377-6000
    Complaints about federally chartered savings and loan groups.

Federal Reserve Board
Division of Consumer Affairs
21 & C Sts., NW
Washington, DC 20551
202-452-3946
    Complaints about state chartered banks (if you're not sure if the bank is state or federal, call them and they will direct you to the proper authority).

Collectibles

American Society of Appraisers
P.O. Box 17265
Washington, DC 20041
703-620-3838

Appraisers Association of America
60 E. 42nd St.
New York, NY 10165
212-867-9775
    For names of appraisers and their specialties, plus general information.

Christie's
502 Park Ave.
New York, NY 10021
212-546-1000
    Free auction estimates.

Sotheby's
1334 York Ave.
New York, NY 10021
212-472-3452
    Free auction estimates.

R. M. Smythe & Co.
24 Broadway
New York, NY 10004
212-943-1880
    For a $20 fee Smythe & Co. will appraise antique stock and bond certificates. Auction services are also available.

Credit

Associated Credit Bureaus
P.O. Box 218300
Houston, TX 77218
713-492-8155
    Complaints about credit bureaus.

Federal Trade Commission
Bureau of Consumer Protection–Credit Practices
Pennsylvania & 6th Sts., NW
Washington, DC 20580
202-523-3727
    For violation of the Truth-in-Lending Act.

National Foundation for Consumer Credit Counseling
8701 Georgia Ave.
Suite 601
Silver Springs, MD 20910
    A consumer credit counseling service (CCCS).

Credit Unions

Credit Union National Association
Public Relations Department
P.O. Box 431
Madison, WI 53701
608-231-4000
    General information and listings of credit unions.

Drugs

Office of Consumer Affairs (HFE-88)
Food and Drug Administration
U.S. Department of Health and Human Services
5600 Fishers Lane
Rockville, MD 20857
301-443-3170
    General information.

Education

American College Testing Program
P.O. Box 168
Iowa City, Iowa 52243
319-337-1038
    ACT provides information on financial aid and also has a Student
    Need Analysis Service to help families determine amount of aid
    they're likely to receive.

226   **Addresses and Phone Numbers**

College Board
888 Seventh Ave.
New York, NY 10106
212-582-6210
    Financial aid and advanced placement exam information.

The Experiment in International Living
Box 676, Kipling Road
Brattleboro, VT 05301
802-257-7751
    Specializes in placing students and adults with families while studying abroad.

Federal/Student Aid Program
Box 84
Washington, DC 20044
800-492-6602 (Maryland)
800-638-6700 (elsewhere)
    General information.

Entrepreneurs

International Franchise Association
1025 Connecticut Ave., NW
Washington, DC 20036
202-659-0790
    General information, as well as lists of association members.

National Venture Capital Association
1730 North Lynn Street
Suite 400
Arlington, VA 22204
703-528-4370

Small Business Administration
1441 L St., NW
Washington, DC 20416
800-368-5855
202-653-7561
    Supplies information on how to start your own business. SBA Office of Advocacy will
    advise and represent small business interests.

U.S. Department of Commerce
Franchise Specialist
Room 4312
Washington, DC 20230
202-377-0342
    General and statistical information.

Public Inquiries
International Franchise Association
1025 Connecticut Ave., NW
Suite 1005
Washington, DC 20036
202-659-0790

Financial Planning

Institute of Certified Financial Planners
3443 S. Galena
Denver, CO 80231
303-751-7600

International Association for Financial Planning
5775 Peachtree-Dunwoody Rd.
Atlanta, GA 30342
404-252-9600
> Both can give you lists of financial planners. The Institute's members have completed a series of courses and use a C.F.P. designation.

Funerals

Continental Association of Funeral and Memorial Societies
Suite 530
2001 S St., NW
Washington, DC 20009
202-745-0634
> Offers guidance and evaluation services.

ThanaCAP
135 W. Wells St.
Milwaukee, WI 53203
414-276-9788
> Contact if you have a dispute you cannot solve with a funeral home. Decisions are binding on both parties.

Furniture

Furniture CAP
Furniture Industry Consumer Advisory Panel's Director of Consumer
Affairs (FICAP)
Box 951
High Point, NC 27261
919-885-5065
> Same as the other CAPs but the decisions are not binding on either party.

Giving

National Charities Information Bureau
19 Union Square West
New York, NY 10003
212-929-6300

Philanthropic Advisory Service,
Council of Better Business Bureau
1515 Wilson Blvd.
Arlington, VA 22209
703-276-0100

   Both provide information on how charities spend their money. Both provide lists of
   charities, the latter also identifies those that do not meet the Better Business Bureau's
   standards.

Government Agencies—General

Council of Better Business Bureaus
1150 17th St., NW
Washington, DC 20036
202-862-1200

Federal Trade Commission, regional offices:

John F. Kennedy Federal Building
Government Center
Boston, MA 02203

55 East Monroe St.
Chicago, IL 60603

Federal Building
26 Federal Plaza
New York, NY 10007

6 Pennsylvania Ave.
Washington, DC 20580

Suite 500
The Mall Building
118 St. Clair Ave.
Cleveland, OH 44114

1718 Peachtree St., NW
Atlanta, GA 30308

2001 Bryan St.
Dallas, TX 75201

450 Golden Gate Ave.
Box 36005
San Francisco, CA 94102

Federal Building
11000 Wilshire Blvd.
Los Angeles, CA 90024

915 Second Ave.
Seattle, WA 98101

1405 Curtis St.
Denver, CO 80202
> The FTC is involved in almost any type of transaction, so if you have a question and don't know where to go, try the FTC near you.

Office of Consumer Affairs
626 Reporters Building
Washington, DC 20201
202-755-8820 (complaints)
202-755-8892 (state and local programs)

Public Citizen Litigation Group
2000 P St., NW—7th floor
Washington, DC 20036
202-785-3704
> Initiates lawsuits on behalf of the public.

Health Care

National Health Information Clearinghouse
U.S. Department of Health and Human Services
P.O. Box 1133
Washington, DC 20013
703-522-2590 (DC, VA, AK, HI)
800-336-4797

Office of Health Maintenance Organizations
Division of Program Promotion
U.S. Department of Health and Human Services
12420 Parklawn Drive
Rockville, MD 20957
301-443-2300
> For general information.

Housing

FHA Loans
Federal Housing Administration
U.S. Department of Housing and Urban Development
Washington, DC 20410
202-755-6600
> Information and assistance.

Insurance

American Council of Life Insurance
Information Services
1850 K St., NW
Washington, DC 20006
202-862-4000

National Insurance Consumers Organization (NICO)
344 Commerce St.
Alexandria, VA 22314
703-549-8050
> Both will answer general questions and supply consumer pamphlets and booklets on life insurance. NICO will analyze the rate of returns on different life insurance policies for a fee. Requests for information and assistance can be directed to the Commissioner of Insurance (in the yellow pages or call your statehouse—insurance is state regulated).

Insurance Information Institute
110 William St.
New York, NY 10038
800-221-4954
> For general information on property and casualty insurance.

Investment Clubs

American Association of Individual Investors
612 N. Michigan Ave.
Chicago, IL 60611
312-280-0170

National Association of Investment Clubs
P.O. Box 220
Royal Oak, MI 48068
313-543-0612
> Both associations give information on how to invest. The National Association will also help you set up your own investment club.

Legal Services

American Bar Association
American Bar Center
1155 E. 60th Street
Chicago, IL 60637
312-947-4000

National Consumers Center for Legal Services
1302 18th St., NW
Washington, DC 20036
202-338-0714

National Resource Center for Consumers of Legal Services
3254 Jones Court, NW
Washington, DC 20007
202-338-0714
> The last two both offer information, however neither give legal advice. For advice, you should call your local bar association.

Mutual Funds

Donoghue's Mutual Funds Almanac
Box 540
Holliston, MA 01746
617-429-5930

Investment Company Institute
(Mutual Fund Fact Book)
1775 K St., NW
Washington, DC 20006
202-293-7700

No-Load Mutual Fund Association
11 Penn Plaza
New York, NY 10001
212-661-8030

All three offer a directory of funds. Only the *Almanac* contains performance statistics on both load and no-load mutual funds. The Investment Company Institute also has pamphlets available on various financial topics.

Real Estate

Home Owners Warranty
2000 L St., NW
Washington, DC 20036
800-841-8000

HOW members must build to certain approved specifications and carry a 10-year warranty against major defects. For a list of members write to the above address.

National Association of Home Builders
Department of Consumer Affairs
15th & M Sts., NW
Washington, DC 20005
202-822-0200

Acts as mediator between builders and buyers.

Retirement

National Council on the Aging
600 Maryland Ave., SW
Washington, DC 20024
202-479-1200

American Association of Retired Persons
1909 K St., NW
Washington, DC 20049
202-872-4700

Both provide information and assistance to older Americans, plus they fight for senior citizens' rights.

Securities

National Association of Securities Dealers
Arbitration Department
2 World Trade Center, 98th Floor
New York, NY 10048
212-839-6244

National Association of Securities Dealers
Customer Complaint Department
1735 K St., NW
Washington, DC 20006
202-728-8000

Securities and Exchange Commission
Office of Consumer Affairs and Information Services
450 Fifth St., NW
Washington, DC 20549
202-272-7440

Securities Investor Protection Corporation (SIPC)
900 17th St., NW
Washington, DC 20006
202-223-8400

> Each of these organizations are set up to handle complaints. If they can't handle your problem, they will direct you to the proper agency.

Stock Exchanges

American Stock Exchange
Rulings and Inquiries Department
86 Trinity Place
New York, NY 10006
212-306-1000

Chicago Board Options Exchange
Communications Department
LaSalle and Van Buren Sts.
Chicago, IL 60605
312-786-7492

New York Stock Exchange
11 Wall Street
New York, NY 10005
212-623-3000

> Just call the above numbers and tell them what your problem or question is and they will connect you to the right department.

Taxes

Internal Revenue Service
—Look in your telephone book under United States Government, Internal Revenue Service:
For information dial 1-800-424-1040
For tax forms & publications dial 1-800-892-0288
For problems with your federal taxes dial 1-800-392-6288
> These are national phone numbers. I recommend you use the tax forms number and get Publication 17 entitled *Your Federal Income Tax*. This booklet can answer many of the questions you may have.

U.S. Tax Court
400 Second St., NW
Washington, DC 20217
202-376-2754
> For small tax battles call the above number for information.

Travel

Airline Discount Club-International
P.O. Box 616
Parker, CO 80134
303-841-4337
> Members ($39 annual fee) of this club can get discounts from 10 to 50 percent off the regular price.

Airline Passengers Association
Consumer Affairs
P.O. Box 220074
Dallas, TX 75222
214-438-8100
800-527-5888
> For problems with air travel.

American Society of Travel Agents
711 Fifth Ave.
New York, NY 10022
202-965-7520
> For problems with your travel agent, tour, or the like.

Bed & Breakfast Registry
P.O. Box 80174
St. Paul, MN 55108-0174
612-646-4238
> For information and lists on bed & breakfast homes in almost every state.

Citizens Counselor Services
Department of State
Room 4811
Washington, DC 20520
202-632-3444   For nonemergencies.
202-632-5225   For emergencies.

234   **Addresses and Phone Numbers**

Warranties

Division of Special Statutes
FTC
Washington, DC 20580
202-523-3598

Appendixes

Appendix 1: Rate of Return (ROR) for Cash Value Life
Insurance

Appendix 2: Life Insurance Comparison

Appendix 3: Sample List of Tax Publications

Appendix 4: 3% *Real* Rate of Return

Appendix 5: IRA Breakeven

Appendix 6: SLYC Funds

Appendix 7: Rule of 72: "How Long to Double Your
Money?"

Appendix 8: 1984 Tax Rate Schedules

Appendix 1

Rate of Return (ROR) for Cash Value Life Insurance

	Cash Value Policy					Buy Term and Invest Difference at 11.0 %							
	(1)	(2)	(3)	(4)	(5)	(6)	(7)	(8)	(9)	(10)	(11)	(12)	(13)	
			End of Year										Side-fund	
Policy Year	Annual Premium	Dividend If Used to Reduce Premium	Cash Value Including Value of Any Dividend Additions	Termination Dividend	Surrender Value (2) + (3) + (4)	Death Benefits Including Dividend Additions Prior Year and (4)*	Annual Outlay: Same as Col. (1)	Amount of term insurance (6) − (11)	Term Rate per $1000†	Cost of Term Insurance	Side-fund Beginning Year (13)* + (7) − (10)	Death Benefit Beginning Year (8) + (11) (=(6))	Side-fund End Year Col. (11) Accumulated @ 11.0%	Annual RORs
1	649.00	0	474	0	474	100000	649.00	99479	1.04	128	521	100000	578	−8.9%
2	649.00	0	1048	0	1048	100000	649.00	98913	1.16	140	1087	100000	1206	6.6
3	649.00	0	1677	0	1677	100000	649.00	98298	1.30	153	1702	100000	1889	8.6
4	649.00	0	2367	0	2367	100000	649.00	97631	1.47	169	2369	100000	2629	9.7
5	649.00	0	3121	0	3121	100000	649.00	96907	1.65	185	3093	100000	3431	10.3
6	649.00	0	3947	0	3947	100000	649.00	96124	1.87	205	3876	100000	4300	10.7
7	649.00	0	4849	0	4849	100000	649.00	95279	2.13	228	4721	100000	5239	11.0
8	649.00	0	5834	0	5834	100000	649.00	94365	2.41	252	5635	100000	6252	11.2
9	649.00	0	6911	0	6911	100000	649.00	93378	2.72	279	6622	100000	7348	11.4
10	649.00	0	8086	0	8086	100000	649.00	92311	3.07	308	7689	100000	8531	11.5
11	649.00	0	9370	0	9370	100000	649.00	91160	3.45	340	8640	100000	9809	11.6
12	649.00	0	10771	0	10771	100000	649.00	89906	3.77	364	10094	100000	11200	11.6
13	649.00	0	12301	0	12301	100000	649.00	88541	4.12	390	11459	100000	12714	11.5
14	649.00	0	13973	0	13973	100000	649.00	87054	4.51	418	12946	100000	14364	11.5
15	649.00	0	15804	0	15804	100000	649.00	85433	4.93	446	14567	100000	16162	11.5
16	649.00	0	17813	0	17813	100000	649.00	83666	5.40	477	16334	100000	18124	11.5
17	649.00	0	20025	0	20025	100000	649.00	81724	5.78	497	18275	100000	20278	11.5
18	649.00	0	22461	0	22461	100000	649.00	79592	6.20	518	20408	100000	22644	11.5
19	649.00	0	25146	0	25146	100000	649.00	77247	6.66	539	22753	100000	25246	11.4
20	649.00	0	28110	0	28110	100000	649.00	74665	7.17	560	25335	100000	28110	11.4

If policy kept	Average Annual RORs		Taxable gain	Marginal RORs (100% ART)
	100% ART	90% ART		
5 years	7.8 %	6.7 %	0	6 thru 10 is: 11.2 %
10 years	10.1	9.4	1596	11 thru 15 is: 11.6
15 years	10.7	10.2	6069	16 thru 20 is: 11.5
20 years	11.0	10.5	15130	

*Means column for prior year.
†Add $25.
1. Insurer: USAA Life.
2. Policy: Universal Life 11%.
3. Face amount: $100,000.
4. Insurance age: 35.
5. Class: male nonsmoker.

An ROR calculation compares the purchase of a cash value policy to the alternative of buying annual renewable term (ART) and investing the premium differences in, say, a bank. The ROR is the interest rate that, based on assumed ART rates, keeps the death benefits of the two programs the same and equates the cash value and the bank account, or side fund, at the end of the period studied. Two sets of RORs are shown: those based on 100% of the rates in col. (9) and those based on 90% of col. (9).
Source: Reprinted with permission from James H. Hunt, director, National Insurance Consumer Organization.

Appendix 2

Life Insurance Comparison

The figures below may hurt your eyes, but they do serve a purpose. These numbers show the amount of money you would have after twenty years if you invested in (1) an annual renewable term (ART) life insurance policy and invested the rest in an IRA or (2) a universal life insurance policy. The main difference between a term policy and a universal life policy is with the universal policy you begin building up a "cash value," similar to putting money in a savings account.

Many insurance agents will show you a computer printout of their insurance policies—so get used to these numbers and make sure you understand each column before you choose an insurance policy. Remember, the National Insurance Consumer Organization (NICO) will help you evaluate various policies. This service costs $25.

Both policies have a $100,000 face amount (meaning they will pay out that amount upon death), for a thirty-five-year-old male nonsmoker. The interest rate of the cash value portion of the universal life policy and that of the IRA is 10 percent for the entire twenty years. Although a constant rate is unlikely, we will use it for our example. If you are in the 35 percent tax bracket and remain in this bracket for the full twenty years:

1. You should compare the net outlay (F) of Table A-1 with the premium paid (B) in Table A-2. Notice these figures are the same after taxes are considered for the IRA deposit.
2. Compare the ending year death benefit in Table A-1 (H) and in Table A-2 (C). The ART/IRA amount is higher than the universal life.
3. The net surrender value in Table A-2 (F) should be compared to the net IRA value (K) in Table A-1. The surrender value is the amount of money you would actually get back if you terminated the policy.
4. The summary (Table A-3) makes it easy to compare the death benefits and net surrender value of each policy at certain points in time.

Table A-1   ART/IRA Package

(A)	(B)	(C)	(D)	(E)	(F)	(G)	(H)	(I)	(J)	(K)
Beginning Year	IRA Deposit	ART Policy	Total Payment (B+C)	Taxes Saved (B×.35)	Net Outlay (D−E)	End Year IRA Value (B×.10)	End Year Death Benefit ($100000 + G)	Tax Due at Death (.35×G)	Net Death Benefit (H−I)	Net IRA Value (.65×G)
1	2000	136	2136	700	1436	2200	102200	770	101430	
2	2000	138	2138	700	1438	4620	104620	1617	103003	
3	2000	142	2142	700	1442	7282	107282	2549	104733	
4	2000	146	2146	700	1446	10210	110210	3574	106636	
5	2000	152	2152	700	1452	13431	113431	4701	108730	
6	2000	158	2158	700	1458	16974	116974	5941	111033	
7	2000	166	2166	700	1466	20872	120872	7305	113567	
8	2000	175	2175	700	1475	25159	125159	8806	116353	
9	2000	185	2185	700	1485	29875	129875	10456	119419	
10	2000	195	2195	700	1495	35062	135062	12272	122790	22790
11	2000	207	2207	700	1507	40769	140769	14269	126500	
12	2000	228	2228	700	1528	47045	147045	16466	130579	
13	2000	252	2252	700	1552	53950	153950	18883	135067	
14	2000	282	2282	700	1582	61545	161545	21541	140004	
15	2000	314	2314	700	1614	69899	169899	24465	145434	
16	2000	353	2353	700	1653	79089	179089	27681	151408	
17	2000	392	2392	700	1692	89198	189198	31219	157979	
18	2000	435	2435	700	1735	100318	200318	35111	165207	
19	2000	481	2481	700	1781	112550	212550	39393	173157	
20	2000	532	2532	700	1832	126005	226005	44102	181903	81903

Source: Reprinted with permission from James H. Hunt, director, National Insurance Consumer Organization (NICO).

Table A-2   Universal Life

(A)	(B)	(C)	(D)	(E)	(F)
Beginning Year	Premium Paid*	End Year Death Benefit	End Year Cash Value	Taxable Gain on Surrender $(D-\Sigma B\dagger)$	Net Cash Value on Surrender $(D-.35(E))$
1	1436	101308	1308	0	1308
2	1438	102795	2795	0	2795
3	1442	104475	4427	111	4388
4	1446	106216	6216	454	6057
5	1452	108178	8178	964	7841
6	1458	110328	10328	1656	9748
7	1466	112686	12686	2548	11794
8	1475	115270	15270	3657	13990
9	1485	118102	18102	5004	16351
10	1495	121204	21204	6611	18890
11	1507	124603	24603	8503	21627
12	1528	128335	28335	10707	24588
13	1552	132435	32435	13255	27796
14	1582	136946	36946	16184	31282
15	1614	141912	41912	19536	35074
16	1653	147382	47382	23353	39208
17	1693	153408	53408	27686	43718
18	1735	160045	60045	32588	48639
19	1781	167354	67354	38116	54013
20	1832	175406	75406	44336	59888

*Same as net outlay for IRA/ART package.

$\dagger\Sigma$ means "sum of." For example, $111 in column (E), row 3, is the result of $4427 — (1436 + 1438 + 1442).

Source: Reprinted with permission from James H. Hunt, director, National Insurance Consumer Organization (NICO).

Table A-3   SUMMARY

Year	Net Death Benefits (After Tax)		Net Surrender Value After Tax	
	IRA/ART	USAA	IRA/ART	USAA
1	101430	101308		
2				
3				
4				
5				
6	111033	110328		
7				
8				
9				
10			22790	18890
11	126500	124603		
12				
13				
14				
15				
16	151408	147382		
17				
18				
19				
20			81903	59888

Source: Reprinted with permission from James H. Hunt, director, National Insurance Consumer Organization (NICO).

Appendix 3

Sample List of Tax Publications*

General Guides

225—Farmer's Tax Guide
334—Tax Guide for Small Business
509—Tax Calendars for 1984
553—Highlights of 1983 Tax Changes
595—Tax Guide for Commercial Fishermen
910—Taxpayer's Guide to IRS Information, Assistance, and Publications

Specialized Publications

15—Employer's Tax Guide (Circular E)
54—Tax Guide for U.S. Citizens and Resident Aliens Abroad
378—Fuel Tax Credits
448—Federal Estate and Gift Taxes
463—Travel, Entertainment, and Gift Expenses
501—Exemptions
502—Medical and Dental Expenses
503—Child and Disabled Dependent Care
504—Tax Information for Divorced or Separated Individuals
505—Tax Withholding and Estimated Tax
506—Income Averaging
508—Educational Expenses
510—Excise Taxes for 1984
513—Tax Information for Visitors to the United States
514—Foreign Tax Credit for U.S. Citizens and Resident Aliens
516—Tax Information for U.S. Government Civilian Employees Stationed Abroad

517—Social Security for Members of the Clergy and Religious Workers
518—Foreign Scholars and Educational and Cultural Exchange Visitors
519—U.S. Tax Guide for Aliens
520—Scholarships and Fellowships
521—Moving Expenses
522—Disability Payments
523—Tax Information on Selling Your Home
524—Credit for the Elderly
525—Taxable and Nontaxable Income
526—Charitable Contributions
527—Rental Property
529—Miscellaneous Deductions
530—Tax Information for Homeowners
531—Reporting Income from Tips
533—Self-Employment Tax
534—Depreciation
535—Business Expenses
536—Net Operating Losses and the At-Risk Limits
537—Installment Sales
538—Accounting Periods and Methods
539—Employment Taxes—Income Tax Withholding, FICA and FUTA, Advance Payments of EIC, Withholding on Gambling Winnings
541—Tax Information on Partnerships
542—Tax Information on Corporations
544—Sales and Other Dispositions of Assets
545—Interest Expense

*Source: Your Federal Income Tax, IRS publication 17 (rev. October 1983).

244   **Appendix 3**

547—Tax Information on Disasters, Casualties, and Thefts
548—Deduction for Bad Debts
549—Condemnations of Private Property for Public Use
550—Investment Income and Expenses
551—Basis of Assets
552—Recordkeeping for Individuals and a List of Tax Publications
554—Tax Benefits for Older Americans
555—Community Property and the Federal Income Tax
556—Examination of Returns, Appeal Rights, and Claims for Refund
557—Tax-Exempt Status for Your Organization
558—Tax Information for Sponsors of Contests and Sporting Events
559—Tax Information for Survivors, Executors, and Administrators
560—Tax Information on Self-Employed Retirement Plans
561—Determining the Value of Donated Property
564—Mutual Fund Distributions
567—U.S. Civil Service Retirement and Disability
570—Tax Guide for U.S. Citizens Employed in U.S. Possessions
571—Tax-Sheltered Annuity Programs for Employees of Public Schools and Certain Tax-Exempt Organizations
572—Investment Credit
575—Pension and Annuity Income
583—Information for Business Taxpayers—Business Taxes, Identification Numbers, Recordkeeping
584—Disaster and Casualty Loss Workbook
585—Voluntary Tax Methods to Help Finance Political Campaigns
586A—The Collection Process (Income Tax Accounts)

587—Business Use of Your Home
588—Condominiums, Cooperative Apartments, and Homeowners Associations
589—Tax Information on S Corporations
590—Individual Retirement Arrangements (IRAs)
593—Income Tax Benefits for U.S. Citizens Who Go Overseas
596—Earned Income Credit
597—Information on the United States—Canada Income Tax Treaty
721—Comprehensive Tax Guide to U.S. Civil Service Retirement Benefits
794—Favorable Determination Letter
901—U.S. Tax Treaties
903—Energy Credits for Individuals
904—Interrelated Computations for Estate and Gift Taxes
905—Tax Information on Unemployment Compensation
906—Jobs and Research Credits
907—Tax Information for Handicapped and Disabled Individuals
908—Bankruptcy
909—Minimum Tax and Alternative Minimum Tax
911—Tax Information for Direct Sellers

Spanish Language Publications

179—Gula contributiva federal para patronos puertorriqueños (Circular PR)
556S—Revisión de las declaraciones de impuesto, derecho de apelación y reclamaciones de devolución
579S—Como preparar la declaración de impuesto federal
586S—Proceso de cobro (Deudas del impuesto sobre ingreso)
850—English-Spanish Glossary of Words and Phrases Used in Publications Issued by the Internal Revenue Service

Appendix 4

3% *Real* Rate of Return*

								Your Tax Bracket									
Present Inflation Rate	20%	22%	23%	24%	25%	26%	28%	30%	32%	33%	34%	35%	38%	42%	45%	48%	50%
5%	10.00	10.26	10.39	10.53	10.67	10.81	11.11	11.43	11.76	11.94	12.12	12.31	12.90	13.79	14.55	15.38	16.00
6%	11.25	11.54	11.69	11.84	12.00	12.16	12.50	12.86	13.24	13.43	13.64	13.85	14.52	15.52	16.36	17.31	18.00
7%	12.50	12.82	12.99	13.16	13.33	13.51	13.89	14.29	14.71	14.93	15.15	15.38	16.13	17.24	18.18	19.23	20.00
8%	13.75	14.10	14.29	14.47	14.67	14.86	15.28	15.71	16.18	16.42	16.67	16.92	17.74	18.97	20.00	21.15	22.00
9%	15.00	15.38	15.58	15.79	16.00	16.22	16.67	17.14	17.65	17.91	18.18	18.46	19.35	20.69	21.82	23.08	24.00
10%	16.25	16.67	16.88	17.11	17.33	17.57	18.06	18.57	19.12	19.40	19.70	20.00	20.97	22.41	23.64	25.00	26.00

*To figure out the rate of return you'll need to attain a real rate of 3%, find the number that coincides with your tax bracket and the inflation rate.

Appendix 5

IRA Breakeven

An IRA can be a great tax-sheltered investment option. Just determine the number of years you must wait to make withdrawals until the tax advantages outweigh the early withdrawal penalty: the breakeven holding period.

Use the table on the following page to find your breakeven holding period if your marginal tax rate will be the *same* at withdrawal as it was when you first put the money into the IRA. (It is important to estimate your marginal tax bracket correctly at the time of withdrawal.) Find the rate closest to your marginal tax rate, then look across to find the average rate you expect your IRA investment to earn each year. So, if you're in the 35 percent tax bracket now and will be when you'd like to take money out of your IRA earning 10 percent, you'll find that you shouldn't make withdrawals for the first 4.77 years. After that, the 10 percent withdrawal penalty will be offset by the combined effect of deferred taxation and compounding of earnings. (See the table on the following page.)

If you anticipate being in a *different* tax bracket at withdrawal than the one you were in when you began your IRA, there is a formula that will give you a more accurate estimate of the breakeven holding period. The formula looks more complicated than it really is. All you need is a calculator that has a natural log function key.

$$\text{Natural logarithm} \times \frac{\dfrac{(1 - \text{tax rate in original year})}{(1 - \text{tax rate at withdrawal} - \text{penalty rate})}}{(\text{Average annual yield}) \ (\text{average annual tax rate}) \ + \ \text{covariance}}$$

Covariance is the number that shows how much returns and taxes vary with one another. For most investors this number is so small it's insignificant. So, for the purposes of estimating, consider the covariance to be zero and leave it out of your calculations.

You will find that an IRA is more advantageous when you invest at a higher tax rate and withdraw at a lower tax rate (exactly the reason it is a useful retirement investment). However, if a breadwinner loses a job or leaves a job, this rule still applies because of the lower income during this time.

Source: Formula and table reprinted with permission from "IRAs and the Breakeven Holding Period," by Donald Smith in *American Association of Individual Investors Journal,* March 1984.

IRA Breakeven Holding Periods (Average Annual Yield to Withdrawal)*

Constant Marginal Tax Rate* (%)	6%	7%	8%	9%	10%	11%	12%	13%	14%	15%	16%	17%
10	19.63	16.83	14.72	13.09	11.78	10.71	9.82	9.06	8.41	7.85	7.36	6.93
15	13.91	11.92	10.43	9.27	8.34	7.59	6.95	6.42	5.96	5.56	5.22	4.91
20	11.13	9.54	8.35	7.42	6.68	6.07	5.56	5.14	4.77	4.45	4.17	3.93
25	9.54	8.18	7.16	6.36	5.72	5.20	4.77	4.40	4.09	3.82	3.58	3.37
30	8.56	7.34	6.42	5.71	5.14	4.67	4.28	3.95	3.67	3.43	3.21	3.02
35	7.96	6.82	5.97	5.30	4.77	4.34	3.98	3.67	3.41	3.18	2.98	2.81
40	7.60	6.51	5.70	5.06	4.56	4.14	3.80	3.51	3.26	3.04	2.85	2.68
45	7.43	6.37	5.57	4.95	4.46	4.05	3.72	3.43	3.19	2.97	2.79	2.62
50	7.44	6.38	5.58	4.96	4.46	4.06	3.72	3.43	3.19	2.98	2.79	2.63

*Rates are continuously compounded for both taxes and average annual yield. Rates not continuously compounded can be substituted for a rough idea of the breakeven point.

Appendix 6

SLYC Funds*

Babson Growth Fund
  D. L. Babson & Co., Inc.
  3 Crown Ctr., 2440 Pershing Road
  Kansas City, MO 64108
  (800) 821-5591

Boston Co. Capital Appreciation Fund
  Boston Company Advisors
  One Boston Place
  Boston, MA 02106
  (800) 225-6190

Bull & Bear Capital Growth Fund
  Bull & Bear Management Corp.
  11 Hanover Square
  New York, NY 10005
  (800) 847-4200

Columbia Growth Fund
  Columbia Management Co.
  P. O. Box 1350
  Portland, OR 97205
  (509) 624-4101

Dreyfus Growth Opportunities Fund
Dreyfus Third Century Fund
  Dreyfus Corporation
  767 Fifth Avenue
  New York, NY 10022
  (800) 223-5682

Fidelity Contrafund
Fidelity Discoverer Fund
  Fidelity Investments Corp.
  82 Devonshire Street
  Boston, MA 02109
  (800) 225-6190

Financial Dynamics Fund
  Financial Programs, Inc.
  P. O. Box 2040
  Denver, CO 80201
  (800) 525-9831

Founders Growth Fund
Founders Special Fund
  Founders Mutual Depositor Corp.
  3033 E. First Avenue, Suite 810
  Denver, CO 80202
  (800) 525-2440

Janus Fund
  Janus Management Corp.
  100 Fillmore Street, Suite 300
  Denver, CO 80216
  (800) 525-3713

Lexington Growth Fund
Lexington Research Fund
  Lexington Management Corp.
  P. O. Box 1515
  Englewood Cliffs, NJ 07632
  (800) 526-4791

*Source: Donoghue's MONEYLETTER and Donoghue's Mutual Fund Almanac.

PRO Services: Medical Technology Fund
PRO Services, Inc.
1107 Bethlehem Pike
Flourtown, PA 19031
(800) 523-0864

SAFECO Growth Fund
SAFECO Asset Management Corp.
SAFECO Plaza
Seattle, WA 98185
(800) 426-6730

Scudder Capital Growth Fund
Scudder Development Fund
Scudder International Fund
Scudder Stevens & Clark
175 Federal Street
Boston, MA 02110
(800) 225-2470

Stein Roe Capital Opportunities Fund
Stein Roe Special Fund
Stein Roe Stock Fund
Stein Roe Universe Fund
Stein Roe & Farnham
150 South Wacker Drive
Chicago, IL 60606
(800) 621-0320

T. Rowe Price Growth Stock Fund
T. Rowe Price International
T. Rowe Price New Era Fund
T. Rowe Price New Horizons Fund
T. Rowe Price Associates, Inc.
100 E. Pratt Street
Baltimore, MD 21202
(800) 638-5660

USAA Mutual Growth Fund
USAA Sun Belt Era
USAA Investment Management Co.
9800 Fredricksburg Road
San Antonio, TX 78288
(800) 531-8181

Value Line Fund
Value Line Leveraged Growth Investors
Value Line Special Situations
Value Line, Inc.
711 Third Avenue
New York, NY 10017
(800) 223-0818

Vanguard Explorer Fund
Vanguard Ivest Fund
Vanguard Morgan Growth Fund
Vanguard Windsor Fund
Vanguard Group
Drummers Lane
Valley Forge, PA 19482
(800) 523-7025

Appendix 7

Rule of 72: "How Long to Double Your Money?"

Interest Rate, %	Years
5.5	13.09
6.0	12.00
6.5	11.08
7.0	10.29
7.5	9.60
8.0	9.00
8.5	8.47
9.0	8.00
9.5	7.58
10.0	7.20
10.5	6.86
11.0	6.55
11.5	6.26
12.0	6.00
12.5	5.76
13.0	5.54
13.5	5.33
14.0	5.14
14.5	4.97
15.0	4.80

$$\frac{72}{\text{Interest rate}} = \text{years to double}$$

To double your money again, just double the years.

Source: Donoghue's MONEYLETTER.

Appendix 8

1984 Tax Rate Schedules

Caution: Do not use these Tax Rate Schedules to figure your 1985 taxes.

SCHEDULE X—Single Taxpayers

If line 5 is: Over—	but not over—	The tax is:	of the amount over—
$0	$2,300	—0—	
2,300	3,400	------- 11%	$2,300
3,400	4,400	$121 + 12%	3,400
4,400	6,500	241 + 14%	4,400
6,500	8,500	535 + 15%	6,500
8,500	10,800	835 + 16%	8,500
10,800	12,900	1,203 + 18%	10,800
12,900	15,000	1,581 + 20%	12,900
15,000	18,200	2,001 + 23%	15,000
18,200	23,500	2,737 + 26%	18,200
23,500	28,800	4,115 + 30%	23,500
28,800	34,100	5,705 + 34%	28,800
34,100	41,500	7,507 + 38%	34,100
41,500	55,300	10,319 + 42%	41,500
55,300	81,800	16,115 + 48%	55,300
81,800	------	28,835 + 50%	81,800

SCHEDULE Z—Heads of Household

If line 5 is: Over—	but not over—	The tax is:	of the amount over—
$0	$2,300	—0—	
2,300	4,400	------- 11%	$2,300
4,400	6,500	$231 + 12%	4,400
6,500	8,700	483 + 14%	6,500
8,700	11,800	791 + 17%	8,700
11,800	15,000	1,318 + 18%	11,800
15,000	18,200	1,894 + 20%	15,000
18,200	23,500	2,534 + 24%	18,200
23,500	28,800	3,806 + 28%	23,500
28,800	34,100	5,290 + 32%	28,800
34,100	44,700	6,986 + 35%	34,100
44,700	60,600	10,696 + 42%	44,700
60,600	81,800	17,374 + 45%	60,600
81,800	108,300	26,914 + 48%	81,800
108,300	------	39,634 + 50%	108,300

SCHEDULE Y—Married Taxpayers and Qualifying Widows and Widowers

Married Filing Joint Returns and Qualifying Widows and Widowers

If line 5 is: Over—	but not over—	The tax is:	of the amount over—
$0	$3,400	—0—	
3,400	5,500	------- 11%	$3,400
5,500	7,600	$231 + 12%	5,500
7,600	11,900	483 + 14%	7,600
11,900	16,000	1,085 + 16%	11,900
16,000	20,200	1,741 + 18%	16,000
20,200	24,600	2,497 + 22%	20,200
24,600	29,900	3,465 + 25%	24,600
29,900	35,200	4,790 + 28%	29,900
35,200	45,800	6,274 + 33%	35,200
45,800	60,000	9,772 + 38%	45,800
60,000	85,600	15,168 + 42%	60,000
85,600	109,400	25,920 + 45%	85,600
109,400	162,400	36,630 + 49%	109,400
162,400	--------	62,600 + 50%	162,400

Married Filing Separate Returns

If line 5 is: Over—	but not over—	The tax is:	of the amount over—
$0	$1,700	—0—	
1,700	2,750	---------- 11%	$1,700
2,750	3,800	$115.50 + 12%	2,750
3,800	5,950	241.50 + 14%	3,800
5,950	8,000	542.50 + 16%	5,950
8,000	10,100	870.50 + 18%	8,000
10,100	12,300	1,248.50 + 22%	10,100
12,300	14,950	1,732.50 + 25%	12,300
14,950	17,600	2,395.00 + 28%	14,950
17,600	22,900	3,137.00 + 33%	17,600
22,900	30,000	4,886.00 + 38%	22,900
30,000	42,800	7,584.00 + 42%	30,000
42,800	54,700	12,960.00 + 45%	42,800
54,700	81,200	18,315.00 + 49%	54,700
81,200	------	31,300.00 + 50%	81,200

Source: Internal Revenue Service.

Index

Accelerated Cost Recovery System
(ACRS), 114
active investors, 199
advertising, 47
of yard sales, 48
aggressive investors, 200
air conditioning costs, 72
airline industry, deregulation of,
155–156
airlines, low-cost, 94
alimony, 85
deduction of, 105, 141
American Automobile Association (AAA),
68
American Capital Reserve Fund, 170
American Express, 92
annuities, 127
defined, 145
fees for, 146
life, 146
variable, 145–146, 147
antiques, regional variations in value of,
46
antique stock certificates, 38–39
appliances, as assets, 44–45

appraisals:
for collectibles, 47–48
free, 45–46
assets, asset liberation, 33–56
inventory of, 35–53
liquid, 35–44
not worth holding onto, 46–47
other, 35, 44–53
requirements of, 33–34
uncollectible, 49
auction houses, free appraisals from, 45–46
audits, 107, 125, 129–131
auto insurance, 68–69, 82
discounts on, 68–69, 84
low-cost companies and, 69
optional coverage of, 68
young drivers and, 69
automobiles, 223
payments for, 81–82
repair of, 92
value of, 44

balance sheets, 34–56
assets side of, 34–53
liabilities side of, 35, 53–55

Band, Richard, 60
bank accounts:
  as liquid assets, 38
  see also checking accounts; money
    market deposit accounts; passbook
    savings accounts
bank credit analysts, 157
banks, 223–224
  competition of, 156, 160, 165–166
  "creative mediocrity" of, 160
  deregulation of, 155–156
  failures of, 156–157, 161, 181
  high interest rates from, 156
  IRAs in, 142, 147, 150
  money funds vs., 175
  service charges of, 90, 108, 161
  uninsured deposits in, 156–157
Barron's, 21, 165
"Be My Guest" certificates, 92
boats, as assets, 46
bonds, bond funds, 2, 9, 29, 127
  corporate, 173
  falling interest rates and, 185–187
  government, 173
  intermediate-term, 172–173, 174
  liberating assets from, 39–40
  long-term, 181, 202–203
  "market rate" structure of, 39
  municipal, 173
  rising interest rates and, 167
  risks of, 120
  short-term, 174
  sold by brokers, 173
  tax-free, 119–120, 187, 194–195
  WPPSS, 120
books, selling of, 48
"break even" mentality, 205
Budget Deficit Reduction Act (1984), 114
budgets:
  importance of, 8
  trimming of, 8, 10
businesses:
  as assets, 49–51
  selling of, 50–51
  value of, 50
business expenditures credit, 111, 114
business expenses, 106, 111, 114, 144
buy low and sell high, as investment
  strategy, 187

cable TV, 83, 94
California, 158, 163
capital gains, 119, 121, 124–125,
    131–133
  IRAs vs., 148–149, 152
  long-term, 124–125, 126, 132, 133,
    189–190
  "net" basis reporting of, 132
  risk and, 125
  short-term, 189
  taxes on, 9, 124, 125, 131–132
capital losses, 131–132, 134
Capital Preservation Fund, 158, 160
car payments, 81–82
car pools, 84, 92
cash-deferred profit-sharing plans, 140
cash flow, income vs., 128, 132–134
cash on hand, uncounted, 37–38
CASHPLAN, 74–97, 193
  family role in, 75–76, 96, 205
  integration of information in, 77, 95–96
  preparation of worksheet in, 76–95
  revision of, 97
  where to cut in, 96–97
casualty losses, 110
catastrophe-proofing, in SLYC system,
    179–181, 202–203
Cates Consulting Associates, Inc., 157
certificates of deposit (CDs), 165, 171,
    181–182
  early withdrawals from, 105–106, 142,
    159, 174
  shopping for, 173–174
charitable contributions, 84, 110, 227–228
charters, 94–95
check-a-month plans, 29, 132–133,
    201–202
checking accounts, 10, 18–25
  free, 8, 19, 21
  liberating assets from, 38, 55
  money fund used as, 26–29
  money market, *see* money market
    deposit accounts
  non-interest-bearing, 22–23
  NOW, 19, 22–23, 38
  proof of payment and, 107
  selected pricing on, 22–23
  Super NOW, 19–20, 22–23, 38, 154
child care credit, 111, 113–114

children:
  assets of, 52–53
  auto insurance for, 69
  education of, 16, 17
  life insurance and, 66–67
  teaching saving habits to, 12
  trust accounts for, 10, 18, 31, 127–128
child support, 85, 105
Christie's Auction House, 46
Christmas clubs, drawbacks of, 6
Christmas gifts, saving money on, 92
Citibank, 173–174
clothing, 91–92
collectibles, 224
  value of, 47–48
commonsense investing, 192–208
  learning to drive car compared to,
    193–194, 204
compounding on a pretax basis, 30,
  137–138
computers:
  cash planning with, 76–77
  documenting business use of, 114
Congress, U.S., 15, 19, 53, 111, 114, 141
  retirement plans created by, 135, 136
  Ways and Means Committee and, 75
conservative investors, 200
Continental Illinois National Bank, 166
Corporate Income Fund—Short-Term
  Series, 172
coupons:
  grocery, 90, 91
  restaurant, 94
credit cards, 10, 18, 29–30, 61–63, 107,
  225
  cash advances on, 29–30
  cash planning and, 84–85
  emergency use of, 29–30, 79
  liabilities and, 53
  promotional circulars included with bills
    for, 63
  proof of payment and, 80–81
  state differences in, 62–63
  value of, 63
credit unions, 198, 225

Deak-Perera, 37–38
Dean Witter, 174
debt, inflation and, 61

deductions, 98–116
  of alimony payments, 105, 141
  of casualty and theft losses, 110
  of charitable contributions, 84, 110
  of educational expenses, 84, 111
  of employee business expenses, 106,
    144
  of interest, 61, 100–102, 107–108, 139,
    141, 150, 196, 197–198
  itemizing of, 103, 106–107, 112
  of medical and dental expenses,
    108–109
  miscellaneous, 110–111
  of moving expenses, 103, 104
  of penalty for early withdrawal of
    savings, 105–106
  proof of payment and, 80–81, 110
  of real estate taxes, 58, 82
  of retirement plans contributions,
    103–105, 108, 137–138, 141–143
  of state and local taxes, 110
  for working, married couples, 105
dental costs, 70, 95
  deduction of, 108–109
depreciation, of business equipment, 114
disability income exclusion, 106
discretionary expenses, 77, 85–95
dollar cost averaging, 10, 188–189
Donoghue Organization, Inc., 165, 176
Donoghue's Money Fund Average, 21, 55,
  67, 169, 182–183, 184
Donoghue's Money Fund Average
  Maturity, 168, 169, 170, 171, 184
Donoghue's Money Fund Table, 21, 24,
  168
Donoghue's MONEYLETTER, 111, 165,
  187, 189, 204
Donoghue's Mutual Fund Almanac, 29,
  187
Dreyfus Liquid Assets, 170–171
drugs, 225
  cutting costs of, 70–71

E bonds, 39
educational expenses, 127, 225–226
  deduction of, 84, 111
EE bonds, 39, 40
emergencies, 85
  SARA plans and, 139

emergencies *(cont.)*
  use of credit cards in, 29–30, 79
  withdrawals from retirement accounts
    in, 43–44
energy audits, 72
energy bills, cutting costs of, 71–72, 93
energy conservation credits, 72, 111–112
energy sources, renewable, 113
entertainment costs, 83, 94, 96–97
entrepreneurs, information sources on,
  226
equity access programs, 44, 134
escrow accounts, for property taxes,
  57–58
estate taxes, 146
expenses:
  discretionary, 77, 85–95
  fixed, 77, 80–85
  major, cutting down, 57–73

Federal Credit Union Share Insurance
    Corporation (FCUSIC), 156
federal deposit insurance, 21, 26,
    156–157, 161, 204
Federal Deposit Insurance Corporation
    (FDIC), 156, 181
Federal Reserve Bank, 128, 172
Federal Savings and Loan Insurance
    Corporation (FSLIC), 156
Fidelity Discoverer Fund, 188
Fidelity Magellan Fund, 188
Fidelity Mercury Fund, 188
financial goals, setting of, 16–18
financial habits, improvement of, 35
financial information, sources of, 7, 29,
    83, 111, 165, 187, 220–234
financial planning, 227
financial revolution, 2
financial tool kits:
  components of, 18–32
  things to leave out of, 31–32
First Trust Money Market Fund, 27
Fitzgerald, F. Scott, 135
fixed expenses, 77, 80–85
  tallying up, 85
flea markets, 48
food costs, 90–91
foreign currency, cashing in, 37–38
Form 1040, 112

Form 3903F, 104
formulas, for tax-free money funds,
    162–163
Form W-2, 140
Form W-4, 100–102
401(k) plans, *see* Salary Reduction
    Accounts
friction costs, 9
funerals, 227
furniture, 227
  as asset, 44–46

garage sales, 48–49
gasoline costs, 92
"Get Rich Quick" Richard, 14
gifts, saving money on, 92
gift taxes, 31, 205
Ginnie Maes (Government National
    Mortgage Association; GNMA), 129
gold bullion:
  as insurance, 179–180
  taxes and, 202–203
gold reserves, storing of, 180
Goodwill Industries, 84
government agencies, addresses and
    phone numbers of, 228–229

Haig, Alexander, 130
Hand, Learned, 117–118
health care, 229
  cutting costs of, 70–71, 95
health maintenance organizations
    (HMOs), 70
Hemingway, Ernest, 135
high-tax-bracket investors, 199–200
hobby equipment, as asset, 44–45, 46
homes and housing, 229
  as asset, 44
  improvement of, as medical deduction,
    109
  insurance of, 69–70, 82
  maintenance of, 71–72, 95
  nonmortgage costs related to, 60–61
  one-time tax exclusion on sale of, 44,
    61, 127, 133–134
  see also mortgages
hyperdeflation, 180–181, 203
hyperinflation, 179–180

IBCA Bank Analysts, Ltd., 157
income, 77–80, 118–129
  adjusted gross, 102, 103–106, 108–109
  capital gains, *see* capital gains
  cash flow vs., 128, 132–134
  deferred, 121, 125–126; *see also* tax
    shelters
  gross, 102, 105
  ordinary, 118–119, 133, 144–145, 146,
    189
  from tax-free investments, 119–124
income averaging, 115
Income Averaging, 115
income-oriented investors, 200
income taxes, 43
  due, 54
  see also deductions
Individual Retirement Accounts (IRAs), 8,
    13, 30, 31, 125–127, 147, 198
  alimony payments as contribution to,
    105, 141
  bank, as trap, 142, 147
  bank account vs., 142
  best place for, 142–143, 147–150
  borrowing for, 150
  borrowing from, 198
  breakeven, 247–248
  commonsense investing and, 195
  deadlines for contributing to, 103, 143
  early withdrawal penalties and, 43, 51,
    136, 142, 150–153
  as liquid asset, 43
  maximum contribution to, 141
  minimum contributions to, 3, 141–142
  other tax shelters compared to,
    137–138, 139, 140, 141, 142, 143,
    144, 148–149
  risks and, 150
  rolling SARAs into, 141
  rolling over of, into variable annuity,
    146
  rollover period for, 43
  tax deduction for, 103–105, 108,
    137–138, 141–143
  unemployed spouses and, 141
  variety of, 51
inflation, 179–180
  debt repayment and, 61

inflation *(cont.)*
  goal setting and, 16–17
  keeping ahead of, 10
  as un-American, 15
insurance, 64–70, 78, 127
  auto, 68–69, 82, 84
  federal deposit, 21, 26, 156–157, 161,
    204
  gold bullion coins as, 179–180
  homeowner's or renter's, 69–70, 82
  information sources on, 229–230
  safety without, 158–159
  see also life insurance
insurance agents, as salespeople, 67
insurance companies:
  as unregulated, 65
  variable annuities and, 145–146, 147
interest, interest rates:
  bond prices and, 167, 173
  falling, best investments for, 10, 133,
    164, 171, 174–176
  highest, 156
  on IRAs, 142, 147–150
  on loans from SARA plans, 139,
    140–141
  on NOW accounts, 19, 38
  refinancing mortgages and, 58–60
  rising, best investment for, 10, 164
  rule of 78s and, 62
  on security deposits, 81
  short-term vs. long-term, 59
  stock market and, 181–182, 183,
    184–185
  on Super NOW accounts, 19–20, 38
  as tax deduction, 61, 100–102,
    107–108, 139, 141, 150, 196,
    197–198
  on tax-free bonds, 119–120
  on Treasury bills, 128–129
  trend indicators for, 167–171
  undeductible, 108
  variable, 54, 59–60, 67, 142, 147–150
Internal Revenue Service (IRS), 99,
    100–102
  business use of computers as viewed
    by, 114
  Individual Revenue Source vs., 117
  penalties levied by, 108

Internal Revenue Service (IRS) *(cont.)*
    publications of, 103, 115, 116,
        243–244
    see also deductions; taxes
investment:
    diversification of, 189
    importance of understanding in,
        203–204
    riskiest approach to, 16
    shelters vs., 51
    as source of cash flow, 79–80
    "substantially identical," 132
    timing of, 164
    when to borrow for, 197–198
    where to borrow for, 198
investment clubs, 230
investment managers:
    becoming your own, 2, 6–7, 15
    stockbrokers vs., 32
investment money, hidden assets as
        source of, 1, 2, 7–10, 33–56
investment strategies, summary of, 10
investment tax credits, 114
investors, typical:
    profiles of, 11–15
    quiz on, 16–17
    Super SLYC, 199–200

jewelry, as asset, 44–46
jobhopping, 78

Keefe Bruyette and Woods, Inc., 157
Kemper Money Market Fund, 161, 170,
        204–205
Keogh plans, 30, 31, 125–127
    borrowing for, 150
    contributions to, 143–144
    deadline for contributing to, 144
    for employees, 144–145
    IRAs compared to, 138, 143, 144
    as liquid asset, 43
    rolling over of, 43, 144, 146
    SARAs compared to, 138, 139, 140
    tax deduction for, 103–105, 108, 138,
        143–145
    types of, 144

Laffer, Arthur, 130
land, *see* real estate
legal services, 230

liabilities:
    current, 53–54
    evaluation of, 53–55
    long-term, 53, 54–55
life annuities, 146
life insurance, 6, 32, 64–67, 108
    cash planning and, 82
    cash value, rate of return (ROR) for,
        236–237
    determining what you really need in,
        65–67
    loans taken out on, 40–41, 42, 64, 198
    mutual fund switching and, 67
    policies compared, 239–242
    term, 64, 66
    "universal life," 64, 65, 67
    variable, 67
    whole, 40–41, 42, 64–65, 66, 198
    worksheet for, 67
liquidity, 164
    of assets, 35–44
    defined, 7, 159
    importance of, 13
    of money funds, 26–27, 159
    of retirement accounts, 43–44
    safety in, 178–179, 203
    in SLYC system, 178–179
loans:
    cash planning and, 84–85
    collateralized, 134, 157
    installment, 54, 61
    interest-free, overwithholding of taxes
        as, 98–99
    as liabilities, 54
    personal, tax deduction of, 107
    repayment provisions of, 62
    from SARA plans, 78, 139, 140–141
    short-term, 54, 59
    uncollectible, 49
    when to repay, 198–199
local taxes, 110, 166
low-load mutual funds, 187–188

market indexes, 218–219
Massachusetts, 111, 163
Mayer, Harold, 130
medical costs, 70–71, 95
    deduction of, 108–109
medical insurance, 70, 109–110
Merrill Lynch, 44, 172, 174

Merrill Lynch Ready Assets Trust
  (MLRAT), 166, 174–176
middlemen, avoidance of, 187
money market:
  changes in, 154
  defined, 25
  getting a handle on trends in, 167–169
  insurance yields vs., 65
  retail, 154, 155
  switching from stock market to,
    182–183
money market deposit accounts
  (MMDAs), 9, 13, 20–21, 25–26, 38,
    51, 192–193
  liquidity of, 159
  lost interest on, 159–160
  money funds vs., 160, 164–165
  safety of, 21
money market investors, 200
money market mutual funds (money
  funds), 2, 9, 10, 18, 25–29
  as assets, 40
  average maturity of, 168–169, 170
  defined, 26
  diversification of, 158
  fees on, 27
  insured, 158, 160
  liquidity of, 26–27, 159
  minimum amount of checks drawn
    against, 27, 28–29
  minimum initial investment in, 3, 4–5,
    12, 27
  purposes of, 118–119
  regulation of, 158
  risks of, 166, 204
  safety of, 26, 158–159, 160
  S&P rating system for, 204
  selection of, 29, 165–166
  SLYC strategy and, 182
  tax-free, 121, 122–123, 162–163, 164
  yield of, 160–161, 175
mortgages, 57–61
  assumable, 54
  as fixed expense, 81
  fixed rate, 54, 60
  GNMA, investment in, 129
  prepayment penalty on, 54, 108
  refinancing of, 58–60, 61
  "reverse," 44
  second, 134

mortgages *(cont.)*
  tax deductions and, 61, 100–102,
    107–108
  variable rate, 54, 59–60
  voluntary contributions of principal on,
    8, 54, 60, 81, 107–108
Mt. Pleasant, Iowa, 157
movies, on pay-TV services, 83, 94
moving:
  expenses of, 103, 104
  tax deductions and, 103, 104
  timing of, 60–61
Municipal Unit Investment Trusts
  (MUITs), 171, 194–195
mutual funds, 51, 119, 231
  as assets, 40
  long-term capital gains distributions of,
    125
  low-load, 187–188
  prospectus of, 204–205
  stock, 2, 3, 9, 29, 133, 150, 182
  variable annuities and, 145, 146
  see also money market mutual funds;
    no-load mutual funds

National Committee for Monetary Reform
  (NCMR), 84
National Consumer Money Market
  Directory, 165–166
National Insurance Consumer
  Organization (NICO), 67
National Life Insurance Association, 41
net worth, 35, 55
New York, N.Y., 200
  bank credit analysts in, 157
  triple tax-free mutual funds in, 119
New York State, 163
  credit cards in, 62–63
no-load mutual mutual funds, 2, 9, 14–15,
    189
  family of, 29, 31
  IRAs in, 142–143, 147–150, 195
  liquidity of, 203
  risks of, 15
nonfriction investing, 9
no-penalty exit clauses, 81
NOW (Negotiable Order of Withdrawal)
  accounts, 19, 22–23, 38

100 Highest Yields, 165, 174

passbook savings accounts, 12, 198
    Christmas clubs as, 6
    drawbacks of, 9, 159–160
    IRAs in, 147
    liberating assets from, 38, 55
    myths about, 79
passive investors, 199
patience, virtue of, 188, 190–191
Patriotic Investing, 15, 189
"pay yourself first," 1, 61, 83, 102, 201
Porter, Sylvia, 72–73
professional support groups, 110
property taxes, *see* real estate taxes
Prudential Bache's MoneyMart Assets,
    170

raises, in salary, 78
real estate, 231
    devalued, sale of, 46–47
    tax-free sale of, 44
    see also homes and housing; mortgages
real estate taxes:
    cash planning and, 82–83
    deduction of, 58, 82
    escrow accounts for, 57–58
    as liabilities, 53
    prepaid, 41–43
    timing of, 58, 82
record keeping, importance of, 8–9,
    106–107, 110
rent:
    as fixed expense, 81
    payment of, 60, 61
    of telephones, 93
renter's insurance, 69–70
repurchase agreements (repos), 156–157
restaurants, cash planning and, 92, 93–94,
    97
retirement planning, 3–6, 18, 30–31,
    135–145, 231
    vested interests in, 51
    see also Individual Retirement
        Accounts; Keogh plans; Salary
        Reduction Accounts
"Rip Van Winkle" investors, 12–13
risk pyramid, 200, 201
risk-reduction strategies, 203–205
Rocky, as investor type, 13–14
Rogers, Will, 181

T. Rowe Price Prime Reserve, 170
Ruff, Howard, 84
rule of 72, 251
rule of 78s ("sum of the digits"), 62

safety:
    importance of, 13, 156–159
    without insurance, 158–159
    liquidity as, 178–179, 203
    in SLYC system, 178–179
salaries, 77–78
Salary Reduction Accounts (SARAs;
    401(k) plans), 30–31, 125–127
    accessibility of, 139
    allowed contribution to, 139–140,
        196–197
    as best shelter, 138–140, 147
    borrowing from, 78, 139, 140–141,
        196, 197
    commonsense investing and, 195–196
    distributions from, 139, 140
    as liquid asset, 43–44, 55'
    matching contributions in, 139, 140,
        196
    rolling over of, 141
    tax deduction for, 103–105, 138–141
    ten-year forward averaging and, 139,
        141
    types of, 140
salary reduction savings plans, 140
sales, 72–73
    garage and yard, 48–49
    post-Christmas, 92
sales taxes:
    deduction of, 110
    on yard sales, 48–49
savings:
    do-it-yourself, 6–7
    Donoghue's rule for, 55
    forced, 6
    monthly, returns on, 3, 5, 7
    right time for, 1
    strategy for, 10
    use of, 80, 85
securities, information sources on, 232
Securities and Exchange Commission
    (SEC), 26, 158
security deposits, interest on, 81
self-employment, retirement plans and, *see*
    Keogh plans

six-month money market certificates, 154, 160

Small Business Administration (SBA), 74–75
  Service Corps of Retired Executives of (SCORE), 50

R. M. Smythe, Inc., 39

Social Security, 18, 136, 145

Sophie the Sensible Saver, 13

Sotheby Parke Bernet, 45

"Sounds Good to Me" Sam, 14

spreadsheet programs, computer, 76–77

Standard & Poor's (S&P) rating system, 204

state taxes, 110, 166

Stein Roe money funds, 204

stockbrokers:
  misuse of, 12–13
  as salespeople, 32

stocks, stock market:
  bull, 192–193
  future value of, 181
  information sources on, 232
  liberating assets from, 38–39
  market price of, 181
  mutual funds of, 2, 3, 9, 29, 133, 150, 182
  net present value of, 181
  rising interest rates and, 183, 184–185
  SLYC system and, 177, 181–182
  switching from money market to, 182–183

stop-loss rule, 184

Super NOW accounts, 19–20, 22–23, 38, 154

Super-SLYC Sallie, 14–15

Super-SLYC (safety, liquidity, yield, and catastrophe-proofing) system, 3–6, 10, 16, 17, 133, 143, 177–191
  advantages of, 184
  catastrophe-proofing in, 179–181, 202–203
  customizing of, 185–186
  don't take the SLY out of, 191
  fund families in, 177–178
  as gear system, 193
  life insurance and, 67
  liquidity and safety of, 178–179
  money funds for, 29, 177, 178, 249–250

Super-SLYC system (cont.)
  risks of, 177
  "super" in, 183–184
  switching in, 178, 182–183, 206, 207
  types of investors in, 199–201
  yields in, 179

Super-SLY (safety, liquidity, and yield) strategy, 6, 10, 13–14, 16, 143, 154–176
  best choices in, 172–173
  as gear system, 193
  money fund as, 27
  one-year wealth-accumulation goals from, 17
  questions and answers for, 165–167
  Super-SLYC compared to, 15, 177

tax audits, 107, 125, 129–131

tax bracket:
  capital gains and, 124
  retirement and, 144–145
  tax-free money funds and, 162–163, 164
  tax-free yields and, 121, 124

tax credits, 72, 111–114

taxes, 10–15, 79, 98–153
  capital gains, 9, 124, 125, 131–132
  estate, 146
  exemptions and, 100–102, 105
  gift, 31, 205
  information sources on, 233
  mortgages and, 61, 100–102
  overwithholding of, 8–9, 77–78, 98–100
  on premature withdrawals from tax shelters, 30, 43
  real estate, 41–43, 53, 57–58, 82–83
  refunds of, 8, 52
  on sale of homes, 44, 61, 127
  sales, 48–49, 110
  state and local, 110, 166
  underpayment of, 52

tax evasion, 107
  tax avoidance vs., 117–118, 189

tax-free equivalent tables, 124

tax-free investments, 119–124
  calculation of worthwhileness of, 121
  diversification of, 120

tax-free money funds, 121, 122–123, 162–163
  double and triple, 163, 164

tax laws, frequency of changes in,
115–116
tax preparers, 116
tax publications, 103, 115, 116, 243–244
tax-qualified investors, 199
tax rate schedules, 253
tax shelters, 30–31, 129–153, 194–198
compounding and, 137–138
investments vs., 51
making the most of, 147
non-tax-deferred investment contrasted
with, 136–137
old-style, 135–136
phony, 107
rate of return on, 147–150
real benefit of, 147
"at risk" requirement of, 131
tricks of, 129–133
variable annuities as, 145–146
for Very Important Investors (VIIs), 136
see also Individual Retirement
Accounts; Keogh plans; Salary
Reduction Accounts
telephone bills, 93
10–20–30 plan, 3–6
theft losses, 110
thrift, virtue of, 1
thrift plans, company, 40, 55, 78,
148–149
IRAs vs., 148–149, 151
pretax, 140
savings bonds in, 39
vested interests in, 51
transportation expenses, 84, 92
as business deduction, 106
as medical deduction, 109
travel agents, use of, 94
The Travelers, 158
traveler's checks, cashing in, 37
travel information, 233
Treasury, U.S., 39, 40

Treasury bills, U.S., 40, 119, 128–129,
171, 172
buying points on the line with, 160
government guarantees of, 158
liquidity of, 159, 166
minimum purchase of, 158
tax-exempt interest on, 166
trust accounts, 10, 18, 31, 127–128
limits on, 128
tuition payments, 84
Twain, Mark, 117

unemployment, 43
Uniform Gifts to Minors Act, 31, 127
union dues, 110
Unit Investment Trusts (UITs), 171, 172

vacations, 94–95
Vanguard, 158

warranties, 234
Washington Public Power Supply System
(WPPSS), 120, 171
wash sales, 132
Weimar Republic, hyperinflation in, 179
William E. Donoghue's Complete Money
Market Guide (Donoghue), 2, 26,
155
William E. Donoghue's No-Load Mutual
Fund Guide (Donoghue), 3,
183–184, 187
wine bars, 94
workplace, selection of, 77

yard sales, 48–49
yields:
guaranteed, 206
real, 17, 176, 245
in SLYC system, 179
in SLY strategy, 13–14, 159, 160–161,
165, 171, 174, 175, 176